THE
ULTIMATE
FISHING
BOOK

THE ULTIMATE FISHING BOOK

Edited by
Lee Eisenberg
and
DeCourcy Taylor

Featuring "A Fisherman's Seasons" by Geoffrey Norman

Galahad Books
New York

First Galahad Books edition published in 1991.

Galahad Books
A Division of Budget Book Service, Inc.
386 Park Avenue South
New York, NY 10016

Galahad Books is a registered trademark of Budget Book Service, Inc.

Published by arrangement with Houghton Mifflin Company.

Library of Congress Catalog Card Number: 81-6605

ISBN: 0-88365-778-3

Printed in China.

Art direction and design: DeCourcy Taylor

Arthur Parton, *Fishing Scene* (1878).

George Inness, *Pompton, New Jersey* (ca. 1865).

CONTENTS

N. C. Wyeth, *A Primitive Spearman* (1913).

Acknowledgments

The editors would like to thank the following for their invaluable help in gathering the art and illustrations for this book: Gordon Wasley, who scouted the sporting galleries and museums of New York City; Paul Schullery and JoAnna Sheridan of the Museum of American Fly Fishing, Manchester, Vermont, who provided access to their fine collections; Jim Merritt, who guided us through the extensive Kienbusch Collection at Princeton University; Major B.D.M. Booth of the Tryon Gallery, London; and Chester Marron, who pointed the way to useful sources of American magazine illustration. Others who were generous in the contribution of paintings and prints were John R. Schoonover of Schoonover Studios, Wilmington, Delaware; Douglas Allen, consultant to *Sports Afield;* William End of the L.L. Bean Company; Jim and Judy Kaiser; Carolyn Wyeth; John Merwin of *Rod and Reel* magazine; Stan Friedman of U.P.I.

We would also like to cite the following galleries and dealers for providing a wide range of artworks: Jack Brewton of Collectors Choice, Santa Ana, California; Fred King of the Sportsman's Edge; John Dodge, Concord, Massachusetts; William Greenbaum, West Gloucester, Massachusetts; Meredith Long, Houston, Texas; Bernard and S. Dean Levy, New York City; the Grand Central Gallery, New York City; the Schweitzer Gallery, New York City; the Hirsch & Adler Galleries, New York City; Coe Kerr Gallery, New York City; the Old Print Shop, New York City; and the Kennedy Galleries, New York City. York City; and the Kennedy Galleries, New York City.

In addition, we are indebted to the following museums for their kind cooperation: the Fogg Museum of Harvard University; the Museum of Fine Arts, Boston; the Delaware Art Museum; and the Adirondack Museum, Blue Mountain Lake, New York.

By giving generously of her time and solid advice, Barbara Wood helped mightily in the development of the text in this book. Her editorial judgment was sound and enlightened throughout. We would also like to thank Priscilla Flood of *Esquire* magazine; and Angus Cameron, who talked to us about writers and writing.

We are grateful to Austin Olney of Houghton Mifflin for his staunch support of *The Ultimate Book* series; and to Dan Okrent and Harris Lewine, co-editors of *The Ultimate Baseball Book,* which set the high standards of text and design that we tried to honor in this volume. We would also like to thank Bruce McCall and agent Liz Darhansoff for their continued encouragement and friendship.

Finally, we would like to offer our appreciation to Geoffrey Norman for helping us arrive at the format of *The Ultimate Fishing Book* and, no less important, for his pleasurable streamside companionship.

INTRODUCTION

During the research for this book, I found myself one afternoon sitting on the floor of an old house in Manchester, Vermont, staring up at shelves that held hundreds of books about fishing. The volumes ranged from Bergman's *Trout* to Schwiebert's *Trout,* from nineteenth-century handwritten diaries to tacky magazines from the thirties, from tomes about bass fishing in the Ozarks to manuals that told boys how to put a worm on a hook and how to get a bluegill off. *Everything has been said,* I thought, not the least perturbed. Everything has been said: elaborated on, argued with, and twisted all around to the point that it had to be said again. And it had been said not only in words as sparklingly clear as a remote Alaskan river, but also in words as malodorously turgid as the Hudson off Battery Park.

The reason for those shelves at the Museum of American Fly Fishing, the reason for those words, is simple enough: given the chance, the passionate fisherman would fish all the time. But he can't. There are deals to close, lawns to mow, turkeys to carve. There are snowstorms in some places, hurricanes in others. The passionate fisherman must get his sport where he can, when he can, even if it's from books, diaries, magazines. Fortunately for him, the printed action is pretty good. As Sparse Grey Hackle first said, as Arnold Gingrich said again, as countless others have parroted, *Some of the best fishing is done in print.* Indeed. So the passionate fisherman (whether he masquerades as a businessman or a gardener or a dad) puts down his pocket calculator or his rake or his serving fork, or comes in out of the snow or rain, and picks up something to read. And it's magic: one minute he's in Pittsburgh; the next he's waist-deep in the Miramichi, having vicariously managed to outfox a twelve-pound Atlantic salmon.

That's one side of the reason, the reader's side. The other side is that some people who fish are never content until they've told others *what* happened, what *didn't* happen, what *might* have happened—a practice that makes this pastime unique among all sports. One minute the writer is knee-deep in the Beaverkill; the next he's up to his ears in sentences—venting his frustrations, trumpeting his conquests, or merely passing on his techniques.

I was delighted to find that there wasn't another book on those shelves quite like this one. The intention here was to bring together a congenial fishing party of nine distinct voices, each to address an aspect of the sport. I was not after fishermen who like to write, but rather writers who love to fish. Only three of the contributors can be said to be professional fishing scribes—and they are three of the best: Schwiebert, Waterman, and Williams (who is not to be confused with that other Ted Williams, the Hall of Famer who has also been known to wet a line). The six other contributors write novels, essays, and book reviews for a living—that is, when they're not out fishing.

The intention was also to gather, then combine in interesting ways, fine art, quality illustration, and rare artifact. Paintings that hang in major museums here and abroad are therefore displayed with drawings taken from century-old fishing catalogs; artwork once used on magazine covers is now united with photographs and objects found in private collections. Designer DeCourcy Taylor, who tirelessly netted the images, now can get back to the fishing he never had time for these past two years.

The material has been arranged according to the seasons. For the fisherman's life—not only within a given year but over *all* his years—*is* so arranged, from the hopeful morning of his springtime to the melancholy dusk of his winter. The saga is told by Geoffrey Norman, whose vision and friendship helped mightily throughout this project.

A final note: Despite its rather grand title, this book does not tell all. It fails to teach the reader how to tie a double nail knot. It contains not a single tip for winning cash prizes in a bass tournament. It offers no recipe for chum. The purpose here is to evoke, not instruct, and to say some of the same old things about fishing—but to say them as beautifully as they've ever been said before.

—L.E.

SPRING

It is the time when a boy's thoughts turn to the mystery and adventure that abound beneath the surface of a nearby pond or stream. And it is the time when a man's thoughts turn again to the feel and the sound of cold, clean water. It is a time of pure expectation.

A Fisherman's Seasons

By Geoffrey Norman

WHEN YOU THINK OF FISHING, you almost inevitably think in seasonal images. The fisherman is nearly as alert to the seasons as the poet. He thinks of spring hatches, summer doldrums, and fall runs. Every fishing story is given a seasonal background. One of the finest works in the literature of fishing is a tetralogy by Roderick Haig-Brown called, simply, *Fisherman's Spring, Fisherman's Summer, Fisherman's Fall,* and *Fisherman's Winter.* To the fisherman, Haig-Brown is not so much using a literary device as thinking about his sport in the obvious way.

So it is convenient to think of the fisherman's life using seasonal metaphor. The fisherman begins as a boy, young and green and eager. He is all enthusiasm and has not had time to learn any of the bad habits that fishermen pick up easily and discard with great pain—fish hogging, for instance. And lying.

This is the spring of a fisherman's life. Perhaps the best thing about it is that there is time to fish, which does not seem like so much to a boy. A surplus resource is nothing special to its owner; probably no Arab holds oil in intrinsically high esteem. But time is precious to the adult fisherman, as the boy will soon learn. *No fisherman ever fishes as much as he wants to*—this is the first great law of fishing, and it explains a world of otherwise inexplicable behavior.

Boys have more time to fish than, say, young men who have conflicting claims on their time. Young families and young careers between them leave almost no time for fishing. When there is time, the weather is impossible, a man's in-laws are coming, or his wife would rather play golf. What fishing the young man manages is done on two-week vacations or weekends or, if he is fortunate enough to live near some good water, for an hour or two before or after work. I know a man who takes his tackle to the office and fishes on his lunch hour. But it is never enough.

When you are young, time seems to glide by, slow and stately, like a spring creek. Failure does not cut so deeply because there is always tomorrow and another tomorrow. With time you can study, experiment, ruminate, and learn. Years later, at a time too distant for you actually to believe in, you will pay money to other men—guides—for their accumulated wisdom and experience. But for now, you build your own fund almost without realizing it.

But where does a boy begin? How does he get started?

Almost all fishermen start fishing as boys. Most learn from a grown man, usually their father, sometimes a relative or friend, and occasionally an older boy, a pal. Hardly anyone learns to fish absolutely alone or from a paid instructor, the way one might learn, say, to ski. Today there are several good fishing schools run by tackle manufacturers or famous fishermen. The schools are probably the answer for an adult who is just starting out; after a certain age it is more comfortable, better for the self-esteem, to keep things on a professional basis. But if you are a boy, it is better to learn from somebody older, and best of all to learn from your father. It is one thing you will be able to share across later generational conflicts. Fishing and its values are more or less constant.

Every fisherman I have spoken to on the subject says that he started fishing in his mind before he ever went out on the water. Perhaps he saw his father's tackle, stored neatly in a closet or study or workshop, and admired it the way a boy admires those material things that speak to him of manhood: razors, pipes, fine leather billfolds, expensive wristwatches. There is a message in fishing tackle. You need only to witness the passion it excites in grown men to believe that. Boys can feel the mystery, the tug, as well.

So a boy might start his life as a fisherman by putting together a tackle box. It is most likely a small metal thing, better suited to carrying nails, screws, and staples and extremely vulnerable to rust. In it he stores those random pieces of equipment he has been able to accumulate. Some of it is gear that his father has discarded, and some he has bought on his own. Some merely appears along the way, which is an unexplained property of fishing tackle known to every fisherman who has ever lived.

I can still remember my own metal tackle box. It stayed in a safe corner of my closet, except when I brought it out to clean and rearrange its contents—

which was almost nightly the first year I owned it. I had a handful of rubber-legged popping bugs for panfish, some leaders that I had tied up according to the formulas in a magazine article, a screwdriver, a pair of needle-nosed pliers, some Mucilin line dressing, and a homemade stringer. There was a scout knife that I had sharpened on a kitchen Carborundum, a pair of dime-store imitation aviator's glasses, a Chap Stick, and a bottle of 6-12 insect repellent. I was ready long before my father ever asked me to go fishing with him.

I was growing up in the South when I put that tackle box together; hence its regional cast. A friend who grew up in the north woods remembers a box full of his father's discarded pike spoons and plugs. Some of them had been real fish catchers, and there were teeth marks in them. He took the treble hooks off the plugs with a tiny Phillips screwdriver and sharpened them with a rat-tail file and an emery board. Then he carefully repainted the balsa-wood bodies with "dope," a thick oil-based paint that was used on model airplanes before it became popular among sniffers. My friend's refinished plugs never looked quite as lifelike as they had when they were new. He couldn't paint scales, and the eyes were never quite right—sort of bug-eyed, and a little deranged, he remembers. But the colors were as vivid as anything that could be found anywhere, and they seemed to attract pike.

My friend remembers coils of piano-wire leader at the bottom of his metal box, some of which had been kinked and straightened. There was a glove in there, and a hickory priest which he had carved himself and intended to use on pike too large to be subdued in any other way. He thinks he may have also carried a few sticks of venison jerky in the box.

A boy whose father fished only for trout would naturally have a different box, full of old dry flies with flattened hackles and wets that had been cast and soaked until they were coming apart. Such a boy would spend time in the kitchen, at the stove, holding those mashed flies over the escaping steam of a hot kettle. If the damage was not too severe, that would restore the flies to a usable condition. He would probably have more odds and ends in the box than the boy whose father fished for bass or pike; the trout fisherman tends to collect miscellany. He buys gadgets to take the temperature of streams and measure the thickness of leaders and pump the stomachs of the fish he catches—and then, the next season, he gets rid of everything in his vest except for one fly box and a spool of tippet. When a trout fisherman feels the urge to simplify, something like a purge follows. So his young son inherits all sorts of specialized devices: gadgets for tying knots in the last ten minutes of twilight, and leader straighteners attached to spring-loaded spools. His tackle box may look more like something that belongs to a seamstress than to a fisherman.

But a boy's tackle box is not a real measure of anything except his desire to fish. The urge to equip is endemic in fishermen, and it reveals itself at an early age. It cannot be extinguished, only disciplined and tempered.

Most young fishermen also begin to read about the sport before they actually practice it. This is another curious but inevitable development, and one that is seldom outgrown. Fishermen continue to read about fishing and tackle until they die. Why is this?

I don't know. Arnold Gingrich, the founder of *Esquire* magazine and a legendary fisherman, used to say that some of the best fishing was done in print. It is true that no sporting activity has produced such a distinguished body of literature or attracted so many literary men. Fishing is both contemplative and tactile, and that makes it appealing to the literary sensibility.

I think another explanation for the vast amount of writing about fishing is buried in that first great rule of fishing: *No fisherman ever fishes as much as he wants to.* Perhaps the next best thing to fishing is reading about it—even if it

L.L.BEAN
MANUFACTURER
FREEPORT-MAINE
SPRING-1933

THE SILVER HOOK

The last resort of a veteran fly fisherman, as depicted
on the cover of the L. L. Bean catalog (1933).

A cartoon (1940) from H. T. Webster's "Life's Darkest Moments"
series, which ran in the *New York Herald Tribune*.

means reading the same story, in outline, over and over again, which is what most youthful readers do. *Field and Stream* is not *Harper's* or *Paris Review*, but it satisfies an urge to experience vicariously what you cannot go out and do.

Outdoor magazines are for enthusiasts, and when one is an enthusiast, he reads everything about his passion. I knew a poet once, a man of rarefied taste and sensibility, who also happened to be a pretty good archer. He read Randall Jarrell and John Dos Passos for relaxation, but he also subscribed to the archery magazines and read them avidly, cover to cover, poring over the most predictable adventure yarns like an adolescent in the grip of Robert Louis Stevenson. When his passion was involved, the poet suspended literary and critical judgments. He simply read everything and loved everything he read.

There is a lot for young fishermen to read, and most of them start with the magazines that publish four-color photographs and easily followed narratives. Most of the "how-to" material is fairly basic and sound. A boy can read it in his room at night, when he should be doing his schoolwork, and actually learn something—the proper way to fish a streamer early in the season, say, when the spring runoff has swollen the river and there is no hope for a dry fly. The essentials of fishing do not change much over the years. But the technology changes all too rapidly, and the magazines are full of advertisements to excite the boy's already active interest in tackle. Every season the advertising pages are full of new tackle lines while the editorial pages remain devoted to the same familiar articles on how to take deepwater bass.

The boy who is ready to go fishing probably has a stack of magazines in his room, well thumbed and studied. He knows tackle brands and essential fishing techniques. He probably knows a few inelegant phrases—calls a smallmouth bass a bronzeback and a largemouth a hog, for instance—but he will probably outgrow that. If he has read the magazines dutifully, he knows some useful woodcraft and first aid, particularly the treatment for snakebite. No good outdoor magazine goes a year without publishing an article on snakebite.

The boy's already excited imagination might have been further stimulated by a reading of the Zane Grey fishing stories. Grey, as prolific in his outdoor writing as in his fiction, wrote dozens of yarns covering everything from floating the Delaware River for bass to trolling off Tahiti for giant black marlin. His fishing was obsessive and—there is no getting around it—the man could tell a tale.

So . . . let's say there is a young boy whose father is a fisherman and who has therefore collected a metal carpenter's box full of cast-off tackle, supplemented by a few items he has bought on his own. He is knowledgeable in an untutored fashion. He probably knows about shooting heads and double hauls before he has even caught his first bluegill on a worm. Above all, he wants to go fishing.

Why? Well, let's just say because boys will be boys and let it go at that. Whenever you poke around motive, you come to a point beyond which everything is speculative and unverifiable. Fishermen fish. They have been doing it for a long time. Not many of them turn out too badly, and with most, fishing is their worst vice.

Most fishing is done with bait. It is the best way to catch fish. It is also the best way to learn how to catch fish with artificial flies and lures. So it is good and proper that most boys, when they start fishing, use bait. One hopes and expects that they will graduate to artificials, just as they will graduate from the sports and the comics to the front page and Joseph Kraft, from R. L. Stevenson to Ernest Hemingway, from *Playboy* to real women. But there is no need to rush things.

There are all kinds of bait: worms, grasshoppers, crickets, hellgrammites, minnows. Every now and then you'll hear about small mice being used. Or frogs. Even birds. Anything that fish eat in nature can be used for bait, and that means almost anything. I once found a nine-inch water moccasin in the stomach of a bass.

Highbrows may sniff at bait fishing and pass it off as boring, unimaginative,

William J. Schaldach, *Spring Note* (1930).

and somehow not quite civilized and fitting. Too many young fishermen who come from the cities believe that the path from Orvis to the Battenkill is Euclidian, a line of no depth and no width from which one does not deviate. To such a boy, brown trout have simply been bred to take Quill Gordons. It is what they *do.* For him, taking fish is a sterile matter of technique, not a question of slipping unobtrusively into the great chain of life and predation and living briefly by those ancient terms. Fishing does not have to begin with a Light Cahill on the Beaverkill and end with a Jock Scott on the Restigouche. Bait is the place to start, and there is no shame in going back to it from time to time. Snobs are made, not born, and most boys are happy to fish with bait and to gather their own. It is a kind of initiation. They learn about things like coffee grounds for keeping worms and a cardboard box with a forty-watt bulb for raising crickets. There is more to bait than buying it in waxed containers.

If you believe that fishing is, among many other things, an avenue to a mature appreciation of nature, you would be pressed hard to defend an opposition to bait. There is much to be learned in a lowly worm bed, not least the smell that is the first whiff most suburban boys ever get of fecund, decaying earth where the end and beginning of life are joined. Grasshoppers are more fun to gather than worms, calling for finesse and technique. If you move too slowly, you will never catch one; but if you use too much force, you will damage or kill those that you do catch. You must be quick but delicate. Catching grasshoppers can be as much fun as fishing with them. By the time a young fisherman leaves the grassy fields and heads for a stream, he almost always has more grasshoppers than he needs, and his fingers are stained with "tobacco juice."

So, with his metal box full of tackle, an old tin can full of coffee grounds and night crawlers, and a rod of some sort, our boy is ready to go fishing, if he can find someone to take him or someplace to go. Let's say he starts out by going with some other boys to a nearby lake or pond, river or creek, bay or bayou.

What the boy sees first is the mask of water. The first time you look at any body of water, it is a mirror. Its surface reveals nothing; it only reflects what is above it. *Where are the fish?*

"I think that is what first hooks you," says a man I know. "It's the challenge, the idea that there is an answer but you've got to figure it out. Find it. The fish are in that river somewhere. Bound to be. But where? It's a mystery, and everybody loves a mystery." Especially boys.

The education of a fisherman truly begins when a boy first stands in front of water with tackle and bait in hand and asks himself where the fish are. This is the first question of any day's fishing. You do not ask what they are feeding on or what sort of cast is most likely to put a hook in front of the fish without spooking them. First you have to know where they are. And even before that, you have to know how to look for them.

"Four-fifths of the earth's surface is covered with water," a fisherman once said, "but only five percent of that is good fishing water. The rest is useless, good only for bathing, drinking, waterskiing, and Niagara Falls. The hardest part of fishing is learning to read water. I can teach any fool to cast and work a fly and the rest of it. But reading water takes sense. And experience."

And in some cases these days, he might have added, sonar comes in handy.

The modern bass fisherman has a depth finder on his boat that not only tells him how much water he is fishing over, but also paints a picture of the bottom and indicates the presence of any schooled fish. The technique he uses—and it isn't as easy as it sounds—was developed and refined on the huge lakes built principally in the South by the Army Corps of Engineers. When the reservoirs first started appearing, fishermen would study topographical maps of the terrain before it had been flooded, then fish over the sites of old barns, roads, cemeteries, and anything else that might still be down there to provide good cover for the small fish that attract the larger fish. Eventually, the fishermen began to use depth finders, borrowed from their saltwater cousins, to help find the

The cover of an equipment catalog published by the Martin L. Bradford Company (ca. 1910).

sunken structures they were looking for. Before long they were calling the technique structure fishing. Then there were tournaments and professional fishermen. All sorts of new tackle came along. A fleet appeared—weekend fishermen in boats rigged out with depth finders, 150-horse engines, trolling motors, electrically lowered thermometers, and all sorts of other technology. Structure fishing for bass replaced bowling, fistfighting, and coon hunting in the affections of southern men with time on their hands. An extreme was reached when Tom Mann, tackle manufacturer and tournament fisherman of note, began teaching a credited course in a junior college in Eufaula, Alabama. The course was called Structure Fishing.

That is one way of reading water if you are faced with acres and acres of flooded farmland upstream of an Army Corps dam. If you are a boy facing a small creek or pond, the magnitude of the problem and the tools for solving it are not the same. The problem, however, is: Where are the fish? Where are the good cover and the food that they need to survive?

One way for a boy to find out is to get into the water, something a trout fisherman in all his dignity would rarely even consider. But that is the best way to find water deep enough to make a swimming—and fishing—hole on a small midwestern river. It is also the best way to determine that the bank downstream from an old sycamore is deeply undercut and a fine cover for smallmouth bass. You can find firm bottoms with gravel and shells in warm southern lakes the same way, then come back later with a cane pole and a bucket of worms and fish for bedding bluegills. When you actually get into a small trout stream, you can feel the cold water of hidden springs when it comes out of the earth. In hot weather, trout come to this cool, oxygen-rich water.

Boys can also simply lie on the bank of a stream and watch, without feeling that they are wasting time. Sooner or later a fish will reveal itself—sometimes only as a shadow moving after an invisible minnow or insect, then dashing back to cover; sometimes as a splashy surface strike. And occasionally a fish will completely clear the water in furious pursuit of some flying thing.

Once a boy knows where to fish—or has an approximate idea—there is nothing left but to go ahead and do it. So he rigs up and puts a line into the water. I think most boys' hands are probably quivering a little when this happens. It is undeniably a large moment in a young life, a fulfillment and a promise as well, a mystery for which most boys lack the vocabulary but not the sensibility.

The water is there, right in front of you, moving, shimmering, and concealing the fish. No matter how long you have studied water, or how well you can read it, there is always something a little foreign and mysterious about it. It is another element, a different medium, and, especially if it is flowing water, it is always changing. A river this moment is not exactly as it was a minute ago or as it will be a moment from now. Moving water is constantly remaking itself, like some form of plasma, and that is its fascination, the reason you can stand and watch it for long periods without becoming bored. You are watching something alive.

And there is life within that life; in the case of a trout stream, more life than you can imagine, a whole system of life in which the fish is only one player. There is microscopic life, vegetable and animal, which sustains all kinds of insects, small fish, and crustaceans. Mayflies, caddis flies, sculpins, dace, shrimp . . . all are food for the trout. These, in turn, sustain the birds and the otters and the occasional larger, cannibalistic trout. There are beavers and muskrats, minks and otters, waterfowl and stalking birds, and larger animals that come to the banks to feed and drink.

It is humbling for a boy—for anyone who has not lost the capacity to be humbled—to stand in the midst of so much life. The experience takes you out of your accustomed position in the center of the universe and puts you into an insignificant crowded orbit along with millions and millions of other creatures. Your feeble impermanence hits you with the force of sheer fact. You are merely one more living creature. If you should actually catch a fish, and hold it in your hand, the connection will be that much firmer.

Gifford Pinchot and his son by a trout stream in the 1930s.
An adviser to Teddy Roosevelt, and known as "the father of the
U.S. Forest Service," Pinchot spent years on the Sawkill River
in Pennsylvania, where, he once wrote, "the colors of sky and
land and water were almost enough to drown the love of fishing."

The best fish to start with, though, is not a trout. Boys should learn about trout after they have learned about girls. Trout, and trout rivers, are sensuous and unpredictable. They frustrate more than they reward, and they have a way of making you feel inadequate. The place to start is with panfish.

For a boy, panfish are as abundant as time. They are not particular about what they eat, and they make fine eating (as the name implies) themselves. They live in all kinds of accessible water. They can survive fishing pressure and the unavoidable pollution that goes with even the best-scrubbed version of modern life. It is as difficult to conceive of panfish as a threatened species as it is to imagine the extinction of armadillos or jackrabbits. Panfish have good shape and color. They are scrappy enough to be justly labeled game fish, and they are not especially temperamental. You can use several different techniques to catch panfish: flies, spinning lures, and all sorts of bait.

Bluegills, yellow perch, crappie—these are all boys' fish. There are plenty of grown men who fish for them with something approaching lust, but they are stalemated fishermen who have never grown in the sport, meat fisherman, generally, for whom the mystery has long since died. Even in fishing you must find a way to grow.

So boys start out on panfish, using crickets or worms. The first fish is not to be believed. He is kept alive on a stringer that is hauled out of the water for repeated study, then lowered reverently into the water again. Then raised for another look. First catch. It could not be more lovely: the faint yellow or red of the breast; the dark ears leading off the gill plates; the puckered mouth; the sturdy, compact body; the smell that is earth and water and something else, something that won't wash off easily. A fine mystery, those small fish. Just right for a boy.

It is important for a boy to be able to catch something. Boys do not see the virtues of a strictly contemplative exercise. Any number of fathers have ruined fishing for their sons by starting them on difficult bass or trout water. The thing seems hard to begin with—all that technique and complicated jargon—and when you don't catch any fish, it becomes another tedious chore, like cutting the grass or washing the car. A boy who starts this way may get discouraged and quit for good.

But all boys can master the rudimentary techniques required for taking panfish. And since the fish are cooperative, the boy who genuinely likes fishing will soon bring home full stringers. It is a grand feeling for a boy to provide supper for the family by his wits and skill. But even that pales eventually, and the boy begins thinking about bigger fish and more exotic techniques. It is a passage, of sorts, though the boy isn't likely to reflect on that very much. But if he has decided to move up from simple bait fishing for panfish to something else—say, casting popping bugs for bass—he is acknowledging another fundamental fishing truth: *There is more to it than merely catching fish.*

You don't have to be Zane Grey to feel a need to expand the scope of your fishing, but his example is instructive. He was a man too driven to be likable, and he could not be satisfied by anything less than an unbeatable world's record for ocean game fish. He wrote touchingly of his days on the Delaware River; there was some proportion and even a little wit in his stories of those early fishing days. He became a very rich man from the sale of his Westerns, and he used his money to fish the most exotic waters of the globe. Grey pioneered some of the basic big-game fishing techniques. Certainly he did more than any man of his time—or any other, perhaps—to generate interest in billfishing. His stories about giant marlin and swordfish are exciting as only the stories of titanic struggles can be. In one of them he tells of battling a fish that he was certain would be a record. After hours of fierce physical effort, he had the fish nearly beaten and at the boat. Then the sharks appeared. The fish was mutilated, but Grey and the crew managed to get it aboard the boat before the sharks devoured it entirely. Even with a couple of hundred pounds of flesh gone, along with most of the blood in its body, the fish weighed over half a ton. It would have been the record that Grey sought so passionately, except

Zane Grey in 1936.

that mutilated fish were not recognized by the authorities of the time. It is an exciting yarn with an extra twist, but it lacks a certain nuance that is present in Grey's reminiscences of days on the Delaware. Fishing, for him, lost something important as he grew obsessed with bigger and more exotic fish. But one suspects that the man had no choice in the matter. We are talking about passion, after all.

Then there was Ernest Hemingway. No other writer has matched his descriptions fishing small rivers for trout. He captured the scene and mood of fishing flawlessly. In his novel of aimless expatriation, *The Sun Also Rises,* there is a brief account of a fishing trip in the mountains of Spain that is as keenly perceived as anything in literature. Yet Hemingway, too, was driven to increasingly larger fish and more brutal methods. His story about a giant fish being devoured by sharks does have feeling, but the fish was not his. He became consumed by big-game fishing almost as he lost his literary gift for subtlety and began to play to his weaknesses as a writer. His tales of marlin fishing off Cuba are spoiled by mock heroics and dubious duty. They seem cheap and easy next to his earlier vivid accounts of fly-fishing on small streams.

Without putting too fine a point on it, I think one could argue that these two men—both giant egos to be sure—lost the sense of proportion that is essential to fishing and, if one is an Aristotelian, to all of life. Instead of willingly taking a small place in the larger scheme, as a boy fishing on a river with worms does, they shut out the world and did lonely battle, one on one, with giant fish. It was combat they sought, and some kind of recognition. Their fishing took an ugly, obsessively competitive turn, and it was, at bottom, unhappy.

There was never a chance that they would stay with crickets, bamboo poles, and panfish. The challenge of bluegills and perch thins with time. *This is easy and anyone can do it,* a boy says to himself. He knows about tackle and other techniques from the magazines, and he is ready to try. It is absolutely inevitable that he will want to catch larger fish and own fine tackle. But there is no sure moral outcome. The possibility of corruption is there. The eager boy may become a bragging, fish-hogging boor who fishes to keep score and prove something. But the other possibility is there, too. He may become a fine fisherman and a man with enough wit to see his sport and even himself for what they are. Salvation lies in keeping part of the boy alive in the maturing man.

John Voelker writes (under the nom de plume Robert Traver) of sitting on the bank of a river as a boy and watching as the man he wanted to become caught a large trout. Voelker, having fished all day with primitive equipment and unpolished technique, was frustrated and impatient, and he had climbed out of the river to rest and think. Maybe it was not going to work out with him and fly-fishing, he thought. Perhaps the ingredients just weren't there. He wasn't doing half as well with tackle as he had always done with bait.

He watched the Michigan river flow slowly past. Then a fish rose to something in the pool just below him: As Voelker watched, the fish rose again. He sighed and got up to try again with his hand-me-down steel fly rod and a discarded streamer, which he describes as a "feathered anvil." The fish rose again. A feeding pattern was apparent, and Voelker was about to step into the stream to take advantage of it when he noticed another fisherman, downstream from him, working his way slowly toward the pool where the solitary fish was rising. Voelker climbed back up the bank and chose a spot from which he could watch the stalk unfold.

The fisherman turned out to be an old man who was casting a dry fly with a delicate, whippy cane rod. He made precise casts and worked each one out all the way before lifting the little fly off the water, drying it with a couple of effortless false casts, then sending it out on the water for another float. The old man worked each likely-looking spot with the same measured and deliberate care; his attention never seemed to waver. Then he looked upstream and saw the rising fish. Instead of passing by the intervening water and going directly upstream to the pool, he turned back to the section of the river where he was standing and fished it carefully and patiently, with no show of haste or urgency.

Ernest Hemingway (right) as a young fisherman
before he went after bigger game.

He came on, casting and following out each cast, false casting to dry the fly, then casting it onto the water again. It was a rhythmic and lulling scene, except for the presence of the fish, which continued to rise in the pool just below the hidden Voelker, who could hardly stand it. That fish was ready; what was the old man waiting for?

As the man came on his deliberate way, Voelker could see that he was truly old—not far from doddering. Voelker was surprised that he could wade at all, much less upstream in the correct dry-fly fashion.

Finally the old man was in range. Voelker could hardly contain his excitement, but the old man was still calm. He inspected his fly and decided to tie on another. He looked through two or three fly boxes before he found the pattern he wanted. He knotted the new fly to his tippet and trimmed the excess gut and hackle. He dressed the fly with a little something to make it float better, and then, when all was ready and everything was back in the proper pocket of his vest, he began false casting and timing the trout's rises. Finally he shot a perfect cast, and the fly landed three or four feet upstream of the fish on a perfect quartering angle. Voelker held his breath as the little speck of hackle and feather rode downstream on the surface film. He almost shouted when the fish took.

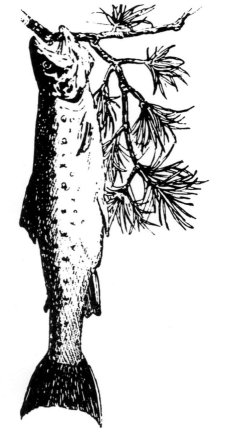

The old man had a time with the fish, which turned out to be a large one. Two or three times he shipped water over the tops of his waders as he changed position to follow the fish. There were several fine runs and splashy attempts to fall back on the leader and break it. But the old man held, and finally he brought the fish in next to his hip and scooped it in his landing net. The fish lay bowed in the fabric sack, too tired to move, as the old man turned his catch from one side to another to admire it. Then he reached down into the net and, with the dainty care of a surgeon, took the hook from the trout's mouth. He picked the tired fish up with gentle hands and lowered it into the water. He held it for a few seconds while its strength returned and its gills began to take in water again. Then he let the fish go. He inspected his fly for damage, found none, began false casting, and once again made his precarious way upstream, working every bit of likely water. Voelker, still watching from his concealed position, decided that was the man he would grow up to be.

All this happened more years ago than Voelker admits. But the lesson took. When I fished with Voelker at his secret pond in north Michigan, he had become that man . . . and a little more. He is a fishing sage who is known best as the author of *Anatomy of a Murder,* but he probably likes that book less than his two volumes of fishing stories collected under the titles *Trout Madness* and *Trout Magic.* Voelker was a justice of the Michigan Supreme Court, then quit when he could afford to, which was after *Anatomy* became a best-seller. (That may be one way of beating the first great law of fishing—*No fisherman ever fishes as much as he wants to*—but it is far from surefire.) In retirement Voelker fishes and writes about fishing and has a fine time. He may have become that man, but he is still that boy, too.

There is no sin in a boy's catching and keeping more panfish than he needs. The point is to catch fish, after all; and if one fish is good, two must be better. If twenty bluegills make a nice stringer, forty are twice as good. The untutored fishing sensibility wants more and bigger fish. And until a boy has caught some fish and put them on a stringer, he probably will not be satisfied with anything less. A boy raised on catch and release probably cannot see the point. The thrill of the release—and it is a thrill—is something that has to be learned.

In a paradoxical way, sport fishing has kept fish populations healthy. As a boy becomes more serious about fishing, there is less of a threat that he will endanger any species. A big score becomes less important. Something else becomes the end of his fishing. It is elusive and not, sadly, for everyone.

The important thing becomes *doing it right.* It has something to do with style and something to do with manners. A lot of it is sheer technique that can be learned only through instruction and application. When a boy is ready to leave panfish, cane poles, and night crawlers, the hard work begins.

Say he wants to learn how to use a fly rod. He knows through reading and perhaps an experience similar to Voelker's that this is where the path will ultimately take him. Before he can do anything, however, he must learn about the tackle and the way it works. It isn't easy. Listen:

"If you have never picked up a fly rod before, you will soon find it factually and theologically true that man by nature is a damn mess. The four-and-a-half-ounce thing in silk wrappings that trembles with the underskin motions of the flesh becomes a stick without brains, refusing anything simple that is wanted of it. All that a rod has to do is lift the line, the leader, and the fly off the water, give them a good toss over the head, and then shoot them forward so they will land in the water without a splash in the following order: fly, transparent leader, and then the line—otherwise the fish will see the fly is a fake and be gone. . . .

"Well until man is redeemed he will always take a fly rod too far back, just as natural man always overswings with an ax or golf club . . . only with a rod it's worse, because the fly often comes so far back it gets caught behind in a bush or a rock. . . .

"Then, since it is natural for man to try to attain power without recovering grace, he whips the line back and forth making it whistle each way, and sometimes even snapping off the fly from the leader, but the power that was going to transport the little fly across the river somehow gets diverted into building a bird's nest of line, leader, and fly that falls out of the air into the water about ten feet in front of the fisherman. If, though, he pictures the round trip of the line, transparent leader, and fly from the time they leave the water until their return, they are easier to cast. They naturally come off the water heavy line first and in front, and light transparent leader and fly trailing behind. But as they pass overhead they have to have a little beat of time so the light transparent leader and fly can catch up to the heavy line now starting forward and again fall behind it; otherwise the line starting on its return trip will collide with the leader and fly still on their way up, and the mess will be the bird's nest that splashes into the water ten feet in front of the fisherman."

And so on, until the author, Norman MacLean, remembers his instructor and his wisdom: "My father was very sure about certain matters pertaining to the universe. To him, all good things—trout as well as eternal salvation—come by grace and grace comes by art and art does not come easy."

It is easier—a little—today. The tackle is better and standards are so subjective in fly-fishing—as in almost everything else—that they have virtually ceased to be standards at all. I was taught to cast by keeping a book tucked between my upper arm and my body, so that only the forearm and wrist operated the rod. Lefty Kreh, top rod among present-day fly casters, uses forearm, upper arm, shoulder, and body in a casting technique that is not so much unorthodox as heretical. The emphasis is on what works for you, in fly-fishing as in too many other things. As long as you can put power to your line and keep a tight loop, you are doing fine. The measure of your ability is whether you can get the fly out where you want it without scaring the fish.

But that is a tall enough order, and whatever system you settle on, it takes practice before you can cast well enough to fish with a fly rod. Many, many boys have spent countless hours practicing on lawns, where things are a little easier without the current of the stream to contend with. Even then it is hard to remember to pause at the top of the cast while the line straightens out behind; to control the slack with the left hand; to keep the rod tip up so that the loop won't collapse on the forward stroke. Clean pickup and shoot the line; over and over again until the vectors smooth and fuse into one dynamic that might look awkward to a bystander but feels fluid and natural to the caster.

But casting is not the end of learning. In fact, it is only the beginning. A boy needs to learn fly patterns. Some boys—those who are good at wood carving and model airplane building—may start tying flies, which almost certainly becomes a lifelong obsession.

Trout fishing calls for stealth and some tactical skills. Wading upstream and casting on a quarter to the river's flow do not come easily and naturally. When you step into running water, you want to walk and cast downstream. But sound methodology and a snobbish Anglo notion of the way things should be done demand that the dry fly—especially the dry fly—be fished upstream. It does come closer to imitating natural conditions than a downstream drift (though that seems less important in this world than in the old one that has passed forever into history, taking with it pocket watches, straight razors, and gentlemen). Handled properly, the dry fly bounces along the surface of the stream free of drag when it is fished upstream; that is, the action of the water on the line is not apparent in the float of the fly, and there is no telltale wake to alert the fish and put them off their feed. Drag is the sworn and constant enemy of the dry-fly fisherman. A boy learns that the first time he steps into a stream.

The feathery intricacy of trout fishing can daunt some boys. One does not have to be a hardened skeptic to doubt the whole proposition. The small fly does not really look like a mayfly at all, or like anything else that occurs in nature. The fine, fragile leaders don't look strong enough to hold a finger-sized bluegill, let alone a two-pound trout. Casting and wading still seem like dubious methods. Better to stay on the bank or get into a boat, to put something alive on the hook and leave it in the water until a fish eats it. Once again, the boy has to be convinced that the thing can be done. He needs to catch some fish.

Best, then, to start on a river that has plenty of fish and perhaps has a few stockers mixed with the natives. There will be plenty of time later for a boy to perfect his disdain for hatchery fish and natural bait. When he is young, all trout look the same, and he isn't concerned about pedigrees.

Even a good stream with a large population of natives and stockers and no-kill regulations is no sure thing, as any trout fisherman will tell you. The best thing that can happen to a young fisherman, then, is to be on a good stream during a major hatch: the Beaverkill during the shad flies; the Ausable during the Hendricksons; the Madison during the salmon flies. In the face of that kind of evidence, all skepticism vanishes. You can catch fish and you can see plainly why it is that you catch fish. Also, you are a witness to the cycle of life in its most intense, accelerated form. There is something frenzied and a little mad about it. It makes an impression on a boy, like watching the migration of thousands and thousands of geese driven by deep, unknowable instinct.

Another, and in some ways better, time to learn about trout fishing with the fly, and to witness the fact that it can be done, is during the hot middle summer. The streams are low then. They are almost naked, and everything is revealed in water that is clear as it is in no other season. This is the best time to learn how to "fish the water."

Also, in the middle of a hot summer day, you can fish big, visible flies that float high and bright instead of tiny mayfly imitations or the underwater nymphs or wets. When a boy locates a dark, shady cut bank with some overhanging grass and puts a Joe's Hopper on a no. 10 hook a few feet upstream of it and gets a solid brown for his trouble, he has learned a lot about trout fishing and has a good reason to stay with it. Furthermore, the early-season hatches can occur on cold and windy days when the fingers are too numb to change flies and a pinhole in your waders feels like a frozen ice pick. In the hot summer, standing hip-high in cold running water feels like just the thing.

There are all sorts of occurrences that can persuade a skeptical boy. I know one man who had been dutifully following his father around from stream to stream for most of one season years ago. He had two or three fish, hooked blind on wet Coachmans, for his trouble. It was late August, and he was ready to quit fly-fishing altogether and go back to Dardevles for pike and worms for bluegills.

He and his father were working their way upstream in a swift little brown river that ran through low, swampy country between walls of leafy tag alders. It was hot, so hot that he was steaming inside his rubber waders. Every few minutes he would take off his old cotton hat and dip it into the stream, then put it back on his head. The cool water dripping down his neck gave him some relief.

William J. Schaldach, *Sunny Run* (1937).

Cumulus clouds building to the west over Lake Michigan billowed and turned dark blue at the edges. Soon they had risen fully twenty thousand feet and turned the color of a day-old bruise. The air went cool and a breeze came up. The sudden drop of pressure was palpable.

There was some lightning and thunder, and the boy's father signaled for him to leave the river and meet him on the bank. The boy acknowledged and, as he was reeling in, felt the frustration of another day of profitless casting. As he was leaving the stream, he noticed some kind of small gray insect pop off the surface of the water. Then another. As he watched, the numbers multiplied, and soon he was witnessing a genuine hatch of some anonymous, late-season mayflies.

Fish began striking as the air became still, the way it does only in the last few minutes before a storm. The boy hastily tied on a fly, something small and gray. He made a cast to the nearest rising fish, which took the fly so eagerly that the boy thought at first it must be a mistake. Perhaps the fish was coming up and the fly had just drifted into its open mouth. He quickly brought in the brown, the nicest he had ever caught, and killed it with the back of a pocket-knife. The fish went into the creel that the boy had never before used. He cast to another rising fish, which took with as much urgency as the first. He played that one out and put it into the creel with the other, feeling that this one was truly earned. And so it went for ten or fifteen minutes. The lightning flashed into the tall cedars on either side of the river. The thunder rolled ponderously. And the boy fished on, putting his first limit of trout into his creel and taking his chances with the storm, which he did not notice anyway. The fishing ended when the rain finally collected and came in sheets, drowning the little insects and putting the feeding fish back down. The boy left the river giddy from the fishing and the storm's ozone. "I wouldn't do it again," he told me years later, "stand out in the middle of a river during an electrical storm with a nine-foot lightning rod in my hand. But I wouldn't trade that one time for anything."

With knowing how to use good tackle comes owning some. A boy's first rod may not be a collector's item and a work of art, but it is something special. He probably does not have to be told to take care of it and to treat it with respect. If he is told, he probably resents it.

This is the best time for him to learn about care and maintenance. He does not have the resources with which to replace rods and reels and the rest once they have fallen apart, and thus he has a strong incentive to take care of them. Taking care of tackle is also a good excuse to get it out and look at it and touch it. There is a kind of tactile fascination in the best tackle. You like to pick it up, even indoors, which is how a lot of rod tips get broken year after year. Ceilings run a close second to car doors and trunks as the rod repairman's best friend.

There was a time, not very long ago, when trout-fishing equipment demanded a great deal of care. All trout men fished with bamboo rods, silk lines, and gut leaders. The rod was varnished and waxed, its ferrules and guides cleaned carefully with soapy water. The silk lines had to be dried and dressed, the gut leaders soaked and kept in moist, soft flannel so that they would stay supple. Today, the average trout fisherman uses a graphite rod, plastic-coated line, and nylon leaders. The equipment is almost indestructible. But it still helps to keep it clean and dry, to store it in a safe place, and to check it for the small breaks and flaws that come with use.

Reels still need to be oiled. Waders need to be dried and patched and stored properly. Hooks need to be sharpened and cleaned from time to time. Rods can be waxed and occasionally rewrapped. But all this simply isn't as important as it once was. You could throw your gear into a closet at the end of the season and never look at it until Opening Day, when it would still be serviceable. But most fishermen still feel an obligation to take care of their tackle. It is a vestigial instinct but a good one, and one that boys should learn, because it is a reminder that fishing is a world of balance and equilibrium, a world that requires attention.

These days it is the fish and the rivers that require the attention. Boys are great at cleaning up stray beer cans and trash from the bottoms of trout streams. In groups they can do much more. In the Midwest once, I saw a troop of boy scouts at work on what they had made their spring project: a trout stream that had fallen into disrepair. Culverts had filled in, blocking the flow of the stream. Vegetation had been cleared from the banks, causing erosion. The stream had been badly bulkheaded and backwaters had developed. The debris of thoughtless picnickers and motorists littered the banks and the bottom.

The scouts got rid of the trash first, including two huge tractor tires and a refrigerator. Then they dredged the culvert, reseeded the banks, and bulk-headed with sandbags. Where the bottom was badly silted, they dredged it with a hand-operated pump and put down crushed limestone to help restore the correct pH. They even brought in some gravel to make spawning beds. When they were finished, after two months of busy Saturdays, the stream was a long way from its natural state, which it would never see again anyway; but it was textbook habitat, and it would hold fish and perhaps even sustain a natural spawning population. Watching those boys work would be enough to make you feel a little ashamed for all you had never done. And a little old, too.

Most things end naturally, if painfully, for a boy. He realizes he will never throw the ball like Bradshaw or hit like Alou. So he puts his toys away.

Fishing is not something you grow out of, but for some reason most boys walk away from it for a while. Automobiles and girls come along to take their time and attention. Boys grow up enough to make fools of themselves and terrify their parents the way they never did when they were digging for worms and going off to some secret pond to fish.

It is impossible to know why boys lose interest in fishing. It is not biology, because some boys never do. But most do and some, sadly, never come back. But it should be counted one of fishing's best features that you can always come back to it. That cannot be said of baseball and football, model airplanes, summer camp, swimming holes, and young flirty girls. As years pass you can recall those things and feel the ache, but you can never have them again. You can pick up a rod and go fishing, and if you haven't completely buried the boy in you, there will be something of the old sweet feeling of awe left. You can feel it long after baseball cards and catcher's mitts and bicycles have become dead objects. Even then, a fishing rod still has a magic feeling, a life. Fishing keeps us—part of us, anyway—boys forever.

Francis Golden, watercolor (1980).

OPENING DAYS:
A Trout Fisherman's Life in Springtime
By Ernest Schwiebert

HE FIRST TIME that I was old enough to join my father and his friends for the opening of trout season, on their annual pilgrimage to the Au Sable or Pere Marquette in northern Michigan, was the spring that he made the apple-tree swing for my birthday. Our family car had developed cardiovascular problems that winter, requiring major surgery on its valves, piston rings, and cylinders, and its malaise threatened our family budget in a year when the nation had not yet recovered from the Great Depression. Our summer vacation in the Wisconsin lakes was in jeopardy too, and birthday presents were simple: the apple-tree swing was born in our basement workshop. Its seat was five-quarter pine with holes carefully bored and sanded smooth, and a rough half-inch rope was snaked through between them to support the wood. It was hung from a high branch that I had been afraid to explore, just as I was frightened of strong currents on the Pere Marquette.

The mechanic who worked on our faithful Oldsmobile was a trout fisherman. His passion seemed strange, because there were no trout near Chicago and his boyhood had been spent in southern Indiana along the sluggish Ohio. His fishing was an obvious symptom of eccentricity and the stubborn disciplines of the born artisan, and he had seldom held a regular job working for the repair shops in town. My mother argued persistently that he drank and that his well-known affection for whiskey and fishing had weakened his character and capacity for work. But the man was such a skilled mechanic that he turned customers away from the oil-stained garage beside the Grand Trunk & Indiana.

My father took me along to the garage during the surgery on the Oldsmobile. Its oil-covered entrails were everywhere. Pistons and spark plugs and other parts lay mixed with generators and fan belts and gaskets. Tools and discarded fenders and tomato cans of bolts covered the floors and workbenches. There was order in the mechanic's work, but its disciplines were hidden in his mind. It was perhaps the secret of his friendship with my father, who could navigate the clutter of his campus office and the labyrinths of Latin and German grammar but was incapable of tuning the radio.

Their friendship flowered over the scattered remains of the Oldsmobile, and later in the week, when the work on the engine was nearly finished, the mechanic started talking about trout fishing and his favorite brook-trout tributaries in the cedar thickets farther north.

"He told us a lot of secrets," I said, as we emerged from the dark little garage beside the railroad tracks.

"He's decided that he likes us," my father explained. "He probably can't afford his regular trip to Michigan this summer and he wants us to fish his places."

"You mean fish them for him?"

"Something like that." My father nodded. "We don't really have the money this year either, but we're going up for Opening Day—would you like to go along this time?"

"You mean it?" I stammered.

"That's right." My father smiled. "We think you're finally big enough to go with us."

Spring comes slowly in trout country, its timid fiddlebacks and marsh marigolds and violets pushing through the winter leaves, while farther south the fruit trees are already bright with blossoms. The winter chill retreats grudgingly from the jack-pine moraines and cedar bogs of northern Michigan. Both wild flowers and flowering orchards are familiar portents of the coming spring, but the secret heart of the trout fisherman is doubtful until Opening Day.

Chicago and the steel mills farther south were somber in the dull spring rain, but the weather improved when we reached Michigan. Entire hillsides were cherry blossoms and flowering apple trees where the old concrete highway wound north along Lake Michigan. Our route passed through Saugatuck and Benton Harbor and Holland, with its fields of flowers. Spirea and yellow forsythia and lilacs filled the streets of big clapboard houses.

The wind from the lake was chill and brisk, but it was almost hot in the towns behind the sheltering dunes. The fresh breeze stirred whitecaps across the bright water, erasing our recent memories of its sullen winter surf. Beyond the jetties and broken pilings at South Haven, where we finally stopped for lunch in the afternoon, the ore boats steamed slowly toward the mills at Chicago or sailed back north, empty and riding high in the water, bound for the iron fields of Lake Superior.

The highway left the lake beyond Muskegon, turning inland through the cornfields and dairy farms and orchards above Grand Rapids. Our pilgrimage crossed the Muskegon at Newaygo, and the pastoral countryside dropped behind. The world of lakes and cedar swamps and forests began there, and spring was but a faint prelude. The rolling farm country and factories were soon forgotten, and the narrow concrete changed to gravel, reaching still farther north into the jack pines. The county roads along the rivers were axle-deep in yellow sand in those years, and beyond the Little Manistee the highway itself dwindled off until it was a sandy incision that wobbled uncertainly north into the scrubby forests. Twilight fog shrouded the lakes and cedar thickets before we reached our campsite, and the tumbling, pale-bottomed trout streams were totally unlike the sluggish silt-yellow rivers farther south.

It snowed the first night on the Little South, and our campfire guttered like a candle and went out, leaving us cold and shivering and struggling to keep warm under summer-weight down. There was a surprising dust of snow on our tents in the morning, and thick snow hung from the north-facing branches of the cedars. We broke camp quickly and abandoned it for the simple cabins near the river on the old Pere Marquette Highway, almost forgetting that it was Opening Day until the musty-smelling cabin was warm, with a brisk fire in the potbellied stove.

Breakfast was not hurried, because fly-fishing would be poor until the sun warmed the rivers and melted the spring snow. The fly hatches are sparse in late April. The old-timers knew that a few struggling *Taeniopteryx* and *Capnia* stone flies might emerge from the gravelly riffles in late morning. Their scattered activity might be mixed with that of some tiny slate-winged *Paraleptophlebia* flies. Sometimes a few trout would rise to these sporadic hatches, but there was still time for several cups of coffee and some last-minute fussing with equipment. The old-timers were secure in the knowledge that the best prospects for dry-fly work waited until well after lunch.

There was even time for the classics professor to dress a few Hendricksons, preening their delicately speckled wings of wood duck, spinning bodies of vixen fox dubbing, and matching a brace of shiny slate-colored hackles from a favorite gamecock cape. These dry flies imitated the best spring hatches of fat *Ephemerella* mayflies, which love warm spring afternoons, typically emerging after two o'clock in good weather. A particularly good hatch can stimulate a fine rise of trout.

Such rises can last as much as two hours when conditions are right, and a light drizzling rain with a steady barometer can trigger a regatta of fluttering *Ephemerella* flies, drying their wings on the current until they look like a flotilla of tiny sailboats. "You've never seen them because you've never fished this early before," the old professor explained while I watched him meticulously complete the fly in his vise, "but they're the best fly hatch of the year."

Good hatches are followed by thick mating swarms after the newly hatched flies have molted in the trees and willows. The dull-colored insects shed their immature skins, drying delicate crystalline wings that sparkle in the sun, and their slim bodies are a rich mahogany elegantly ringed in primrose. The males gather high above the river in the late afternoon, often attracting squadrons of hungry swallows, and they are finally joined in their rising and falling dance by the egg-filled females. Mating occurs over the river in mid-flight, and the graceful ballet ends at twilight, when the dipping females flutter low to wash their butter-colored eggs into the current.

"Sometimes the mating swarms produce good fishing, too." The classics professor concluded his lecture and smiled. "But it usually takes a warm evening with no wind."

Our leisurely schedule allowed my father to take me fishing in the mornings that weekend, limiting his fishing time to the late afternoon fly hatches, and we searched out some of the secret places described by our friend in the car-repair shop. His shrines were solitary places in the brushy creeks and headwaters, where a swift current worked over the bright gravel into dark little holes under the logs and willows. There was no room for fly-fishing

such streams, but my father stopped at Baldwin to buy some worms in a tomato can of rich loam.

Our first expedition led north past Government Lake to fish the Little Manistee above Peacock. We left the Oldsmobile where the logging trace stopped in a cedar thicket, and we circled the bog downstream through an abandoned farm. There were deer beds in the matted winter grass. The river flowed through another dense copse of cedars, and there were a few marsh marigolds mixed with the dead cattails in its bottoms. The current was still tea-colored with spring flowages from its headwater bogs, and it felt cold when we slipped into the shallows above a labyrinth of tangled logs. I swung the freshly baited hook out and dropped it into the current; it drifted deep until it tumbled along the bottom in the darkness under the logjam. My fingers were shaking with excitement, and there was a strong, throbbing tug when a trout darted from the shadows to gobble the wriggling worm. The fish were hungry in spite of the weather, and I took a limit of small brook trout and hatchery rainbows before we started back.

"Worms work pretty well this early," my father said as he stared past the windshield wipers into a chill spring rain, "but I don't believe the boys will find much dry-fly fishing this afternoon—you'll have to serve as quartermaster and supply the trout for suppers."

His dour prediction proved correct, although my father and his friends took a few good fish on wet flies and streamers along the Little South and the headwater riffles of the Pere Marquette itself, fish-ing their flies deep along the deadfalls and willows on undressed lines of British silk. Their bulging fly books were filled with old favorites. The retired doctor still fished a traditional three-fly cast and preferred a somber Dark Cahill, a Leadwing Coachman, and a small Black Gnat for early season. "I've gotten to the age when I like old things best," he explained over a tumbler of sour-mash whiskey, "and I like the look of those old flies."

"They're too much like a funeral parlor," the young pediatrician responded teasingly. "I like flies with more color—like the Royal Coachman and Parmachene Belle and Silver Doctor!"

"Taxi dancers!" the classics professor observed grumpily. "Painted ladies for foolish brookies and hatchery fish!"

Their good-natured challenges and joking lasted well into the night, with a roaring fire in our pot-bellied stove, but finally I fell asleep in spite of their laughter. My father drove north again on the second morning, and when we left the cottage the classics professor was singing hymns while he mixed a second batch of pancakes. "It's Sunday morning and a little psalm singing can't hurt this crowd much!"

"Prayers could help the fishing," the old doctor agreed in mock solemnity.

"The fish-truck boys are a better bet." The old professor stopped singing and flipped a pancake expertly. "But we've got to give them time to give the fish lobotomies before stocking—and then they teach them how to swim again."

My father was still laughing when we reached

Winslow Homer, untitled oil painting on a fan blade
(late nineteenth century).

Winslow Homer, *Casting for a Rise* (1889).

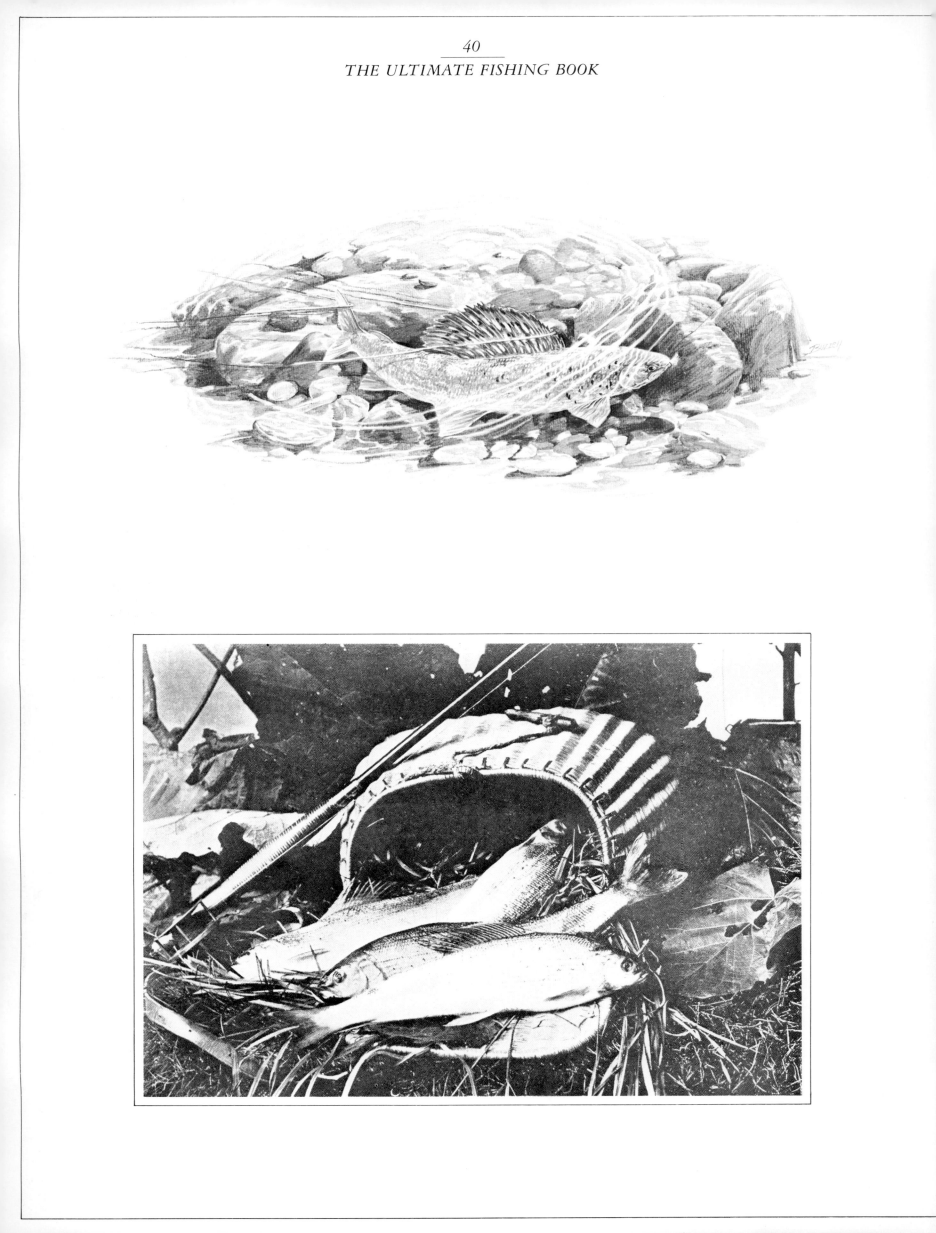

The Michigan grayling was a prized sport fish in the latter part
of the nineteenth century, though it would be virtually
extinct by 1900. According to Thaddeus Norris, writing in 1883,
the grayling was known locally as "white" or "Crawford County"
trout. On the facing page, grayling are depicted in a drawing
by Russell Buzzell and in a vintage photograph. Above, a painting
of a Michigan grayling taken from S. A. Kilburne's *Game Fishes
of the United States* (1878).

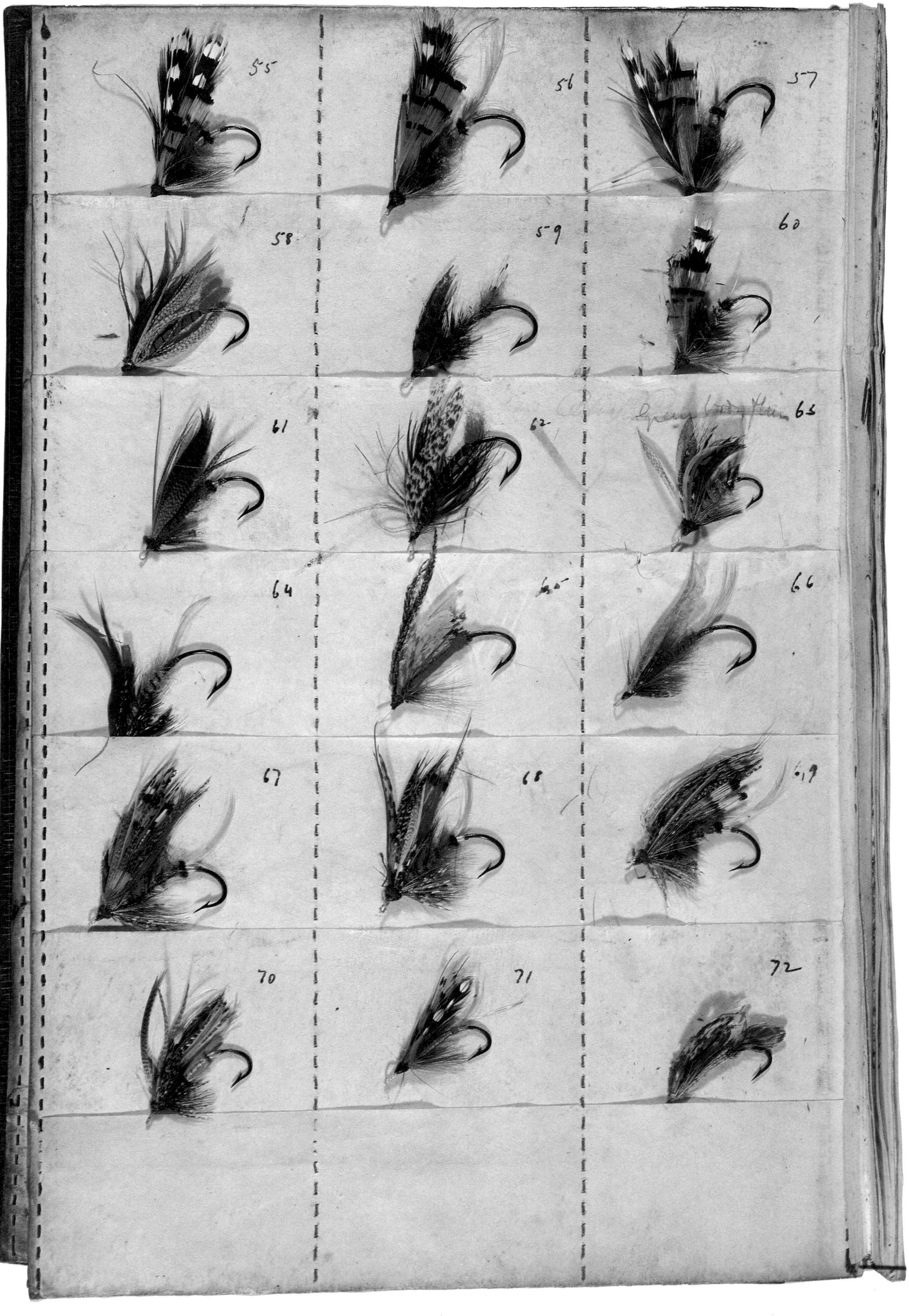
55
56
57
58
59
60
61
62
63
64
65
66
67
68
69
70
71
72

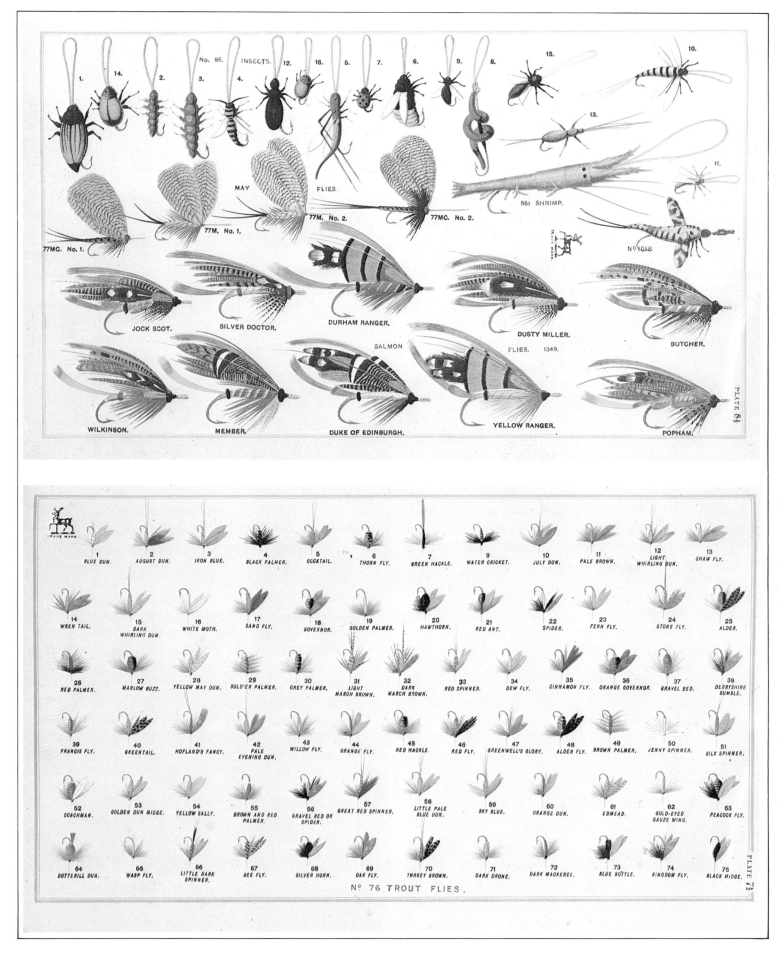

On the facing page, a parchment book of salmon flies from
turn-of-the-century Britain. Above, color plates showing an array of
artificials taken from the S. Allcock & Co. catalog (1887), England.

the highway, although he was a properly solemn worshipper almost every Sunday, looking grave and singing woefully off-key. We left the highway where the concrete ended east of Peacock and explored sandy traces that crossed creeks and rivers on rusty trusswork bridges. Pale gravel and fine sand sifted through their rattling floorboards as we passed in the resurrected Oldsmobile, until we finally reached the bridge across the Pine that our mechanic friend had recommended.

The Pine dropped swiftly from the cedars that choked its channel above the bridge, circling west into a series of serpentine bends that wound through an old hayfield where deer were browsing. Its currents were a little frightening that spring, sucking and throbbing through the fallen trees that lined its steep banks. Fountain mosses flowed with the currents, bright accents on the deadfalls lying deep in the bends. The river felt colder than the other streams, and it held only brook trout in those years, eager fish that waited lazily under the jack-straw tangles. The fish took my worms greedily under the logjams, pink-fleshed and fattened on sedge larvae, their sides shining with opals and tiny ruby spots and moonstones.

We filled my little split-willow creel with layered trout and fresh spring-bog mint and ferns. It rained hard again that afternoon, and my father stayed in our cabin struggling with galley proofs, while the classics professor taught me to dress Cahills.

We fished the crystalline Middle Branch several miles above the Forks Pool, where it joins the swamp-dark currents of the Little South to form the Pere Marquette itself. Its bends downstream from the culvert crossing were a series of brushy holes, and I simply stripped line downstream under the logs and willows to feed my worms along the bottom. There were freshly planted rainbows in every hole, and when my bait drifted and hung there briefly, it was quickly taken with an eager strike. The trout were guileless and greedy, and I creeled a limit of pale, red-striped fish in twenty minutes.

"They're not much fun!" I protested that my day's fishing was finished so quickly. "Hatchery rainbows are too easy!"

"We'll try some brown trout tomorrow," my father said.

Our last morning it rained hard, and we found the Little South roily and a little high when we drove upstream toward the Powers' Bridge.

"Our friend at the garage talked about big browns around Powers' Bridge"—I remembered our winter conversations—"particularly in the deep holes under the trees."

"Brown trout are pretty hard to catch." He smiled.

"I hope I can catch them," I sighed.

"They're the most difficult fish," my father suggested gently, "but with the river running a little

high and milky—you just might get a few browns this morning."

I fished downstream from the bridge, patiently working my worms through each likely-looking place. The trout were still eager after the rain, and I took several wild brookies in the shallows before I hooked a strong fish under the trees. It threshed wildly along the deadfalls there, its dark spotted sides above a butter-colored belly, and then it bolted deep under the logs.

It's a big brown! I thought wildly.

The trout bulldogged angrily, raking the leader along the logs on the bottom. Its surprising strength frightened me, and when I tried to stop its struggles, it easily broke the gut leader. The fish was gone, and I sat on a fallen tree, staring unhappily at the milky current, before I felt like fishing again. It was many years before I fully understood the importance of such failure in the sweetness of success.

Our first opening weekend together was past, and we drove back south through the sleeping villages and farms along the lake, arriving home long after midnight. The fly hatches had been poor, but my father and his friends seemed happy in spite of their luck, and there was a lot of merciless joking about needing a worm-fishing boy to supply the trout for their kitchen.

The other men in the party are all gone, although my father, at eighty-five, still fishes a little with me along the Brodheads in Pennsylvania. Since that April expedition before the Second World War, the memories of its fishing have strangely faded. Other things about our trip seem more important now. Good fellowship and stories and the perfume of fine pipe tobacco persist in my thoughts of that time. The fishing talk taught me a lifetime of secrets about trout and seeking them, and about how to feel about fishing. The sparsely tied dry flies that were miraculously given life in the skilled fingers of the classics professor, with their elegant wings and perfectly dressed hackles and classic British hooks, still influence the character and proportions of my own flies. I remember the effortless grace of the retired doctor's casting and the patient ballet of his amber silk working in the rain. But the most important lessons were the men's obvious affection and mutual respect, the unique dovetailing of their characters, and the fierce competition between them that was utterly without malice.

Time has also taught me imperceptibly that a first Opening Day is capable of spinning its silken web until facts and memories gradually embroider themselves into designs and patterns of impossible symmetry.

Opening Day has always been something more than the beginning of trout season. Serious fishermen have always believed that it is a better benchmark of springtime than the equinox itself, although its fickle weather often finds colonies of

Spring Trout Fishing in the Adirondacks: An Odious Comparison of Weights

Frederic Remington's drawing of early-season Adirondack trout
fishing (date unknown) originally appeared as a magazine illustration.
It was rendered in black-and-white, and color was later added in the engraving process.

Arthur Fitzwilliam Tait, born in Liverpool, came to America in 1850 and shortly thereafter discovered the beauty of the Adirondacks. He lived and painted in Chateaugay, Rainbow Lake, Paul Smith's, and Loon Lake. Below, Tait's *American Speckled Brook Trout* (1863) depicts fine equipment of the time, including a German silver reel seat and a solid butt of ash or lancewood.

C. E. Monroe, *Trout Fishing* (1979).

A Gallery of American Masters

Rod builder Hiram Leonard

Dry fly pioneer Theodore Gordon

Author Roderick Haig-Brown

THE ULTIMATE FISHING BOOK

Author Joe Brooks

Fly fisherman Lee Wulff

Author Ernest Schwiebert

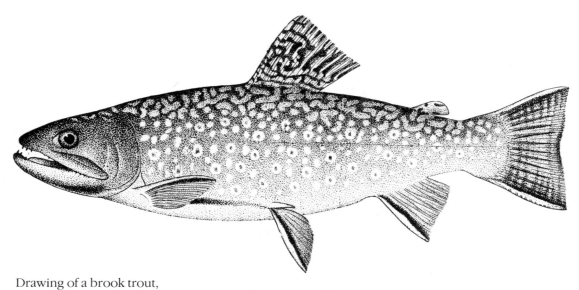

Drawing of a brook trout,
taken from *American Game Fishes,* edited by G. O. Shields (1892).

somber winter stone flies on streamside snowbanks in our eastern mountains. The currents are bitterly cold and breath blossoms in the wind. Frozen reels and guides clogged with ice crystals are perhaps a better measure of its weather than a thermometer, since our eastern trout fishing starts earlier than the seasons farther west, and the faithful carry flasks and coffee jugs and gather around gravel-bar fires.

"Don't expect fish," the late Arnold Gingrich observed on Opening Day on the Brodheads in Pennsylvania. "The first days of trout fishing are like Oriental philosophy—more fishing than fish!"

Opening Day ceremonies are still observed in several states, signaling a vernal migration of trout fishermen to their favorite waters, but weather conditions usually make their sport an act of faith and stubborn affirmation and habit. Late snow remains in the birch and hemlock thickets. Delicate veneers of ice persist in the margins of ponds and backwaters and reservoirs. Beaver colonies are often completely sheathed in April ice, their springheads mere seepages among the brittle sticks and saplings. Trout awaken slowly from their winter doldrums.

Our eastern rivers awaken slowly too, flowing black and almost silent among the rocks. The conifers are dark accents of color in bare forests of rattling branches. The timid willows stir first, their swelling buds a faint prologue to the coming spring, long before winter has displayed any trace of ebbing. Coltsfoot and skunk cabbage and violets sprout in the sheltered places. Pale colonies of may apples rise from the winter forests. The swift rivers of the Adirondacks and Appalachians are still sullen and cold, tumbling through granite and ledgerock of sandstone and slate, and seeping tea-brown from their headwater springs and bogs. Fishermen

search their pools on Opening Day for trout still sluggish with the bitter temperatures of February, their spotted flanks as cold as the frost-chilled gleam of a Manhattan cocktail shaker.

Opening Day is invariably an anticlimax after weeks and weeks of anticipation, and the waiting is invariably sweeter than the day itself. Fishing is seldom far from the thoughts of a serious angler, and the first pianissimo notes in the prelude to Opening Day are probably heard in the weeks before Thanksgiving.

Tackle has been recently stored then, and Christmas lists are the first obvious symptoms. Clumsy hints are offered for family consideration, although an angler probably knows that a split-cane rod and fine British reel are beyond most family budgets, pieces of equipment he must purchase himself and conceal their actual cost. Fishing gifts at Christmas are usually disappointing, and the tackle shops and mail-order houses always report a spate of purchases in January, when fishermen clandestinely acquire the things they really wanted. Books become important after Christmas, too, and favorite fishing titles are searched out and taken down from their shelves.

"Books keep our fishing alive through the winter." Arnold Gingrich enjoyed an excellent library of classic fishing books. "Books are a kind of surrogate stream and have the magic of erasing time, and the best fishing is always found in books and saloons!"

Fishing collections are usually filled with books about technique and tactics, but there are better themes for passing a winter's night. John Waller Hills is among the best choices, and his book *A Summer on the Test,* graced with the etchings of Norman Wilkinson, transports readers to the chalk downs of Hampshire. Romilly Fedden was a land-

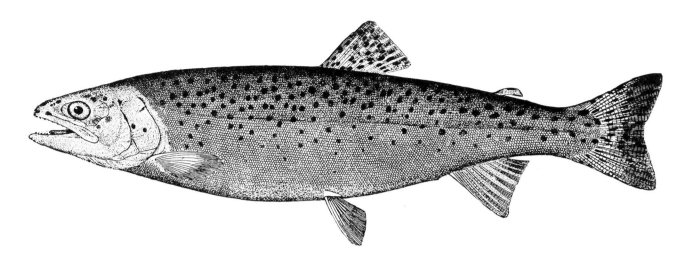

Drawing of a cutthroat trout, from *American Game Fishes* (1892).

scape painter who recuperated from his wounds on the battlefields of Flanders with thoughts of fishing in Brittany, and his lyric *Golden Days* describes both art and sport. Odell Shepherd was an American angler who described his fishing in *Thy Rod and Thy Creel,* on the classic British streams at the threshold of the Great Depression. Plunkett Greene was a famous British singer, but he is better remembered today for his charming *Where the Bright Waters Meet,* which recounts several years of sport on the little Bourne at Hurstbourne Priors. Roderick Haig-Brown was a British expatriate who lived and wrote in British Columbia, and his books include several titles devoted to fishing; his anthology *A River Never Sleeps* is a perennial favorite. Its pages carry us into the forest rivers of his province, searching out summer-run steelhead on the Stamp, catching coin-bright cutthroats on his beloved Campbell in late winter at the foot of his orchard, and fighting the stern currents of the wild Nimpkish in winter. Counting the calendar is much easier with books of such character waiting on the night table.

"We think our fishing in British Columbia is getting crowded too," Haig-Brown observed in his cluttered library a few months before his unexpected death, "but from the American papers and journals I see these days, your people fish armpit to armpit when the season opens on some of your streams."

"Truck followers." I nodded.

Our fledgling trout hatcheries first evolved in the late nineteenth century, starting with facilities at Cold Spring Harbor and Caledonia in New York. Their emerging technology coincided with our growing awareness that the rapacity and pace of our timber cutting were stripping the forests.

"Fish culture seemed like a workable solution."

Haig-Brown shook his head sadly that afternoon. "Our biologists actually believed that fish hatcheries could compensate for clear-cutting our forests and destroying the watersheds that drain into our streams."

"It's called mitigation today," I said.

"That's what the politicians and dam builders and lumbermen call it." Haig-Brown nodded thoughtfully. "*Mitigation* is a perfect example of the perfect weasel word, but it has hoodwinked generations and generations of fishermen into thinking that we could destroy habitat and simply compensate with tame hatchery trout."

Since those mistaken beginnings, we have bred hatchery strains of fish we hoped would produce the most trout in the shortest time at the lowest cost. Such obviously high-minded efficiency has seldom been challenged in the past fifty years, but our perspective suggests that hatchery programs were most successful in political terms and have been a tragic shotgun marriage between biology and poultry farming and the mentality of a bottom-line manager. Biology itself accepted the wedding, with a few grudgingly doubtful voices of dissent, and the results have often proved tragic.

Hatchery rainbows have literally become artificially bred hybrids that display some disconcerting qualities. "Frankenstein would have recognized our hatchery fish!" Haig-Brown observed wryly in his library. "But they should have the monster's bolts behind their eyes, because they're not really trout—they're like clones!"

Such hatchery strains display surprisingly rapid growth, but the price for that bottom-line performance has proved complex. Wild trout often survive for between six and ten years, but hatchery rainbows seldom live three seasons. Brook trout were bred selectively at Caledonia to reach early maturity, with the goal of increasingly rapid reproduction, but the tragic result has been stunted fish breeding successive generations of stunted fish, and such genetic pollution has been distributed throughout the United States. The brown trout introduced from Europe has suffered from less genetic tinkering, although hatchery brood stocks of this species also display less wildness and suspicion than their progenitors. Fish culturists dislike brown trout because they are difficult and costly to propagate.

The remarkably few hatchery trout that survive to spawn pose other serious problems. The ripe females have few eggs, and surprising numbers of their ova are infertile. Survival rates of the fingerlings hatched are minuscule. Hatchery strains have also been selected for early maturity and ripening eggs, until our hybrid rainbows often display a tragicomic urge to spawn during autumn. Such fall-spawning rainbows have few potential mates, since most hatchery strains and their wild cousins still spawn in the spring. Hybrids that successfully pair off in the fall are forced to compete for spawning grounds with brook and brown trout populations, which are autumnal spawners in nature. Hatchery strains that do survive to spawn with wild mates pose serious problems, too, since current studies demonstrate that such matches merely dilute the genetic integrity of surviving wild stocks, weakening the entire trout population.

Hatchery trout are like poultry, except that poultry are wrapped in cellophane and sold at supermarkets. Poultry are not distributed along our rural rights-of-way and hunted in the following weeks. Like poultry, however, our hatchery trout have been protected and pampered until they cannot recognize their natural foods and predators. People have coddled and fed them regularly until the fish trucks transport them to the streams, when people are suddenly transformed into enemies. The fishing public should not be surprised when hatchery trout are swiftly decimated after stocking, because these fish are like foolish chickens abandoned in a hostile world of coyotes and foxes.

The supermarket crowds that engulf our trout streams on Opening Day are triggered by the marriage of hatchery technology and politics. The rod-swinging crowds that line the beautiful little Amawalk and Croton just outside New York, and the regiments that attack the Musconetcong in northern New Jersey with a macramé of tangled hooks and frayed tempers, are hatchery products too. Wild trout would never cooperate in such a piscatorial circus, and without such willing victims from our hatcheries, the modern desecration of an ancient and honorable sport would prove utterly unworkable.

Fish trucks disgorge their flopping cargo at bridge after bridge on our famous streams, filling their riffles and pools with more trout than they can actually support. Crowds literally encircle entire pools, standing in the shallows and fishing between their boots. Politics has transformed Opening Day into a shabby carnival, and fights are common among competing fishermen. Such tumult shames trout fishing itself, stripping both its solitude and its poetry, until it is reduced to the summer throngs horsing in blowfish and baby flounder on breakwaters from Montauk to Barnegat.

But hatcheries and fish trucks played no role in the beginnings of our Opening Day traditions. There were trout streams everywhere when the colonial settlements were founded in Massachusetts, and there were even brook-trout tributaries on Manhattan itself, when New York was a bustling little seaport lined with slips' masts and rigging from Trinity churchyard to the Battery fortifications.

The prosperous Dutch patroons who settled the Hudson watershed in the seventeenth century found good sport in its tributaries too, and there is still decent fishing on the Kaaterskill and Roeliff Jansen Kill and Kinderhook. Long Island boasted excellent trout fishing at Suffolk and Massapequa and Smithtown. The trout clubs at Suffolk and South Side and Wyandanch had memberships filled with both café society and the social register.

Several elegant fishing clubs were established on the trout ponds of Maine after the Civil War, and their memberships were largely formed of the principal families of Boston and New York and Philadelphia. They gathered in surprisingly urbane quarters, considering that no roads connected their clubhouses and remote shelters and cottages with civilization. The clubhouses and outbuildings were framed of smooth-peeled logs. Their roofs were sheathed in rough hand-split shingles, but their rustic character sheltered wine cellars that held some memorable vintages of claret and champagne and sauterne. Supplies were entirely transported in freight canoes and wagons, and the members reached Maine in private railway cars from Boston, dining on champagne and lobster and pastry-wrapped Beef Wellington.

Other famous clubs and private fishing preserves were formed in our eastern mountains in those years. The freshly powerful royalty of industry and investment banking houses and railroads acquired extensive forest acreages. Such people were constantly in the public eye. Their lives seemed almost touched with magic, and the public hungrily watched them camping and trout fishing and enjoying long canoe trips through their private wilderness tracts. The example of such celebrated figures had a considerable impact on the status of trout fishing in America, shaping in large measure our traditions of Opening Day.

Our heritage of important fishing writers perhaps begins with George Washington Bethune and Thaddeus Norris, who fished the little Brodheads

Turn-of-the-century photographs taken at Camp Garfield on Moosehead Lake, Maine, where hunting and fishing went on simultaneously. In the fall, sportsmen pursued trout and landlocked salmon, as well as woodcock and partridge.

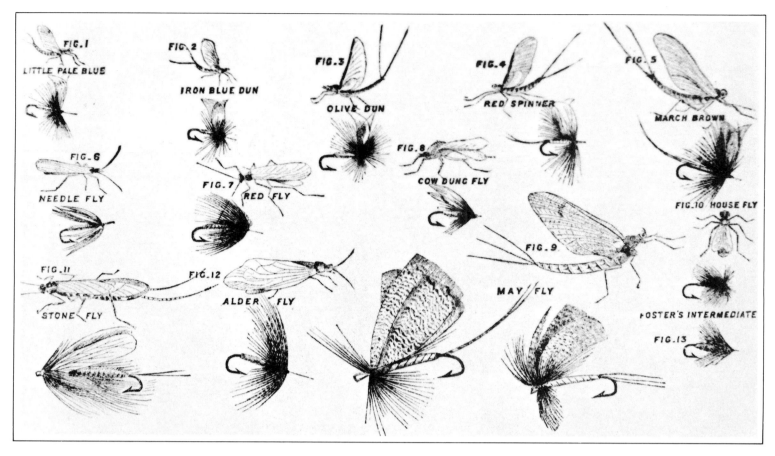

Naturals and their imitations, from *The Scientific Angler* (1833).

from Henryville House before the Civil War. Bethune was responsible for the first American edition of *The Compleat Angler,* and his surprisingly large appendix was actually a book itself, its pages filled with information on American waters and fishing. Norris was a widely traveled fisherman from Philadelphia, and the publication in 1864 of his *American Angler's Book* established his position as our Walton. The famous Brooklyn Flyfishers, whose membership was largely composed of wealthy brewers and bankers who built the elegant mansions at Brooklyn Heights, were founded at Henryville on the Brodheads in 1895.

Its circle of membership provided the cadre that later became the prestigious Anglers' Club of New York, whose charming quarters are found above Fraunces Tavern near Wall Street. The Brooklyn Flyfishers found their Boswell in *The Lotus Eaters,* the famous story by the equally celebrated Sparse Grey Hackle, who still presides like a venerable bulldog guarding the Broad Street quarters of the Anglers' Club. Both timber cutting and overfishing finally decimated the brook-trout fishing on the Brodheads, and the Brooklyn Flyfishers left the Henryville water after the season of 1897. Several members observed sadly that the fishing on their favorite river had declined, and the august clan emigrated north to acquire fishing rights at the Hardenburgh property on the Beaverkill. The Brooklyn Flyfishers remain there after eighty-odd

years, and these earlier Brodheads fishermen played a major role in the swiftly growing reputation of the Beaverkill and its sister rivers.

The Catskills are acknowledged as the birthplace of dry-fly fishing in America, and almost legendary characters like Theodore Gordon have evolved into the patron saints of rivers like the Beaverkill and Willowemoc. Gordon passed his fly-dressing skills grudgingly to other fishermen like Herman Christian and Roy Steenrod in the Neversink country where he spent his last years, dressing his elegant dry flies in the lamplight at the old Anson Knight farmhouse. The fly-fishing historian John McDonald has lovingly assembled his memorabilia in his book *The Compleat Flyfisher: The Notes and Letters of Theodore Gordon,* and the Theodore Gordon Flyfishers have grown into a major organization devoted to the preservation of both their sport and the swift-flowing rivers where it is practiced.

Reuben Cross also knew Gordon in those early Catskill years, when the old fisherman was losing his fight with the tuberculosis that ultimately led to his death in 1915, in a late spring snow that had blighted the fly hatches expected on Opening Day. Cross was among the finest fly dressers who ever lived, and his techniques were translated into books like *Tying American Trout Lures* and the subsequent little *Fur, Feathers and Steel,* which was published in 1940. Cross performed his magic with wood duck and gamecock capes and silk in a simple

In May 1865, a group of New York doctors who called themselves "the Fishicians" took a Catskills angling holiday on the Neversink. Their expedition was chronicled in an illustrated, handwritten journal, pages of which are shown here. The keeper of the log, Dr. Walter de Forest Day, recounted preparations for the trip: "Flasks and pipes, and wind-defying matches are not likely to be forgotten, nor the stores for lunch, nor the wading shoes, full of memories, perchance of holes, half-hobless, and dented all over with honorable scars...."

Labor of Love

farmhouse on the upper Beaverkill at Lew Beach.

Although it was Cross who codified the principles of the Catskill style of fly-making, still younger tiers like Walter Dette and Harry Darbee have carried its tradition of elegant rolled-wing dressings into our time. Darbee is perhaps better known, and the biography simply titled *Catskill Fly Tier* is testimony to his craft, but Dette is cut from similar cloth. Both men still dress the sparse dry flies typical of the Catskill style beside the Willowemoc and Beaverkill, and tiers like William Chandler, who created the classic Light Cahill on the Neversink, were pillars of the same philosophy. Arthur Flick is the consummate master of the Schoharie, which drains the northern summits of the Catskills, and his famous *Streamside Guide* contains his observations of its fly hatches over many seasons. The fishing and painstakingly tied flies and philosophy of these pioneers, from the frail Theodore Gordon dressing his patterns with winter-chilled fingers at his potbellied stove to the monastic elegance of the sparse dry flies that Flick still ties in the farmhouse under the mountain at West Kill, have evolved into the rich tapestry of the Catskill School.

On the Catskill rivers Opening Day is something between religion and sport, and their character is so compelling that I have happily traveled north from Princeton for more than twenty seasons to fish them in blizzards and April weather as bracing and clear as a perfectly chilled bottle of Pouilly-Fuissé.

There are many memories of the Catskills in early spring. There were camping trips to celebrate Opening Day in my student years, and later times in the old Campbell Inn, with its sprawling porches across the valley from Ferdon's Pool. There have been other times at the Antrim Lodge, and times when we merely stopped for a late supper there, or tried to warm our river-chilled bodies with a drink at its bottle-lined Home Pool, where fishermen have bought each other rounds and told fishing stories for more than fifty years. April stone flies were hatching in the long riffle below the bridge at Craigie Clare, and we fished from the old Renner farmhouse at the foot of the mountain. The good times tumble through the mind like the river itself.

Other years we fished with friends like Robert Abbett at the famous Beaverkill Club farther upstream, with its hemlock-sheltered Home Pool down the meadow across the old country road. Its simple rooms were under a canopy of elms, where robins were nesting when the first fly hatches were coming, and we walked to the other house with its second-floor dormitory and tackle-hung porches.

The Beaverkill is perhaps more famous than its Catskill sisters, and in many ways it fully deserves its affection and respect, but my best memories of fishing on Opening Day in the Catskills are probably those of the Schoharie farther north.

Art Flick was the proprietor of the charming West Kill Tavern in those years, and his quiet inn was a rambling structure with sheltering gables and slate roofs and white clapboard. Its hallways and steep staircases were a labyrinth that held a virtual museum of paintings and sporting prints and needlepoint. There were remarkable examples of old taxidermy, woodcock and ruffed grouse and quail, all displayed in their elegant nineteenth-century glass covers. The food and drink and companionship were excellent, although the proprietor never kept the tiny bar open as late as his regulars wanted. It was perhaps the best fishing inn anywhere in the Catskills.

The Schoharie is still a native brook-trout fishery in its headwaters on the timbered summits of Indianhead. Its gathering currents riffle over ledges there, through vast thickets of rhododendron and the overgrown walls of abandoned colonial farms, and it tumbles through huge boulders in other places. The swift runs and pools above Hunter are classic Catskill water, and in the valley at Lexington it becomes a series of sweeping riffles and smooth flats. There are deep ledgerock pools downstream, and before the Gilboa Reservoir warmed its lower mileages, the old-timers told us, there had been excellent trout fishing as far downstream as the covered bridge at Blenheim.

Its watershed has witnessed a formidable parade of famous anglers over the years. Preston Jennings did extensive fieldwork and some of the writing for *A Book of Trout Flies* while fishing from the West Kill Tavern. His pioneer studies were the first disciplined American attempt to classify and imitate our fly hatches, just as British fishing writers like Alfred Ronalds and Frederic Halford had begun during the nineteenth century. Leslie Thompson, another regular on the Schoharie in those days, later published *Fishing in New England*, which is filled with delicate prose and watercolors. Raymond Camp was the outdoor writer at the *New York Times* after the Second World War, and it was Thompson and Camp who badgered a reluctant Art Flick into writing his *Streamside Guide*, helping with the fieldwork along the river, and Thompson painted exquisite watercolors of the insects they collected over the years. His delicate brushwork was hung in a place of honor in the quiet little corner bar. Dana Storrs Lamb both fished and hunted grouse from the West Kill Tavern, and I first met him there with his sons in woodcock season. Lamb has since written a charming shelf of particularly lyric fishing books, and titles like *Pink Ladies and Green Highlanders* and *Woodsmoke and Watercress* and *Where the Pools Are Bright and Deep* are among his best work. Several of these men became treasured friends in later years.

Opening Day that first season on the Schoharie offered surprisingly good fishing in spite of the

William J. Schaldach, *Barnhardt's Pool* (1929).

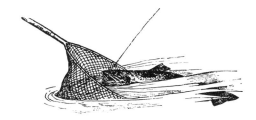

weather. It had been raining when I stopped for dinner with Jim Rikhoff on the Sawmill River Parkway, and it was colder when we drove along the Esopus toward Phoenicia. The rain changed to snow where the county road crosses the mountains at Bushnellsville, and the fields were already white farther north.

It was still cold at breakfast in the West Kill Tavern. Richard Wolters and John Falk had joined us there, and we sat staring unhappily at the weather. The raw wind sighed past the roof slates and eaves. Winter leaves still scuttled in the county road, and a chambermaid had been adding logs to the fireplace when we came downstairs.

"It's cold!" Rikhoff groaned.

Art Flick stoked the fire expertly and joined us, bringing an extra coffee cup from the sideboard. "Well, boys"—Flick smiled and shook his head—"the best thing about our April fly hatches is they're not too early—particularly on days like this!"

"Thank God!" Rikhoff shuddered melodramatically.

"What hatches might be coming?" I asked.

"Provided anything decides to come out in this weather!" Wolters interjected dryly. "Bugs would be crazy to hatch in this blizzard!"

"It might be potluck out there," Flick admitted grudgingly, "but you could see our early mayflies after midday—and there might be sporadic hatches of early stone flies too."

"Frostbite before noon!" Rikhoff predicted.

The brief journey down the little valley into Lexington offered little hope. Snow flurries were mixed with freezing rain. When we crossed the iron bridge into Lexington, the river was covered with whitecaps and sleet rattled across the windshield.

"This is getting ridiculous!" I laughed.

Rikhoff studied the hailstones thoughtfully. "The weather is trying to tell us something," he suggested. "Maybe it's time to think this through over some Irish coffee!"

"But it's ten o'clock in the morning!" I protested weakly.

"Perfect!" He grinned.

The fierce wind buffeted the narrow streets. We ducked our heads into the squall and dashed clumsily into the Lexington Inn. Its dining room was empty and the bar seemed closed, but the proprietor was busily tending his fireplace.

"Irish coffee!" Rikhoff announced grandly.

The proprietor stoked the fire and wiped his hands. "Gentlemen"—he shook his head and laughed—"that's the first intelligent thing anybody's said all morning!"

The weather seemed a little better after an hour of Irish coffee at the Lexington Inn, and although the proprietor suggested it might be only an illusion sustained by his hospitality, we decided to drive upstream toward Hunter. We studied the pools along the river and circled in through the cemetery to find water that was not being fished, to wait for the worst squalls to pass.

There are fine-looking pools above Lexington, where the Schoharie dances through stands of hardwoods and birches, with a few white pines rising tall and somber among the pale, bare-branched trees. Swift runs tumble over bedrock ledges. There is beautiful pocket water below the county bridge, and there are several fine pools behind the old camp buildings at Jeanette.

We drove slowly through Hunter and dropped down to cross the river there. The bad weather had emptied the river of other fishermen. Rikhoff dropped me at the county bridge and circled back along the unpaved township road to leave the car downstream.

The Schoharie seemed lifeless at first. It is a particularly beautiful reach of water, but my stream thermometer registered forty-four degrees, and the current felt bitter cold. There were no insects hatching from the riffles and pools below the bridge. When the chill wind finally dropped, the sun filtered weakly through the wintry overcast, and I discovered a few little *Taeniopteryx* flies struggling to emerge in a shallow backwater.

There's a fish working! I thought excitedly.

Trout started rising fitfully at midday, and we took a few decent fish in the pools and flats. The tiny stone flies ebbed and flowed and ebbed again in sporadic flurries of activity. The fish took them hungrily when the flies were coming well, and when the fluttering insects stopped hatching, the trout stopped rising too.

We started back through the woods toward the car when the first dark-winged *Epeorus* mayflies began sailboating down the swift riffles behind the outbuildings at Jeanette. "We can't stop and eat!" I started back with excitement. "Just when the Gordon Quills start coming—it's really going to get the fish going!"

Our optimism was justified for several minutes. The dark-winged duns were coming in good numbers, and several good fish were soon working greedily. It was still cold in spite of the faint sun, but my fingers were not shaking because of the weather, and I finally succeeded in clinch-knotting a delicate Gordon Quill to my tippet. The first trout took the fly with an excited splash, and it bored swiftly upstream, with sweet ratchet music spilling from the reel.

The light suddenly dropped as another squall lashed along the river. Huge snowflakes gusted wetly on the wind. The trees and buildings and fields were quickly covered with fresh snow, and the flies stopped hatching. The river flowed black and silent between its snow-covered banks and boulders. It was almost impossible to see across the river when another squall struck, and we retreated through the driving snow.

A selection of naturals, from *A Book of Angling* by Francis Francis (1867).

Scenes from the Sport of Presidents

Calvin Coolidge at Squaw Creek in the Black Hills of South Dakota.

Harry S. Truman on a lake near Sun Valley, Idaho.

Jimmy Carter on a stream near Camp David, Maryland.

Herbert Hoover on the Housatonic near Sheffield, Massachusetts.

Dwight D. Eisenhower at Swan Ranch near Denver, Colorado.

Opening Day had proved fickle again, and the following morning we tried the Schoolhouse and Cemetery Pool and Blue Bell water farther downstream toward Lexington. The bad weather persisted through the night, and the headstones in the churchyard were wearing white caps when I walked down through the wintry meadow. The fly hatches failed to come again through the entire week, and fishing remained poor until the last days of April, when spring finally awakened the stubborn earth and the Catskill rivers came alive.

There were fine fly hatches that season, and we had several days of excellent sport, but it was later that year when we heard that the old West Kill Tavern was gone. It was lost in a tragic chimney fire that swiftly engulfed its century-old frame, licking at its antimacassars and tiger-maple sideboard and ladderback chairs, smoldering in the faded Oriental carpets and stair runners, and melting the elegant nineteenth-century glass cases of grouse and woodcock.

Wyandanch was the setting for another memorable Opening Day, and it seemed strange to drive there through the barren cityscapes of western Long Island, with its tasteless billboards and grim, prisonlike apartment buildings and pasteboard tract housing.

Wyandanch traced its genesis to the fishing expeditions of Daniel Webster and his friends, and its clubhouse grounds and the carefully preserved acreages that concealed its trout ponds and the fishing beats along the Nissequogue were another world. The clubhouse seemed immense in its sheltering stand of giant elms, surrounded with sweeping lawns and porches, and its interiors were an intricate puzzle of comfortable sleeping rooms and labyrinthine hallways and staircases. Rare prints and paintings and antique decoys were everywhere, and photographs of famous members and fishing guests watched silently from its dining-room walls. Exquisite mahogany cabinets and lockers, each with its brass locks and engraved nameplates, held the tackle and liquor of each member. Some lockers held a few bottles of surprisingly old port, and during the weekend there was a remarkable century-old Madeira that was shared among several members.

Between the card room, which was hung with original Ripley and Pleissner watercolors, and the antique pool table that filled the tackle room like an Egyptian sarcophagus were the rod racks.

The rods were assembled and fitted with costly Hardy and Walker and Bogdan trout reels. Some were graced with antique Leonard and Conroy reels, and a particularly old Leonard displayed a gleaming Meek reel of German silver. The rods themselves were a museum of old craftsmanship. There were relatively new bamboo rods from Orvis in Vermont, mixed with a few butter-colored Leon-

ards of recent vintage, but others were startling. There were several Garrisons, with their ascetic sense of fittings and grip design and clear silk wrappings, and a dark flame-tempered Young Perfectionist. Several were early Thomas and Edwards and Gillum rods, and there was a single Halstead with a skeleton reel seat that had miraculously survived the short-lived glues habitually mixed by its maker. It seemed a mistake to fish with such equipment. Several were more than half a century old, including some lovely old Leonards made before the First World War, and their cane was probably brittle and dried out after so many seasons. There was a single white-glass Shakespeare as seemingly out of place as a Brooklyn cocktail waitress at a Boston cotillion.

Dinner was a revelation, too. The cuisine that appeared on the Long Table at Wyandanch seemed better suited to some highly rated country restaurant in Provence, with its constellation of stars in the *Guide Michelin.* The menu should not have been startling, since the membership maintained the family traditions of the same captains of commerce and industry who had earlier created feudal kingdoms in the Catskills and Adirondacks.

Breakfast the next morning featured rolling dice from a leather cup to assign the beats on the trout ponds and on the six stream beats along the Nissequogue itself. Each beat consisted of a specific length of stream assigned to those with the successively best combinations of dice; such fishing-beat systems are in the European tradition. The bottom beat was usually fished with a canoe, and there were duckboard walkways in the marshy bottoms to the other water.

My host was the late Lester Brion, and when he rolled the highest number from the leather cup, his choice of the best beat was graciously assigned to me. "It's our finest water," Brion explained as the fleet of costly automobiles drifted silently out under the elms to reach the river beats and trout ponds. "It's always held some large wild brown trout—and I'm curious to watch you fish it."

"I'm curious too," I said.

Beat Five was a serpentine piece of water with marshy borders. We found dogtooth violets mixed with skunk cabbage and marsh marigolds and shadbush along the duckboards in the woods. Arrowheads and water plantain and cattails shaped the still currents of the Nissequogue. There were bright buds on the swamp maples upstream, where the redwing blackbirds were busily mating.

Okra-lee-o! Their cries filled the marsh.

The fishing was surprisingly good. The trout were largely hatchery fish planted for Opening Day. There were a few fat *Leptophlebia* duns emerging from the quiet flow, and an occasional trout took one splashily on the surface. The flies were soon hatching in good numbers, but the fish did not increase their activity to harvest them, and I

The Professor Landing a Double drawn by J. H. Cocks (1863).

stopped casting to observe the backwater where they were emerging.

We've got a pretty good hatch going here, I thought, *but the fish must be taking nymphs along the bottom —they've got to work with so many flies available.*

These particular mayflies love such still-water flowages, and before their actual emergence, the maturing nymphs often display a unique schooling behavior. Large colonies migrate upstream like schools of tiny fish, and the trout often discover and follow these schools to gorge themselves.

It seemed likely that the backwaters and currents producing the most hatching flies were sheltering the principal concentrations of their nymphs, and perhaps the fish had discovered them too. There were several chocolate-colored nymphs in my fly books, dressed with fringed peacock to suggest the densely layered gills of the *Leptophlebia* genus. Since these nymphs can swim rhythmically, I decided to cast my imitation upstream and let it sink a few moments before starting a deliberate, teasing retrieve.

The first attempt dropped along the willows at the canoe landing, where the current quickened slightly and had scoured a clean run in the gravel bottom. Several mayflies had hatched there while I had been observing the emerging insects. The fat nymph sank quickly, and I had just started a teasing retrieve when a boil telegraphed up through the current, and I tightened at the strong pull. *It worked!* I thought happily, checking the fat brook trout when it threatened to tangle the leader in the arrowheads and cattails. *They've found the school of hatching nymphs and they're taking them!*

Sometimes a puzzle falls suddenly into place, and that early spring morning on the Nissequogue was such a time. Several other brookies took the quiet retrieve before I hooked a surprising two-pound rainbow that cartwheeled past the canoe landing in the weak sunlight. Several other hatchery trout succumbed in the backwater upstream and in a deep springhole under the willows, before I covered the gravelly channel upstream and my retrieve was intercepted by a sullen strike.

It was a beautiful sixteen-inch brown trout, richly spotted above its ocher belly, and I admired its wild beauty in the net meshes before releasing it. Other brook trout followed in the sweeping bend above, and a brace of good browns took the nymph along some mossy logs. The fifty yards above those deadfalls was a sandy shallows that held no trout, but farther upstream there was a soft rise under an overhanging willow. The trout was unmistakably taking the hatching *Leptophlebia* flies, and its bulge suggested size, so I checked the leader for casting knots and changed to a dry Dark Hendrickson.

The dry fly dropped nicely just above the rising fish, floated briefly, and disappeared in a soft little dimple. When I tightened, the trout exploded the still current and bolted upstream.

Good fish! I thought happily.

It was another wild brown, and it was several minutes before it surrendered to the straining little Leonard. It measured almost twenty inches, and when my host called from the duckboards where my beat ended, I nursed it gently upstream in the net for his inspection. We admired its ruby-bright spotting, like the fierce color on the shoulder of the male redwings, and released it.

Wyandanch was a remarkable club, and its beautiful grounds and trout ponds and river mileage have since been purchased as a state park, its fishing made available to the public. Its forest walkways, spring-bog ponds, and river beats along the gentle Nissequogue are a world of fishing ghosts. Its character echoed a sense of style that is virtually gone in these demotic times. But its fishing was tinged with sadness, since its feudal world was clearly ending. Versailles was perhaps like that on the eve of the guillotine, and the parkway traffic was perhaps the equivalent of the sound of tumbrels in the Paris streets. Its sport was sustained by costly transfusions of hatchery trout each Thursday, stocked to perpetuate the comfortable illusion, in spite of the backyard conversations and power mowers that could be heard in the tract housing beyond the trees, that its members were enjoying a remote brook-trout bogan on the Allagash and could really fish.

Opening Day in our northern Rocky Mountains is utterly different. Outsiders are sometimes grudgingly tolerated, but they have little effect on the unique liturgies of Opening Eve, ceremonies performed against a background of country music with echoes of our frontier.

Fishing country there still has saloons crowded with miners and sheepherders and cowboys. Fishing guides and boatmen are mixed with such older western trades these days, in a changing cast that mirrors the circling seasons of the mountain country, their beards and stovepipe jeans and Frye boots mingling perfectly with the natives around the bars. It is still a relatively simple life, although it conceals its complications and peculiar demons behind a stoicism that reflects a fiercely held code, its truths and commandments often overlooked or misunderstood by outsiders. Its drinking habits are simple too, with a fulcrum of beer and bourbon whiskey to fuel such serious work, and esoteric choices like the ten-to-one Beefeater martini with a twist of lemon to baptize the rim of its glass are certain to generate suspicion and outright hostility. Local fishermen have started fights over less obvious points of conflict, and solitary men like sheepherders and hardrock miners and cowboys can wax belligerent over a Cheviot tweed jacket or a rumpled Connemara fishing hat.

Butte and Livingston and Dillon are still tough Montana towns of miners and cattlemen and railroaders, and their bars are legendary in the northern Rockies. Bad whiskey and beer chasers are standard fare, and Butte is famous for its pork-chop sandwiches. Female bartenders who worked the cribs and bordellos fifty years ago, and still have tongues as salty as that of any Parris Island drill instructor, are common characters throughout these mountains.

Some western fisheries remain open throughout the winter months, but there are still many places that celebrate the rituals of Opening Eve in their favorite saloons. Fishermen gather in such places, from Taos in northern New Mexico to towns like Cut Bank and Kalispell, farther north in the Montana border country. The famous Red Onion in Aspen, and the Frontier on the Frying Pan in Basalt, have sheltered more than their share of trout fishermen.

Other anglers can be observed at Steamboat Springs, in temples like the Shortbranch and Tugboat, and the Parshall bar is a favorite with the regulars who fish the upper Colorado between Kremmling and Hot Sulphur Springs. Jackson Hole has its Silver Dollar in the old Wort Hotel, and its colorful old Cowboy Bar, which boasts saddles instead of barstools. There is the poorly lighted bar at Pond's Lodge on the Henry's Fork in eastern Idaho, its gravel parking lots filled with jeeps and riverboat trailers, and the old log-framed main building and bar at Henry's Lake Lodge, which was frequented by Theodore Roosevelt before the First World War. Sun Valley has its famous Pioneer and the Cedars Yacht Club and Ore House, and anglers looking for serious cow-country color might try saloons like Slavey's in Ketchum, or migrate across the Galena Summit to the storied little hotel bar at Stanley, in the beautiful Sawtooth basin.

Montana has its beer-and-whiskey meccas too. Fishing pilgrims fill saloons like Grogan's and the Wise River Club beside its famous Big Hole watershed, along with the colorful Quack-Quack Café at Melrose. Other anglers crowd into West Yellowstone, with its honky-tonk atmosphere of bars and restaurants and motels all competing with enough neon signs to suggest that the designers of pinball machines and jukeboxes have gone into city planning and architecture. Its fishing bars include the Totem and Stagecoach and Frontier, where there is gambling to pass the hours before fishing season starts again. Other fishing centers include Emigrant and Pray, with their Pine Creek store and Livery Stable saloon, as well as Chico Hot Springs, which boasts a surprisingly sophisticated dining room and

wine cellar so celebrated that the owners of small airplanes often land on its county road to have dinner there. It is not unusual to find ranch aircraft in its parking lot, until it seems like an airport apron filled with Pipers and Beechcrafts and Cessnas bearing registrations from Missoula to the Gulf of Mexico.

The northern Rocky Mountains are filled with many such places to spend an Opening Eve, and anyone familiar with the quixotic moods of weather in the high country should expect anything when the fishing starts the following morning. The horse wranglers and hay-cutting crews who worked for my mother's family in the Arkansas headwaters in Colorado had spent their lives warily observing its weather and were constantly talking about its fickle character when they straddled the corral fences behind their bunkhouses.

"You ain't got no weather back there!" The men ragged the summer people good-naturedly and considered anyplace beyond Kansas City suspiciously eastern and effete, just as the lobstermen at Kennebunkport believe the population of Hartford might still harbor Confederate supporters. "We got just two seasons out here in Colorado— past six thousand feet we got Coors and firecrackers and high-school bands to get things started in July— and we got winter!"

There are many obvious choices for an Opening Day pilgrimage in the northern Rockies, but the mecca is perhaps the famous Harriman water on the Henry's Fork in eastern Idaho. It drains the mountains and forest-covered plateaus and fertile lava outcroppings beyond the Teton country in western Wyoming, from its source at Henry's Lake and its giant springheads in the Yellowstone escarpment to its junction with the Snake at Idaho Falls. Its pilgrims include serious fishermen from the entire United States, mixed with knowledgeable anglers from Europe, and its headquarters lie at Last Chance.

Since its fly hatches are among the most varied and prolific in the world, and its big rainbows are found free-rising steadily throughout the season, the river is justly famous. Its beautiful meadows on the Harriman stretch are governed by special regulations restricting that mileage to fly-fishing, and its season does not start until the middle of June. The trout rise with frustrating dimples and soft porpoising rolls, and their feeding continues steadily, but these fish are so picky and selective that fishing for them, compared with fishing in other streams, has correctly been described as the difference between chess and Chinese checkers.

Since the motels and lodges at Last Chance are typically crowded for its Opening Day, Dan Callaghan and I often choose to stay in West Yellowstone. The Henry's Fork is just a brief trip across the Targhee Pass into Idaho.

The last time we fished the Harriman water on its Opening Day, we had dinner at the Totem in West Yellowstone and walked down in the surprising cold to the Stagecoach, looking for a fishing friend from Oregon. Its downstairs bar was crowded, but the tiny bandstand stood silent, its guitars and music stands and drums catching reflections in their brightly polished fittings.

"He's not here," Callaghan announced, "and it's going to get pretty noisy when that crew starts playing again—let's try the little bar around the corner upstairs."

Our friend had still not returned from the spring creeks near Livingston at two o'clock. The bartender switched off the lights over the faded pool tables, while the waitress collected the empty bottles and glasses from the tables and chair seats and windowsills. The bartender washed and rinsed his glasses and stacked them swiftly against the mirrors, where their gleaming surfaces caught the flickering lights of the jukebox and beer signs. The waitress finished clearing the tables, chewing gum in time with driving guitars on the jukebox, and a few last-call patrons sat nursing their drinks. There was an old sheepherder sleeping with his face in his arms, his darkly stained hat covering his head and his shabby boots hooked in the barstool.

"Fishing tomorrow?" the bartender asked.

"That's right." We grudgingly surrendered our half-finished drinks. "We're fishing the Henry's Fork at Last Chance."

"Those rainbows are tough," he said.

The young bartender let us out the street door and carefully closed the blinds. The waitress wrapped her chewing gum in a cocktail napkin and switched off the jukebox and pinball machines. The bartender finished his last sinkful of glasses and wiped down the bar before trying to wake the old sheepherder.

It was almost three o'clock when we finally went to bed at the Roundup. We fell asleep almost immediately, and I found myself dreaming fitfully of other times on the Henry's Fork. There was the first really big rainbow with Andre Puyans during an August swarm of tiny slate-colored sedges, and the piranhalike sipping rhythms of entire schools of big trout that followed the early mating swarms of minute *Tricorythodes* mayflies. The dreams included a huge fish that was taking a hatch of slate-winged duns along a grassy bank, took my little olive-bodied dry fly, and bolted downstream, cartwheeling high past the startled face of a fishing friend and showering his sunglasses with water. There was another immense rainbow hooked at Battleship Row, the immense flat in the bend below the old Harriman ranch and its red-roofed outbuildings, and the giant rainbow that Dan Callaghan took during a float with Jack Hemingway. The restless dreaming finally came to the monster rainbow that took my spent sedge softly, when I was fishing with Michael Lawson near Last Chance, and simply started downstream slowly with awesome strength.

"You're running out of backing!" Lawson warned, and shook his head in futility. "You're really in trouble!"

"You're right," I said helplessly.

The big trout shook itself with a kind of bored lethargy, its entire length gleaming in the evening light. Its spotted tail rolled lazily, showing above the current with its surprisingly large dorsal fin, and started downstream again. It gathered speed and strength slowly until the protesting reel was completely empty.

The fishing dreams ended mercifully with the giant rainbow still hooked and the backing line gone, thrashing on the still surface of the river far downstream in spite of the straining rod.

"It's six-thirty!" Callaghan was pounding at my door. "Let's get rolling!"

We stopped for breakfast at Huck's Diner, and Callaghan devoured an awesome double omelet with hash-brown potatoes and sausages. It was still cold, and ragged layers of mist drifted through the lodgepoles when we left West Yellowstone and climbed steadily past the South Fork toward Targhee Pass. Wild cutthroats were dimpling in the beaver ponds beyond the summit, and the still expanse of Henry's Lake lay polished like old Sheffield in the early morning. The sky seemed dark and sullen farther west, behind the Centennial Mountains.

Callaghan pointed. "Winter gives up slowly."

The lake bottoms beyond the pass were alive with antelope and sandhill cranes and cattle. The dark lodgepoles at Island Park on the horizon defined the shorelines of a primordial glacier lagoon, and the highway crossed the bunch-grass flats into the trees. The lava formations under those tree-covered ridges provide the immense aquifers and springheads that give birth to the Henry's Fork itself. We crossed the river at Mack's Inn, several miles below the gargantuan springs that add more than ninety thousand gallons per minute to its swelling currents, spilling from fissures in the lava cliffs into a crystalline lagoon of watercress. We stopped at the Henry's Fork Anglers to talk and purchase Idaho fishing licenses and rummage through the fly drawers that Michael Lawson works through the winter to fill.

"The river looks pretty good," Lawson observed with a laconic drawl that matched the cadences of horse-opera actors like Slim Pickens and Chill Wills, sounding more like the Oklahoma panhandle than eastern Idaho. "But that sky beyond Pilot

A fishing party in Yellowstone Park (1901).

Mountain still looks a little like snow."

"Snow?" we asked. "Snow?"

"July and winter." Lawson shook his head and grinned. "You fellows know how the weather works out here!"

The parking fields at Last Chance were crowded, and the famous shallow flats downstream were crowded with fishermen too, staking out their claims along the best banks and currents. The fishermen were already an army of cranes and cattle egrets and herons. "It looks," Callaghan observed wryly, "like we've got company!"

We clambered over the rail fence in our waders and walked down through the water meadows, crossing the irrigation ditches there and stopping to watch for rising trout. Beyond the single tree in the pale wheatgrass and hawksbill and lupine downstream, where the scarlet flowers of Indian paintbrush were mixed with colonies of fescue, we found a few pale *Ephemerella* flies hatching. We waited and watched the smooth current, hoping the trout would discover them, and finally there was a sucking dimple against the grass.

Several large trout were soon bulging for nymphs along the bank, sliding back in the current to sip a few of the fluttering yellow-bodied mayflies. Callaghan was still fussing with his tackle and the immense duffel of cameras that he habitually takes fishing when I worked stealthily into casting position. The hatching flies were coming steadily now, and more and more fish were rising. The best-looking rises bulged steadily, triggering a series of undulating waves that washed along the trailing grass, and I watched several of the little mayflies disappear in porpoising swirls.

Here goes, I thought hopefully.

The big trout drifted under my delicate fly, inspecting it critically for a moment, before its snout pushed through the surface film and softly inhaled the floating confection of feathers. The fish bolted straight upstream along the bank, rooting under its grassy overhangs, and I felt the leader catch and come free. The leader caught again, and the fragile tippet parted when a fierce squall came sweeping down the river, driving the huge snowflakes on the wind.

It was impossible to see the opposite bank through the snow, and the temperature and barometer both plummeted. Callaghan quickly gathered his equipment. Snow had already covered the meadows by the time we reached his jeep, and later we stood in Lawson's tackle shop watching the blizzard and its drifting snow.

"Winter already!" I groaned.

"We didn't even get to July this summer"—Callaghan laughed ruefully—"and my teeth are still chattering!"

"Let's get back while we can still get across Targhee," I suggested. "We can celebrate Opening Day with some of that pot-still whisky from the Isle of Skye."

"Worth getting frozen," Callaghan said.

It was still snowing hard when we fishtailed the jeep past the summit of Targhee Pass and dropped gingerly through its surprising drifts toward West Yellowstone. Heavy snow was still falling there

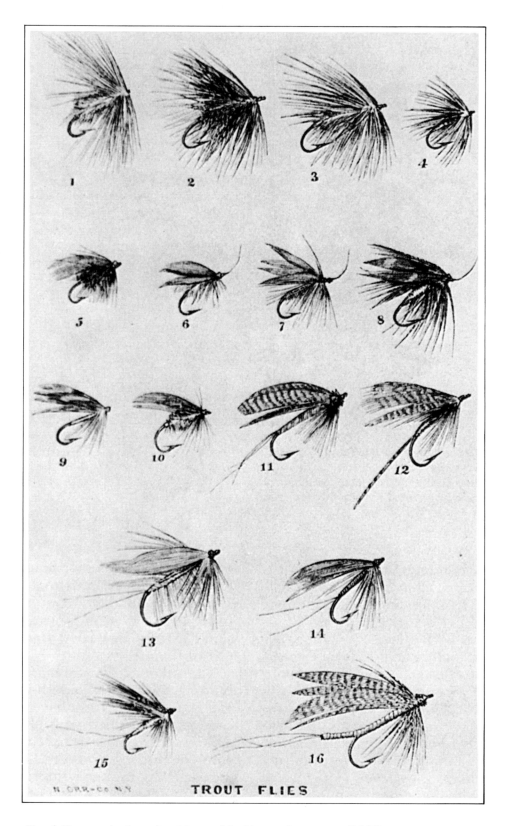

TROUT FLIES

Frank Forester's *Complete Manual for Young Sportsmen* (1856)
offered a selection of sixteen trout flies, including one
that was rather erroneously named "the Winged Larva of Mr. Blacker."

William H. H. Murray's *Adventures in the Wilderness* (1869) contained
a tale in which a fisherman is ferociously attacked by a wild trout.
The caption for this illustration reads: "When, high in mid-air,
he shook himself, the crystal drops were flung into my very face."

too, muting its garish buildings and signs.

"Forgot the tire chains when I left home," Callaghan muttered. "When we start talking about Opening Day again next year, remind me about this weather and do us both a favor!"

Forty-odd years of failure and success, mixed with spates of bad weather and snow, have taught me that the muses of Opening Day are hopelessly fickle and bad-tempered. Optimism in trout fishermen is typically rooted in romanticism, like that of some lover too often betrayed by life but completely incapable of stilling his timorous heart. Such hope is a little like spring fever.

Opening Day is often disappointing, but our bittersweet mixture of hope and patience is forgiving too. Fishing can completely possess the daydreams, and its anticipatory echoes and preludes are so filled with such daydreaming that we forget our past failures.

Recently I have returned to fish in Michigan again, celebrating a kind of Two-Hearted pilgrimage that Opening Day and traveling farther north in search of both boyhood and sport. The fishing was only fair, although the rivers were still beautiful in the stretches that remained relatively free

of cottages and summer houses. The cedar sweepers have been cleared from many reaches of the Au Sable, and their trout-hiding labyrinths have been replaced with putting-green lawns better suited to the tree-lined streets of Winnetka and Grosse Pointe.

The other rivers were changed too. The cedar bottoms along the smooth-flowing mouth of the Big Two-Hearted itself have been transformed into a campground filled with tents and motor homes and campers. There are fireplaces and picnic tables along the little Fox, where I once hiked like Hemingway along the sandy moraines above Seney and dropped down into its thickets of cedars and marsh marigolds to fish. Hemingway caught his first trout on Horton's Creek in lower Michigan, and there is a family photograph of a serious five-year-old fishing among its cedar deadfalls, wearing a floppy straw hat with an immense split-willow creel. The little creek still drains the hill country above Lake Charlevoix, flowing icily toward the estuary where Hemingway once fished for trout from the beaches and boardinghouse piers that provided the setting for stories like "The End of Something" and the unhappy "Up in Michigan," but its lower currents today lie behind platoons of no-trespassing signs and cottages.

Time has scarred other places since that first Opening Day. The logging traces and sandy back-country roads we traveled to fish the Pine and Pere Marquette and Manistee are paved now, like the cottage-lined country road that once passed the Bacon farmhouse, where the Hemingway family built the summer place they christened Windemere on the north shore of Walloon Lake.

The little Michigan towns are changed too. Simple houses have had their honest siding sheathed in false aluminum facades, and the brickwork stores on the main streets have been thoughtlessly remodeled with false roof cornices and plastic window mullions and cheap factory-made shingles. Shopping centers and car dealers and drive-ins are drowning their quiet character in the ugliness of electric signs and plastic pennants, fluttering in the clean wind that still comes briskly from Lake Michigan. Motels that seem manufactured, in some giant factory that shapes them with the uniformity of a gargantuan cookie cutter, are spreading like tumors outside towns and highway interchanges. The boyhood campsites and clapboard lakefront hotels and cottages are largely gone, and when I searched this spring for the cabins where we had retreated from the April snow that first Opening Day, there were only their broken foundations in the saplings and winter leaves and trilliums.

The mind remembers that other Opening Day morning years ago with the late Arnold Gingrich, standing beside his antique Bentley in the April rain at Henryville. "Don't expect much fishing." His wisdom is a gentle echo across the seasons since his death. "Opening Day is more pilgrimage than fishing."

The fishing is often predictable and poor, but it was Gingrich who also observed that fishing itself is perhaps the least important thing about fishing.

Such philosophy seems as threatened as many endangered species. Opening Day is already hopelessly changed, reduced to people who religiously follow the fish-truck schedules and rivers trampled under armpit-to-armpit legions fishing noisily with canned corn and cheap supermarket cheese.

Serious anglers who learned to revere their craft in more gentle times, taught patiently by older fishermen schooled in rumpled tweeds and elegant split-cane rods and flies, seldom participate in those cacophonic rites. Such anglers seemingly have the patina of old fishing tackle themselves, like vintage rods with actions sweetened after years on familiar streams. But such streams are tragically changed too, bringing a terrible wisdom to the perceptions of young Thomas Wolfe, coming home to Asheville with a cloying sense of loss.

Opening Day is not the sole casualty in these times of willful change, and perhaps it is foolish to expect otherwise, since the lost iconography of childhood cannot last.

The streets and houses of those early years seem curiously shrunk today, almost toylike in their diminished scale, and the memories of those summers are threatened. It is seldom the children's games that I remember now, since my thoughts often return to our fathers in those troubled years, sitting in their porch swings and talking behind the bedroom walls.

The men stood silently in the evenings, watering grass and gardens parched in the baseball weather of August. Our street of sheltering elms is changed, stripped of its trees in storms and seasons of blight. The big clapboard house, with its attic secrets and bay windows staring into the ice-wagon heat of summer, is sadly gone too. Its intricate porch railings and rose trellises are memories, where there were daydreams of that first Opening Day, and there are only fire-blackened foundations with no trace of the apple-tree swing.

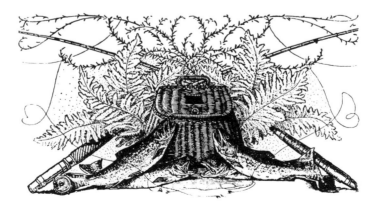

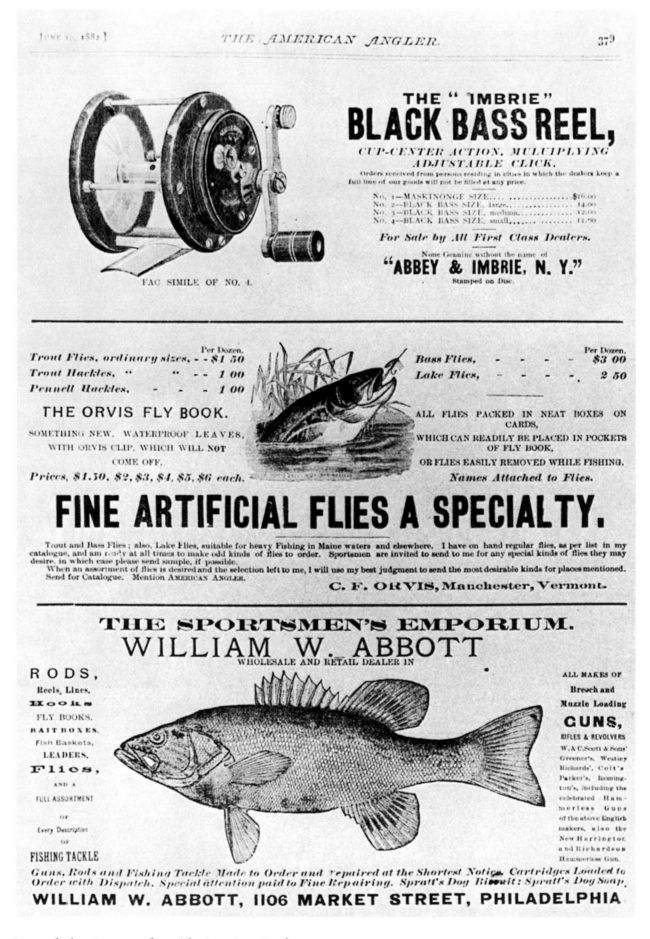

Pages of advertisements from *The American Angler,* a
newspaper for fishermen published in New York (1882).

Illustration by Russell Buzzell (1981).

FISHING THE RUN:
Close Call on the Brazos
By John Graves

'D MADE the mistake, the evening before, of mentioning to my younger daughter that I'd heard the crappie and sand bass were running in the Brazos. Therefore that Saturday morning, a clear and soft and lovely one of the sort our Texas Februaries sometimes offer in promise of coming spring, filled with the tentative piping of wrens and redbirds, I managed to get in only about an hour and a half's work in my office at the rear of the barn before she showed up there, a certain mulish set to her jaw and eyelids indicating she had a goal in mind and expected some opposition.

I said I needed to stay awhile longer at the typewriter and afterward had to go patch a piece of netwire boundary fence in the Booker pasture, shredded by a neighbor's horned bull while wrangling through it with my own Angus herd sire. She reminded me that the winter before we had missed the best crappie day in local memory because I'd had something else to do, one somewhat greedy fellow whom we knew having brought home eighty-three in a tow sack. She was fifteen and it struck me sometimes, though not to the point of neurosis, that maybe she deserved to have been born to a younger, less preoccupied father. In answer to what she said I raised some other negative points but without any great conviction, for I was arguing less against her than against a very strong part of myself that wanted badly to go fishing too.

The trouble was that those two or three weeks of late winter when the crappie and the sandies move up the Brazos out of the Whitney Reservoir, in preparation for spawning, can provide some of the most pleasant angling of the year in our region on the fringes of dry West Texas, where creeks and rivers flow tricklingly if at all during the warmer parts of a normal year. Even when low, of course, the good ones have holes and pools with fair numbers of black bass and bream and catfish, and I've been fishing them all my life with enjoyment. But it's not the same flavor of enjoyment that a hard-flowing stream can give, and those of us who have acquired—usually elsewhere—a penchant for live waters indulge it, if we've got the time and money, on trips to the mountain states and look forward with special feeling to those times when our local waters choose to tumble and roll and our fish change their ways in accordance.

The Brazos in this section, my own personal river of rivers if only because I've known it and used it for so long, is a sleepy catfishing stream most of the time, a place to go at night with friends and sit beneath great oaks and pecans, talking and drinking beer or coffee and watching a fire burn low while barred owls and hoot owls brag across the bottomlands, getting up occasionally to go out with a flashlight and check the baited throw lines and trotlines that have been set. Its winter run of sand bass and crappie is dependable only when there's been plenty of rain and the upstream impoundments at Granbury and Possum Kingdom are releasing a good flow of water to make riffles and rapids run full and strong, an avenue up which the fish swim in their hundreds of thousands. To catch them in drouthy winters you have to drive down to Whitney's headwaters above the Kimball Bend, where the Chisholm Trail used to cross the river and the ruins of stone factory buildings recall old Jacob De Cordova's misplaced dream of water-powered empire, back in the 1860s. But that is lake fishing, best done from a boat and short on the concentrated excitement that a strong current full of avid live things can give.

Generally you fish the river run blind, choosing a likely spot where fast water spews into a slow pool, casting across the flow and letting it sweep your lure or fly in a long arc downstream to slack water near the shore, working it in with what you hope are enticing twitches and jerks and pauses, then casting again. It is the venerable pattern still most often used with Atlantic salmon and the west coast's steelhead, though our local quarry is far less impressive than those patrician species, since a pound-and-a-half crappie is a good one and the sandies—more properly known as white bass—only occasionally exceed a couple of pounds or so. There are plenty of them when a good run is on, though, and unless you overmatch them with heavy stiff tackle they can put up a reasonable fight in the strong water. For that matter there's always an outside chance of hooking a big striped bass, a marine cousin of the sandy introduced to the salty Brazos reservoirs in recent years and reaching fifteen or eighteen pounds or more. To have a horse like that on a light rig is quite an emotional experience, at least if you're of the tribe that derives emotion from angling, but the end result is not ordinarily triumphant. The annoyed striper hauls tail swiftly and irresistibly downriver while you hang onto your doubled, bucking rod and listen to the squall of your little reel yielding line, and when all the line has run out it breaks, at the fish's end if you're lucky, at the reel if you're not.

I've never been happy fishing in crowds, and after word of a run of fish has seeped around our county the accessible areas along the river can be pretty heavily populated, especially on weekends in good weather and even more especially at the exact riverbank locations most worth trying. So that morning when without much resistance I had let Younger Daughter argue me down, I got the canoe out, hosed off its accumulation of old mud-dauber nests and barn dust, and lashed it atop the cattle frame on the pickup. If needed, it would let us cross over to an opposite, unpeopled shore or drop downriver to some other good place with no one at all in sight.

After that had been done and after we had rooted about the house and outbuildings in search of the nooks where bits of requisite tackle had hidden themselves during a winter's disuse, the morning was gone and so was the promise of spring. A plains norther had blown in, in northers' sudden fashion, and the pretty day had turned raw. By the time we'd wolfed down lunch and driven out to the Brazos, heavy clouds were scudding southeastward overhead and there was an occasional spit of thin, frigid rain. This unpleasantness did have at least one bright side, though. When we'd paid our dollar entrance fee to a farmer and had parked on high firm ground above the river, we looked down at a gravel beach beside some rapids and the head of a deep long pool, a prime spot, and saw only one stocky figure there, casting toward the carved gray limestone cliff that formed the other bank. There would be no point in using the canoe unless more people showed up, and that seemed unlikely with the threatening sky and the cold probing wind, which was shoving upriver in such gusts that, with a twinge of the usual shame, I decided to use a spinning rig.

Like many others who've known stream trout at some time in their lives, I derive about twice as much irrational satisfaction from taking fish on fly tackle as I do from alternative methods. I even keep a few streamers intended for the crappie and white bass run, some of them bead-headed and most a bit gaudy in aspect. One that has served well on occasion, to the point of disgruntling nearby plug and minnow hurlers, is a personal pattern called the Old English Sheep Dog, which has a tinsel chenille body, a sparse crimson throat hackle, and a wing formed of long white neck hairs from the amiable friend for whom the concoction is named, who placidly snores and snuffles close by my chair on fly-tying evenings in winter and brooks without demur an occasional snip of the scissors in his coat. Hooks in sizes 4 and 6 seem usually to be about right, and I suppose a sinking or sink-tip line would be best for presentation if you keep a full array of such items with you, which I usually don't. . . .

But such is the corruption engendered by dwelling in an area full of worm-stick wielders and trotline types, where fly-fishing is still widely viewed as effete and there are no salmonids to give it full meaning, that increasingly these days I find myself switching to other tackle when conditions seem to say to. And I knew now that trying to roll a six-weight tapered line across that angry air would lead to one sorry tangle after another.

We put our gear together and walked down to the beach, where the lone fisherman looked around and greeted us affably enough, though without slowing or speeding his careful retrieve of a lure. A full-fleshed, big-headed, rather short man with a rosy Pickwickian face, in his middle or late sixties perhaps, he was clearly enough no local. Instead of the stained and rumpled workaday attire that most of us hereabouts favor for such outings, he had on good chest waders, a tan fishing vest whose multiple pouch pockets bulged discreetly here and there, and a neat little tweed porkpie hat that ought to have seemed ridiculous above that large pink face but managed somehow to look just right, jaunty and self-sufficient and good-humored. He was using a dainty graphite rod and a diminutive free-spool casting reel, the sort of stuff you get because you know what you want and are willing to pay for it, and when he cast again, sending a tiny white-feathered spinner bait nearly to the cliff across the way with only a flirt of the rod, I saw that he used them well.

Raising my voice against the rapids' hiss and chatter, I asked him, "Are they hitting?"

"Not bad," he answered, still fishing. "It was slow this morning when the weather was nice, but that front coming through got things popping a little. Barometric change, I guess."

It wasn't the barometer but the wind that had me wishing I'd mustered the sense to change to heavier clothing when the soft morning disappeared. It ruffled the pool's water darkly, working against the surface current. Younger Daughter, I recalled, had cagily put on a down jacket, and when I looked around for her she was already thirty yards down the beach and casting with absorption, for she was and still is disinclined toward talk when water needs to be worked. My Pickwickian friend being evidently of the same persuasion, I intended to pester him no further, though I did wonder whether he'd been catching a preponderance of

Etching of a crappie by Sandy Scott (1980).

crappie or of sand bass and searched about with my eyes for a live bag or stringer, but saw none. When I glanced up again he had paused in his casting and was watching me with a wry, half-guilty expression much like one I myself employ when country neighbors have caught me in some alien aberration such as fly-fishing or speaking with appreciation about the howls of coyotes.

"I hardly ever keep any," he said. "I just like fishing for them."

I said I usually put the sandies back too, but not crappie, whose delicate white flesh my clan prizes above that of all other local species for the table and, if there are many, for tucking away in freezer packets against a time of shortage. He observed that he'd caught no crappie at all. "Ah," I said, a bilked gourmet. Then, liking the man and feeling I ought to, I asked if our fishing there would bother him.

"No, hell, no," said Mr. Pickwick. "There's lots of room, and anyhow I'm moving on up the river. Don't like to fish in one spot too long. I'm an itchy sort."

That being the kind of thing I might have said too had I been enjoying myself there alone when other people barged in, I felt a prick of conscience as I watched him work his way alongside the main rapids, standing in water up to his rubber-clad calves near the shore, casting and retrieving a few times from each spot before sloshing a bit farther

upstream. It was rough loud water of a type in which I have seldom had much luck on that river. But then I saw him shoot his spinner bug out across the wind and drop it with precision into a small slick just below a boulder, where a good thrashing sand bass promptly grabbed it, and watched him let the current and the rod's lithe spring wear the fish down before he brought it to slack shallow shore water and reached down to twist the hook deftly from its jaw so that it could drift away. That was damned sure not blind fishing. He knew what he was doing, and I quit worrying about our intrusion on the beach.

By that time Younger Daughter, unruffled by such niceties, had caught and released a small sandy or two herself at the head of the pool, and as I walked down to join her, she beached another and held it up with a smile to shame my indolence before dropping it back into the water. I'd been fishing for more than three times as many years as she had been on earth, but she often caught more than I because she stayed with the job, whereas I have a longstanding tendency to stare at birds in willow trees, or study currents and rocks, or chew platitudes with other anglers randomly encountered.

"You better get cracking," she said. "That puts me three up."

I looked at the sky, which was uglier than it had been. "What *you'd* better do," I told her, "is find the right bait and bag a few crappie for supper pretty fast. This weather is getting ready to go to pieces."

"Any weather's good when you're catching fish," she said, quoting a dictum I'd once voiced to her while clad in something more warmly waterproof than my present cotton flannel shirt and poplin golfer's jacket. Nevertheless she was right, so I tied on a small marabou horsehead jig with a spinner—a white one, in part because that was the hue jaunty old Mr. Pickwick had been using with such skill, but mainly because most of the time with sand bass, in Henry Fordish parlance, any color's fine as long as it's white. Except that some days they like a preponderance of yellow, and once I saw a man winch them in numerously with a saltwater rod and reel and a huge plug that from a distance looked to be lingerie pink. . . .

I started casting far enough up the beach from Younger Daughter that our lines would not get crossed. The northwest wind shoved hard and cold and the thin rain seemed to be flicking more steadily against my numbing cheeks and hands. But then the horsehead jig found its way into some sort of magical pocket along the line where the rapids' forceful long tongue rubbed against eddy water drifting up from the pool. Stout sand bass were holding there, eager and aggressive, and without exactly forgetting the weather I was able for a long while to ignore it. I caught three fish in three casts, lost the feel of the pocket's whereabouts for a time before locating it again and catching two more, then moved on to look for another such place and found it, and afterward found some others still. I gave the fish back to the river, or gave it back to them: shapely, fork-tailed, bright silver creatures with thin dark parallel striping along their sides, gaping rhythmically from the struggle's exhaustion as they eased away backward from my hand in the slow shallows.

I didn't wish they were crappie, to be stowed in the mesh live bag and carried off home as food. If it wasn't a crappie day, it wasn't, and if satisfactory preparation of the sandies' rather coarse flesh involves some kitchen mystery from which our family's cooks have been excluded, the fact remains that they're quite a bit more pleasant to catch than crappie—stronger and quicker and more desperately resistant to being led shoreward on a threadlike line or a leader. In my own form of piscatorial snobbery, I've never much liked the sort of fishing often done for them on reservoirs, where motorboaters race converging on a surfaced feeding school to cast furiously toward its center for a few minutes until it disappears, then wait around for another roaring, rooster-tailed race when that school or another surfaces somewhere else. But my basic snobbery—or trouble, or whatever you want to call it—is not much liking reservoir fishing itself, except sometimes with a canoe in covish

waters at dawn, when all good rooster-tailers and water-skiers and other motorized hypermanics are virtuously still abed, storing up energy for another day of loud wave-making pleasure.

In truth, until a few years ago I more or less despised the sand bass as an alien introduced species fit only for such mechanized pursuit in such artificial waters. But in a live stream on light tackle they subvert that sort of purism, snapping up flies or lures or live minnows with abandon and battling all the way. It isn't a scholarly sort of angling. Taking them has in it little or none of the taut careful fascination, the studious delicacy of lure and presentation, that go with stalking individual good trout, or even sometimes black bass and bream; but it's clean, fine fishing for all that.

Checking my watch, I found with the common angler's surprise that nearly three hours had gone a-glimmering since our arrival at the beach, for it was after four. Younger Daughter and I had hardly spoken during that time, drifting closer together or farther apart while we followed our separate hunches as to where fish might be lying. At this point, though, I heard her yell where she stood a hundred yards or so downshore, and when I looked toward her through the rain—real rain now, if light, that gave her figure in its green jacket a pointillist haziness—I saw she was leaning backward with her rod's doubled-down tip aimed toward something far out in the deep pool, something that was pulling hard.

If she had a mature striper on her frail outfit, there wasn't much prayer that she'd bring him in. But I wanted to be present for the tussle that would take place before she lost him, and I hurried toward her, shouting disjointed, unnecessary advice. She was handling the fish well, giving him line when he demanded it and taking some back when he sulked in the depths, by pumping slowly upward with the rod and reeling in fast as she lowered it again. She lost all that gained line and more when he made an upriver dash, and he'd nearly reached the main rapids before we decided he might not stop there and set off at a jog trot to catch up, Younger Daughter reeling hard all the way to take in slack. But the run against the current tired him, and in a few minutes she brought him to the beach at about the point where we'd met Mr. Pickwick. It was a sand bass rather than a striper, but a very good one for the river. I had no scale along, but estimated the fish would go three and a half pounds easily, maybe nearly four.

"I'm going to keep him," she said. "We can boil him and freeze him in batches for Kitty, the way Mother did one time. Kitty liked it."

"All right," I said, knowing she meant she felt a need to show the rest of the family what she'd caught but didn't want to waste it. The wind, I noticed, had abated somewhat, but the cold rain made up for the lack. "Listen," I said. "I'm pretty

WHITE BASS. (ROCCUS CHRYSOPS. Rafinesque.)

White Bass by S. F. Denton from *South Side Sportsmen's Club* (1896).

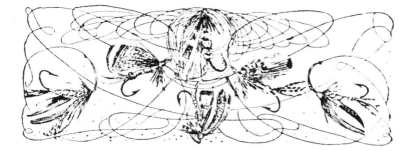

wet and my teeth are starting to chatter. Aren't you about ready to quit?"

A hint of mulishness ridged up along her jawline. "You could go sit in the truck with the heater and play the radio," she said.

I gave vent to a low opinion of that particular idea.

"There's his hat," she said. "The man's."

Sure enough, there it came, the tweed porkpie, shooting down the rapids upside down and half submerged like a leaky, small, crewless boat and no longer looking very jaunty. It must have blown off our friend's head somewhere upriver. Riding the fast tongue of current to where the pool grew deep, it slowed, and I went down and cast at it with a treble-hooked floating plug till I snagged it and reeled it in.

"I guess we can drive up and down and find his car, if we don't find him," I said. "It's a pretty nice hat."

She said in strange reply, "Oh!"

The reason turned out to be that Mr. Pickwick was cruising downriver along the same swift route his hat had taken, but quite a bit more soggily, since his heavy chest waders, swamped full of water, were pulling him toward the bottom as he came. He was in the lower, deepening part of the rapids above us, floating backward in the current— or rather not floating, for as I watched I saw him vanish beneath surging water for five or six long seconds, then surface enormously again as his large pink bald head and his shoulders and rowing arms broke into sight and he took deep gasps of air, maintaining himself symmetrically fore and aft in the river's heavy shove. He stayed up only a few moments before being pulled under again, then reappeared and sucked in more great drafts of air. It had a rhythmic pattern, I could see. He was bending his legs as he sank and kicking hard upward when he touched bottom, and by staying aligned in the current he was keeping it from seizing and tumbling him. He was in control, for the moment at any rate, and I felt the same admiration for him that I'd felt earlier while watching him fish.

I felt also a flash of odd but quite potent reluctance to meddle in the least with his competent, private, downriver progress, or even for that matter to let him know we were witnesses to his plight. Except that, of course, very shortly he was going to be navigating in twelve or fifteen feet of slowing water at the head of the pool, with the waders still dragging him down, and it seemed improbable that any pattern he might work out at that extremely private point was going to do him much good.

Because of the queer reluctance I put an absurd question to the back of his pink pate when it next rose into view. I shouted above the hoarse voice of the water, "Are you all right?"

Still concentrating on his fore-and-aftness and sucking hard for air, he gave no sign of having heard before he once more sounded, but on his next upward heave he gulped in a breath and rolled his head aside to glare at me over his shoulder, out of one long blue bloodshot eye. Shaping the word with care, he yelled from the depths of his throat, "No!"

And went promptly under again.

Trying to gauge water speed and depth and distances, I ran a few steps down the beach and charged in, waving Younger Daughter back when she made a move to follow. I'm not a powerful swimmer even when stripped down, and I knew I'd have to grab him with my boots planted on the bottom if I could. Nor will I deny feeling a touch of panic when I got to the edge of the gentle eddy water, up to my nipples and spookily light-footed with my body's buoyancy, and was brushed by the edge of the rapids' violent tongue and sensed the gravel riverbed's sudden downward slant. No heroics were required, though—fortunately, for they'd likely have drowned us both, with the help of those deadweight waders. Mr. Pickwick made one of his mighty, hippolike surfacings not eight feet upriver from me and only an arm's length outward in the bad tongue water, and as he sailed logily past I snatched a hold on the collar of his many-pocketed vest and let the current swing him around till he too was in the slack eddy, much as one fishes a lure or a fly in such places. Then I towed him in.

Ashore, he sat crumpled on a big rock and stared wide-eyed at his feet and drank up air in huge, sobbing, grateful gasps. All his pinkness had gone gray blue, no jauntiness was in sight, and he even seemed less full-fleshed now, shrunken, his wet fringe of gray hair plastered vertically down beside gray ears. Younger Daughter hovered near him and made the subdued cooing sounds she uses with puppies and baby goats, but I stared at the stone cliff across the Brazos through the haze of thin rain, waiting with more than a tinge of embarrassment for his breathing to grow less labored. I had only a snap notion of what this man was like, but it told me he didn't deserve being watched while he was helpless. Maybe no one does.

He said at last, "I never had that happen before."

I said, "It's a pretty tough river when it's up."

"They all are," he answered shortly, and breathed a little more, still staring down.

He said, "It was my knees. I was crossing at the head of this chute, coming back downriver. They just buckled in the current and whoosh, by God, there we went."

"We've got your hat," Younger Daughter told him, as though she hoped that might set things right.

"Thank you, sweet lady," he said, and smiled as best he could.

"That was some beautiful tackle you lost," I said. "At least I guess it's lost."

"It's lost, all right," said Mr. Pickwick. "Good-bye to it. It doesn't amount to much when you think what I . . ."

But that was a direction I somehow didn't want the talk to take, nor did I think he wanted it to go there either. I was god-awfully cold in my soaked, clinging, skimpy clothes and knew he must be even colder, exhausted as he was. I said I wished I had a drink to offer him. He said he appreciated the thought but he could and would offer me one if we could get to his car a quarter-mile down the shore, and I sent Young Daughter trotting off with his keys to drive it back to where we were. The whiskey was nice sour-mash stuff, though corrosive Skid Row swill would have tasted fine just then. We peeled him out of the deadly waders and got him into some insulated coveralls that were in his car, and after a little he began to pinken up again, but still with the crumpled, shrunken look.

He and I talked for a bit, sipping the good whiskey straight from plastic cups. He was a retired grain dealer from Kentucky, and what he did mainly now was fish. He and his wife had a travel trailer in which they usually wintered on the Texas coast near Padre Island, where he worked the red-fish and speckled trout of the bays with popping gear or sometimes a fly rod when the wind and water were right. Then in February they would start a slow zigzag journey north to bring them home for spring. He'd even fished steelhead in British Columbia—the prettiest of all, he said, the high green wooded mountains dropping steeply to fjords and the cold strong rivers flowing in from their narrow valleys. . . .

When we parted, he came as close as he could to saying the thing that neither he nor I wanted him to have to say. He said, "I want . . . Damn, I never had that happen to me before." And stopped. Then he said, "Jesus, I'm glad you were there."

"You'd have been all right," I said. "You were doing fine."

But he shook his strangely shrunken pink head without smiling, and when I turned away, he clapped my shoulder and briefly gripped it.

In the pickup as we drove toward home, Younger Daughter was very quiet for a while. I was thinking about the terrible swiftness with which old age could descend, for that was what we'd been watching even if I'd tried not to know it. I felt intensely the health and strength of my own solid body, warmed now by the whiskey and by a fine blast from the pickup's heater fan. If on the whole I hadn't treated it as carefully as I might have over the years, this body, and if in consequence it was a little battered and overweight and had had a few things wrong with it from time to time, it had nonetheless served me and served me well, and was still doing so. It housed whatever brains and abilities I could claim to have and carried out their dictates, and it functioned for the physical things I liked to do, fishing and hunting and country work and the rest. It had been and was a very satisfactory body.

But it was only ten or twelve years younger than the old grain dealer's, at most, and I had to wonder now what sort of sickness or accident or other disruption of function—what buckling of knee, what tremor of hand, what milkiness of vision, what fragility of bone, what thinness of artery wall— would be needed, when the time came, to push me over into knowledge that I myself was old. Having to admit it, that was the thing. . . .

Then, with the astonishment the young bring to a recognition that tired, solemn, ancient phrases have meaning, my daughter uttered what I hadn't wanted to hear the old man say. She said, "You saved his life!"

"Maybe so," I said. "We just happened to be on hand."

She was silent for a time longer, staring out the window at the rain that fell on passing fields and woods. Finally she said, "That's a good fish I caught."

"Damn right it is," I said.

SUMMER

*The fisherman's condition couldn't be better.
His eyes are sharp, his aim is true, he's got his
timing down. He is yet another natural element
among those that swim beneath and flutter above him.
He's aware of every one. The fisherman is all business now.*

Young men of summer are generally proud and often arrogant. It is part of their hubris to think they can beat the system. Any system. There are no obstacles that cannot be overcome, in their thinking, if you are determined enough and strong enough. You can even reverse the first law of fishing: *No fisherman ever fishes as much as he wants to.*

The man who believes he can break the grip of this law is not necessarily idly rich or insane. He merely believes he can satisfy his urge to fish by fishing *harder.* He arrives at the river earlier and leaves later than other men. He doesn't stop for lunch. When he comes to fish, his tackle is in order. His leader and line are joined by a perfect nail knot that was tied the night before and reinforced with some epoxy. His flies are sorted and stored by pattern and size, and he has enough reel spools to hold line for virtually any fishing occasion: floating, sinking, sink-tip, fast-sinking, Hi-D, shooting heads. There is a place for everything in his vest, and everything is in its place. The idea is to *fish,* not to waste time looking through accumulated tackle for the right fly. And since he's come to fish, he gets started early and covers a lot of water. He changes flies and tactics if he doesn't catch anything. He keeps moving, working, thinking, trying things. Fishing *hard.* Getting *mad* at those fish.

Most people I know have fished like that, at least for a little while. The most extreme case I have ever known was a man who left his office every single Friday during trout season and, without even going home to change clothes, drove seven hours to the nearest good fishing river where he had leased a cabin. He would unpack, eat something, change out of his business suit and into his fishing clothes. Around two in the morning he would be in the swift black water of that river, testing each step and false casting until he was in position to work a big streamer through a pool for one large, night-feeding brown trout.

He kept it up until dawn, when he changed to a large wet fly, hoping to imitate a dead moth or some other nocturnal insect that had drowned and was being carried downstream. He would change flies again, as the day warmed, according to the season and the activity along the river. He seldom quit before breakfast. He carried some oranges and wrapped sausages in his vest and left a thermos of coffee hidden somewhere on the bank for needed mid-morning stimulation.

There were those days, in the late spring and early summer, when four or five different mayflies would be hatching—or likely to hatch—during the course of a day. Then he might start out with blue-winged Olives, go to March Browns, through Sulphurs and Drakes, and finish with a fall of the previous day's hatched insects. There could feasibly be insects on the surface of the water—and fish feeding on them—*all day long.* He could not chance missing a hatch merely for two or three hours of sleep. He wouldn't have been able to sleep anyway. So he stayed on the river all day, dragging himself wearily back to the cabin and climbing out of his waders, which by then felt like a body bag, two or three hours after sunset on Saturday night.

Though by this time he was too tired to have much appetite, he would cook something hearty, knowing that he needed to be restored. While the chili or beef stew warmed, he would stand under a hot shower and slowly soap his weary body. When he had shaved his sunburned face and dressed in clean clothes, he would sit down to two bowls of hot food and a coffee cup of Jack Daniel's. Then he would go to bed and sleep for five hours, hearing all the time the sound of the river just beyond his window. He would be up before sunrise on Sunday and would fish all day, climbing out of the river only after sunset, when he would return once again to his cabin.

He could not afford to eat heartily then, because he would be driving. He would pack, fill a thermos with coffee, change back into the business suit, and drive seven hours with the vent window cocked at forty-five degrees so that a stream of air would play across his face and keep his eyes opened. The wind and the black coffee were always enough, and he would arrive at his office on Monday morning still smelling vaguely of insect repellent, fish, and the river. Sometimes, he said, he would be sitting at his desk, talking on the phone, and

Louis Rhead, *The End of a Stiff Fight* (1902).

Winslow Homer, *Ouananiche Fishing:
Lake Saint John* (1897).

suddenly he would feel the river flowing around his hips and between his legs, much like the seaman home from a long voyage who feels the roll of the ship while sitting in his chair at home. It would be Wednesday before he felt completely right again.

On one of those marathon weekends, after a week that included two enervating business trips complete with overnights in strange hotels, he got out of the river at four o'clock Saturday morning because he could not take anymore. He was so tired he felt vertiginous, like a man standing on the edge of a cliff. He knew that any minute he was going to lose his footing and fall into the dark river, fill up his waders, and perhaps even drown, all because he was so tired he simply did not know which way was up.

He made his way to the bank, sliding his feet carefully along the gravel bottom—shuffling, almost. Once he was on dry land, he sat down and leaned against the trunk of a large tree. He was too tired to go back to the cabin, or even to the spot where he had cached his coffee thermos. He fell asleep almost immediately, still wearing his waders.

The sun had risen when he woke up. He opened his eyes and saw a fisherman standing in the river where he had been the night before. The man was looking back at him, puzzled and a little alarmed. My sleeping friend probably looked dead, and if you had merely stumbled on him, you might have concluded that he'd suffered a coronary and had barely made it out of the river before his heart failed completely.

He waved to the worried fisherman, who waved back, then immediately turned away and began working his way upstream without so much as a look back. "Once I'd established that I was not dead," my friend said, "he probably figured I was drunk. That was the only other good explanation for why I was lying up under that tree with my eyes closed and my mouth open."

He ached everywhere, and every part of his body that was not covered with clothing had been mosquito-bitten. "My face and hands looked like the inside of a watermelon," he said. "I had bites on bites. One ear was swollen up as thick as your thumb. I was a sight. If I had come across somebody like that in the woods, I might have just backed off and never mentioned it."

He stood and splashed some river water on his face, which made him feel a little better. Then he stumbled downstream to the place where he had left his coffee, and after a cup he felt a *lot* better. He decided that there was no point in going back to the cabin. "What was I going to do in there? Place didn't even have a radio. The only thing you could do in that cabin was sleep, and I'd been asleep for almost four hours." So he stepped into the river and started fishing again. "The worst part," he said, "was the bites. Next time I'm that tired, I'll remember to load up with the Cutter's and wear one of those hats with a mosquito net rolled up under it. Then I'll be set."

Fishing isn't quite a game; it is too serious. You care too much. And it isn't a sport, because there is no good way to keep score. Nobody wins or loses. This is true in spite of the fact that there are all sorts of fishing tournaments these days, complete with cash prizes and beauty queens. In the case of southern bass fishing, there is even a race of professional fishermen who travel from tournament to tournament, living on their winnings and the fees they charge for endorsements. Just like golfers. This all seems to miss the point; but no matter. It is here, and here to stay. It exists simply because that's the way people are—or have become.

It is hard for most of us to know satisfaction in nonrelative terms. It requires too much lonely self-confidence simply to be happy by one's own lights. Thoreau's advice is easy to understand but damned hard to follow. We need to know not merely that we are rich, but *richer* than so and so. Or younger, prettier, sexier, wiser, more saintly. Or a better nymph fisherman.

It is comic on the one hand and ugly on the other. There is no way, no way at all, to measure fishing success. The empirical standards are all insufficient. It is not necessarily how many fish you catch—you could use a net. Or how large—you could use a harpoon. Or how difficult the means—you could use a

Oliver Kemp, who died in 1934 at age forty-eight, was perhaps the best-known outdoors artist of his time. Kemp contributed numerous covers to *The Saturday Evening Post.*

George Luks, *Trout Fishing* (1919).

straight pin and cotton thread that tested at less than a pound. The essence of fishing cannot be quantified or categorized. Its values come from a sense of proportion and unities that are almost spiritual. Once you understand that, a six-inch brook trout can mean as much as a five-pound brown if the context is right.

But if you spend enough time trout fishing, you hear a lot of talk that makes trout fishing sound like baseball or tennis. One evening I was fishing in the Battenkill, sharing a pool with another fisherman, and I observed the competitive urge.

The other fisherman and I were far enough apart that we weren't interfering with each other, but we were close enough to study each other. That's not the best situation in a trout stream, but the celebrated Battenkill draws pilgrims from New York and Boston for whom sharing a trout pool is the height of solitude. I live near the river and would have gone looking for another pool, but it was late, and there were some fish rising, and I had to get home soon. So . . . we shared the pool in silence, casting and changing flies and watching as the fish began to feed more actively.

The other man was wearing a bright green shirt and one of those Irish tweed hats. His equipment was in mint condition, and he handled the fly rod deftly. He was a serious fisherman and no rookie.

There were, I noticed, some spinners on the water. I knew to look for them because a friend had seen them the night before and hit pay dirt on a small polywing imitation he tied and sold to me along with the information. So I quickly caught three or four fish. The man in the hat called across the pool to ask what I was using. I told him. He tried something from his box with no success, so I made my way over to him and gave him a couple of the little flies. He thanked me and was playing a fish before I left the pool.

I was out of my waders and behind the wheel of my car when he came up the path from the river. His partner was waiting there for him. "Great fishing," he said. "I go three nice ones."

"Oh, yeah?" the man I had shared the pool with said. "That's great."

"How did you do?"

"Not bad. I caught twelve."

Twelve? Not while I was looking. It was a lie and a lie out of all proportion, a lie that was tinged with a kind of nasty smugness that made me want to step out of the gloom and witness the truth.

I didn't, of course, but I thought about that little episode as I drove home, and I have thought about it a lot since then. There was no reason for the man to lie. He had not been skunked, which is the great fear of every fisherman. To read the books and magazines, you would think that it never happens, that no man who is knowledgeable enough and well enough outfitted ever spends a day on the water and catches nothing. But it happens all the time. Even so, it is a shameful thing, especially when you are trying to explain to a nonfisherman why it is you fish. Most fishermen lie about being skunked. My fanatical friend who went to sleep in the woods used to tell people that he'd caught a "couple of little rainbows" whenever he was skunked. That was, I thought, a perfectly proportioned lie. Most of the time you *could* catch a couple of rainbows in the streams he fished. It was nothing to be proud of. So when he lied, his intentions weren't all *that* bad.

There are horrible times when you are skunked and there is no face-saving way around it. I saw this happen to the celebrated Doug Swisher, coauthor of *Selective Trout* and *Fly Fishing Strategy*. He was holding a fishing seminar on the Beaverkill on a lovely spring day. It was time for all sorts of hatches, between the March Browns and Green Drakes, as I recall. The water was clear and swift. It was a fine time to be fishing and, according to the book, a likely day for catching fish. But no matter how hard Swisher tried, he could not interest a single trout in that fabled river. Nor could his students. By the end of the day Swisher had nothing to show for his time except a sunburn. And there was no plausible lie; there were too many witnesses. He was embarrassed, but I took great comfort in that episode. If it could happen to him, it could happen to anyone.

George Marples, *On the Feed* (1924).

Winslow Homer, *The Mink Pond* (1891).

Winslow Homer, *Leaping Trout* (ca. 1889).

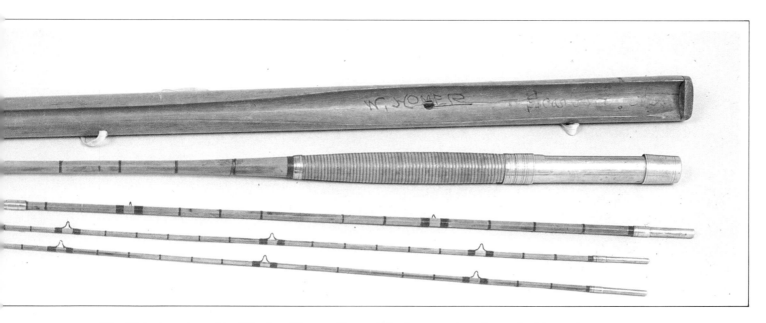

The Nichols rod used by Winslow Homer. The artist's signature is at the end of the rod case.

Robert Nisbet, untitled etching (ca. 1955).

But the man in the green shirt and tweed hat had not been skunked. He'd caught at least one fish, and not a bad one at that. He could have told it like that: "Only managed to get one up, but he was a nice fish." No shame in that, especially on the Battenkill.

Nor would telling the truth have made him look feeble. Three to one is not a rout in hockey or soccer or fishing. If the man's partner had announced that he'd caught thirty fish, that might have been a different matter. A lie of some

George Marples, *Mayfly Time* (1924).

sort would have been called for, sheerly in self-defense. "Thirty," he might have said, "that's great. I didn't get nearly that many. But I got one that was real nice."

However, the man was not lying to avoid humiliation, rather to inflict it. Why? And why settle on twelve? Why not fifteen? Or ten? Why not double his partner's catch and merely say six? Why lie to your partner at all? Your wife, perhaps. The people in the office, certainly. But your *partner*?

It had to be a case of sheer frustrated competitiveness, unless the men were related and there was a lifetime of motive in the lie. If they were friends, they should have been doing something else together—playing golf or tennis, perhaps, and keeping a running score, paying off bets in beer.

That sort of thing has its place in the world, to be sure. The fact is, its place seems more and more to be everywhere. Women are rated on a scale of one to ten. On a percentage or two in the television ratings hang the fates of hundreds of high-priced men with ulcers. We keep track, obsessively, of who is ahead and who is behind, largely by the bloodless abstract method of looking at the numbers. That sort of obsession is what you go fishing to escape, however temporarily. Some men, especially young ones, don't understand that.

Phillip Little, *White River Run* (1929).

A mechanic I knew was working on a stubborn generator in a hot garage one summer afternoon. He'd eaten a big lunch of greens and black-eyed peas, corn bread and buttermilk. He was tired and everything felt heavy. The best thing that generator could have done for him was to turn into a pillow. But there it was, mute and ugly, fighting him all the way. Finally, it came down to one small screw, the head of which was hidden by a steel flange with a wicked corner. The mechanic found a screwdriver with a shaft a foot long, and he was able to get just enough angle to fit the head of it into the slot of the screw. He applied pressure, and the screw turned slowly. The mechanic was sweating and impatient. He applied more pressure, and the screw made another turn. Then the bit slipped from the slot, his slick hand slipped off the handle, and his meaty knuckle hit the corner of the flange with the force of a good right cross. The mechanic came up with every knuckle of his greasy right hand skinned and bleeding.

"Use the right tool," an old man who was sitting in the shop said, "and you won't skin your knuckles. You need to get you an offset screwdriver." He was right—and old enough to get away with saying it—and I have thought about that advice often. Especially as it applies to fishing, and justifies owning an excessive amount of equipment.

An engraving from *The American Turf Register and Sporting Magazine* (1839).

Winch in Butt.

Foster's Steel-centred Fly Rod.

Pike Rod.

General Rod.

Ash Trolling Rod.

New Style of Pike Rod

Bottom Ferrule of Walking-stick Rod.

Walking-stick Rod.

This sampling of antique rods was published in J. H. Keane's *Fishing Tackle* (1885).
In his treatise the author judges bamboo to be the superior material for a rod,
while arguing strongly against cedar. The latter "is only fit for a *dilettante* [*sic*]
angler who fishes open water where there is no danger of a foul on his back cast,
and who is ever on his guard to give the fish no opportunity to strike his fly
when the rod is approaching the perpendicular."

One hundred years of trout gear. The reels, from left to right: a rare English model (1870); another unsigned reel (late 1870s); the Martin automatic (1926); the Clinton fly reel (1890); an inexpensive reel (1890s); the Kosmic multiplying reel (1890s); a design by Edward von Hofe (1883); a design by Leonard Mills (1920s). The rods, from

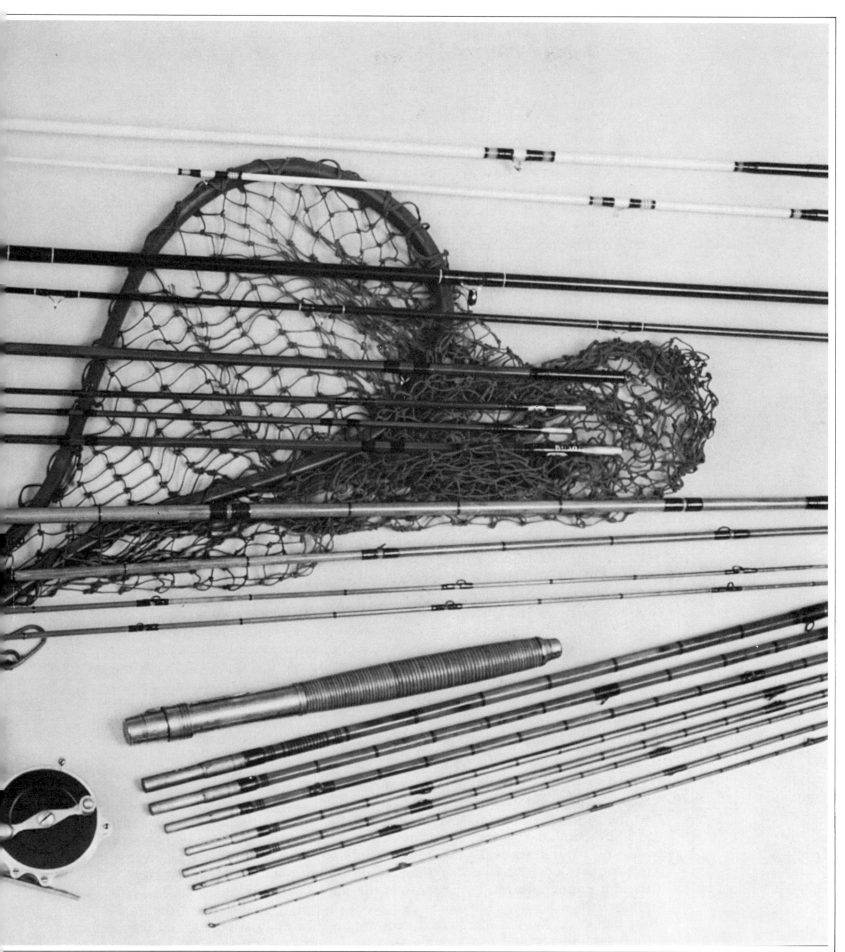

top to bottom: the Shakespeare "Wonderod" (1950s); Fenwick
graphite prototype (1974); an F. E. Thomas three-piece fly rod (1920);
a Thomas Chubb lancewood rod (1890); an H. L. Leonard valise rod
(1880). Both the creel and the landing net date from the 1920s.

The Orvis Company offers for sale more than one hundred different fly rods. If you owned them all, you would not be a fisherman or even a collector; you would be a fanatic. But if you eliminated duplication of materials—there is no reason to have the same rod in glass, graphite, and bamboo—and close duplication of function, you could still justify owning around thirty different fly rods by saying that each served a particular purpose. A man, after all, cannot be expected to fish brushy New England creeks for brook trout and Florida mangrove islands for snook with the same rod. There is no all-purpose fly rod. But nobody really needs to own thirty fly rods, either. There is some prudent middle ground.

But a young buck wants all thirty. I have known men who owned all thirty and were on the lookout for the rod that they did not own: the little four-piece midge rod, tapered especially for spring creeks, say, that would round out the collection once and for all.

My theory is that a passion for equipment, which by the evidence hits young men with special force, is a sublimation. If there is not ever enough time to fish, even if you fish hard, there is at least enough money to buy all the tackle and to experience the vicarious thrill of holding a five-hundred-dollar Leonard rod in your hand when you are stuck in some high-rise apartment or suburban two-story with garage and patio. The catalogs come in the mail all year long, and the closest some men get to fishing for months at a time is studying those glossy pages and writing checks, then waiting for the rod to come. It is just the thing, they think as they fondle it for the first time, for next year at Henry's Fork. Just the thing.

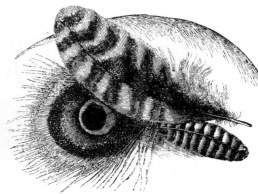

Almost every fisherman is fascinated by tackle. In the general sense, tackle includes everything from little goosenecked flashlights that clip onto your vest and help you see to change your flies in the last gray light of day or at night, to stomach pumps for trout that enable you to see what the fish was eating without killing him. (I for one have never really understood that one and find it almost obscene. If you caught the thing, he was obviously feeding, or willing to feed, on whatever you were using.) In the case of tackle, a part may very well stand for the whole, and in the case of fly fishermen, that part is rods. Nothing excites a fly fisherman like the prospect of owning a fine new rod—or, for that matter, a fine *old* rod.

That is not to say that he doesn't get excited about other things. He does. I have a friend who was obsessive about fly boxes. He simply had to own the perfect fly box. He began as many serious equipment fanatics do, with those lovely aluminum boxes by Wheatley. They are very precise and well machined, very English. They open on a smooth hinge, and inside there are tiny clips for wets and nymphs, and small windowed compartments for dries; lovely things, really, but on the heavy side, my friend decided. He wanted something lighter and went to a Scientific Anglers plastic box with little slots inside that gripped the hook so that each fly stood up smartly for inspection. It was much lighter than the Wheatley box and satisfactory—except that you had to open the box to see if the fly you wanted was inside. Maybe one of those clear plastic boxes was the answer. So he got a bunch of them from Leonard. Then he decided that the business of having several different fly boxes rattling around in his vest was impractical and inefficient, so he ordered an apparatus from Abercrombie that hung around his neck and looked something like a miniature tool chest. It had compartmented drawers that you could pull out and study, and it had space for enough flies to cover most of the major patterns and some idiosyncratic personal favorites. It was at that point that my friend decided the entire thing had gone too far. He started keeping his flies in cigar boxes, and before he left home he would pick out a dozen or so and stick them in the sheepskin band of his hat. "I was beginning to feel like a librarian," he said.

Fly boxes were his minor passion, however. Like that of other fly fishermen, his grand obsession was with rods. A rod is the indispensable tool of the art and the vessel of all its mysteries. Craft and skill and tradition are built into the best rods.

There are rods and there are *rods,* manufacturers and builders. And master builders. Standards are as elusive as Oriental ethics, and there is—beyond a certain minimal point—no objective standard by which one can judge a rod. It comes down to personal preference. Still, grown men seriously dispute the qualities of a good, or even a sublime, fly rod. They write whole books about it. The estimable Arnold Gingrich argued for the short rod, for instance, preferring those that were six feet or less. He was especially fond of one that was four feet and some inches, not really very much longer than his arm. On the other hand, the equally estimable Leonard Wright believes that long rods, the nine-plus-footers, do best what a rod should do. There is no resolution to this argument, which becomes, at times, as arcane as the conflicts of scholastic theology. Fine fishermen have prospered with short rods, and fine fishermen have also prospered with long rods—which does not mean, sadly, that the difference is unimportant.

It gets still more involved. There is much more to it than length. But before getting into the details, a few things should be established. First, a rod is just a fishing pole. Cheap will catch fish, and so will expensive. The all-around trout rod is still eight feet long and carries a six-weight line. The all-around bass rod is eight and a half feet long and carries an eight-weight line. You could own both in fiberglass, a couple of Pflueger Medalist reels with an extra spool or two for the trick lines you will need from time to time, some flies and bugs, leaders, and a few odds and ends, and . . . if you did your homework and learned how to cast and read water, you would probably catch just as many fish as the man who has invested twenty or thirty times what you've spent. But the truth is, you probably don't exist. Fooling around with tackle is a big part of fishing, and if you don't like that part of it, chances are you don't much like the rest of it either.

So when you begin to dabble in rods, the first thing you notice is that the most obvious difference between one rod and another is the material from which each is constructed. Some materials are cheap and others are preciously expensive. Fiberglass is the cheapest material, and glass rods are good, fundamental tools. You could fish a lifetime with glass rods and not die deprived—provided you used rods from good companies, such as Fenwick, Scientific Anglers, or Berkley, or bought from a good builder, some of whom make glass rods that match the performance and the price of rods built from more expensive materials. Nobody has anything really bad to say about glass rods. They tend to be heavy, and they wobble more than the perfect rod should, so you can get something like a sine wave running the length of your cast if you aren't careful. But if you are a good caster, you will do fine with a glass rod, and if you are learning to cast, you won't be threatening some delicate instrument. Glass rods are sturdy, and some very fine anglers prefer them for that reason, especially the men who fish for steelhead with heavy lines. Glass rods are as reliable and unpretentious as canned beer.

Few fishermen fall undyingly in love with them. Most fishermen who start on glass soon want to move up to something better. A young man with money to spend begins looking fondly at bamboo and graphite.

Bamboo is for classicists. The great rods of history were made with Tonkin cane, and there are people who carry on the tradition today—tradition, incidentally, that almost perished during the cold war. Before Richard Nixon reopened the gates of China, it was almost impossible for rod builders to acquire cane. Some of them used the poles that Oriental rugs were wrapped around—these by way of England—or disassembled rattan furniture. Chinese cane is unique and there is no natural substitute for it. Devotees argue that there is no substitute for it at all, though the graphite manufacturers shake their heads over such quaint sentimenality.

The traditional split-bamboo rod is a little more than a century old, and the man who made the first one was, appropriately, a violin maker. What he did, essentially, was to take four strips from a stalk of bamboo, which he mitered down to a predetermined taper. He glued the bamboo strips together and let the glue set under pressure. The result was a remarkably tough rod with deep, continuous action, the sort of flexibility that enables bamboo plants to grow one hundred feet tall and still survive typhoon winds.

The split-bamboo rod was a breakthrough. An angler could use it to cast distances that were out of the question with rods made of solid woods such as greenheart. Bamboo also opened up a new field to craftsmen with the patience and the skills to build the rods. The demand was there, and the suppliers soon followed.

The most noted was Hiram Leonard, an independent and resourceful man from Maine who loved the outdoors and lamented the things that were being done to it. He was a guide, but he wanted to do something else. Rod building was the alternative he settled on.

He improved the early split-cane rods, making the tapers more subtle, using nickel silver ferrules, wire guides with fine red silk wrappings, and rattan reel seats. His rods were clean and elegant, light but strong. They performed beautifully.

As the demand for his rods increased, he expanded his rod-building operation and brought in men who later went out on their own and whose names, along with Leonard's, make up the roll call of the best builders in history. Those rods were, and still are, the purest expressions of the art. Nothing in split cane is done any better than it was in the glory days of Hiram Leonard, Everett Garrison, and Jim Payne. The glues are now synthetic and easier to work with than the old animal glues, and they are more resistant to mildew and dampness. Some bamboo is now heat-treated for better temper. Orvis impregnates its rods with an epoxy, a process that was as much a boon to the Orvis Company as it was to rod building. The government gave Orvis the contract on ski poles during the Second World War. The poles were to be made of impregnated bamboo, just like the Orvis rods, and so the company was able to acquire bamboo on a priority basis while other builders had to get by on prewar inventories. When peace came, Orvis had a significant jump on the competition, which it still held at the time of the embargo on products from mainland China. This is not to say that Orvis does not make a fine rod. My favorite rod is an Orvis eight-footer with a sweet, slow action that I have not been able to find in any other rod. In fact, I have a short, quick Orvis rod that I like very much, too.

The apogee of the age of cane came in the first three decades of the twentieth century. Then the great makers grew older, supplies of cane dried up, and glass came along. After the Second World War cane rods became almost a novelty.

In the past ten or fifteen years, however, there has been a renaissance. The Leonard Company in Central Valley, New York, still makes fine rods, and so does the Orvis Company in Manchester, Vermont. Several other manufacturers produce quality split-cane rods, and a few individual builders custom-make rods for their customers. The market in classic rods has boomed enormously. Vintage Paynes and Garrisons sell for more than five hundred dollars in some cases and, every so often in the case of an exceptional rod, more than that.

What is it, finally, about cane? Putting aside for a moment the legends of the great makers and the few thousand rods they were able to build by painstaking methods, let's consider this question: Does cane make a better rod? And why does cane appeal to men like Hoagy Carmichael, Jr. (son of the entertainer), who dedicates himself to making rods strictly by hand the way he learned from the late Everett Garrison, a master who made only eight hundred rods during his life? And why will a fisherman pay Carmichael several hundred dollars for a rod that takes more than two weeks to build? The rod will not (repeat, *not*) catch any more fish than a glass or graphite rod. It is more fragile and more easily broken. Is it snobbery, or is there something about cane?

I must think that there is something special about cane, because I seem to leave the house time after time carrying a cane rod, especially when I am going fishing for trout. I own a four-piece glass rod that I use for bass and a couple of graphite rods in trout tapers that I use from time to time. But I still like something about cane that I call the "feel," because that is what most people say they like about cane rods and I can't really come up with anything better.

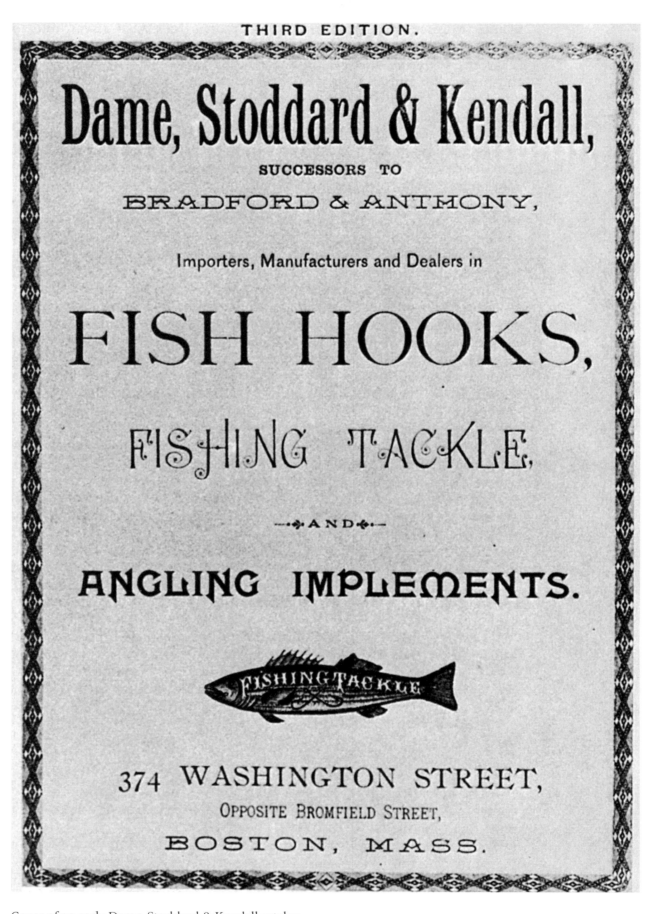

THIRD EDITION.

Dame, Stoddard & Kendall,

SUCCESSORS TO

BRADFORD & ANTHONY,

Importers, Manufacturers and Dealers in

FISH HOOKS,

FISHING TACKLE,

— AND —

ANGLING IMPLEMENTS.

FISHING TACKLE

374 WASHINGTON STREET,

OPPOSITE BROMFIELD STREET,

BOSTON, MASS.

Cover of an early Dame, Stoddard & Kendall catalog.
Considered the oldest tackle shop in the United States, Stoddard's began
operations in 1800 under the name Samuel Bradford's. Over the
decades the establishment outfitted Boston's upper crust with
custom-made reels, lancewood rods, and handmade rods by such as
Hiram Leonard and Charles Murphy.

Also, I am enchanted by the idea of the thing—the stripping and mitering and gluing. I don't own many fine things, but I count my five cane rods among them. And there is something about owning a fine thing that you can also *use* that I find alluring. The world of instant collectibles and priceless antiques seems to me to belong to museums. A cane rod is different. It is built to be fished; it derives its value from the fact that it does what it was built to do very well and satisfies aesthetic considerations as well. It is almost unique that way.

By any scientific measure, however, cane is probably not the best all-around rod-building material. Classicists may argue, but graphite rods probably do more of the things that a rod should do and come closer to doing them with Platonic perfection.

Like fiberglass rods, those built from graphite are manufactured, not made by hand. They do not lend themselves to craftsmanship. A graphite rod is constructed by spinning fibers and epoxy around a mandrel to make a blank. The fibers, in this case, are carbon and glass—graphite—and the result is a rod that is tougher and lighter than a glass rod and has a much faster recovery, the speed with which the rod steadies after action has been put to it. Ideally, a rod should stabilize almost immediately after taking one deep bend. There should be no residual vibration. Graphite and cane are about equal in this regard; glass falls behind.

Graphite rods are tough. When they first came along, they were too tough—brittle, in fact—and they tended to break under heavy use. But the technology has advanced since then, and the rods are still tough but more pliable. Where graphite is clearly superior to both cane and glass is in weight-to-strength ratio. A general-purpose trout rod in graphite might weigh two ounces or less, whereas it would run almost four ounces in bamboo and nearly six in glass. That makes a marginal difference in artful eastern trout fishing. When you move up to bass or salmon fishing, however, the difference becomes significant. Graphite is less fatiguing and therefore makes for better casting over the course of a day; this makes things more pleasant all the way around and probably means more fish, too. It's as simple as that.

The scientific and pragmatic arguments for graphite have obviously persuaded many anglers, because you see more and more black rods on any stream you fish. Even some notably conservative fly fishermen have made the switch to graphite from cane, among them John Voelker and Charles Fox, the unofficial keeper of the Letort. He likes graphite because he can get a great deal of length in a light rod, and a nine-foot rod keeps his back cast out of the bushes. Voelker simply admits to casting better with graphite but says that he will probably go back to cane in spite of that. He hates to concede anything to the modern age.

John Merwin, who is the editor of *Rod and Reel* magazine, also likes graphite. Merwin is an unusual specimen—a perfectionist with a sense of humor. He is a first-rate fisherman, photographer, and fly tier who does not confuse the things one does on a river with the search for the Grail. He still fishes for the fun of it. We fish the Battenkill together from time to time, and when we are rigging up, he always asks, "You still using cane?" Merwin casts better than I can, and he catches more fish. But although he has wit, he does not understand about the feel of cane. And I pity him.

A young fisherman, even if he is not prosperous enough to buy a ten- or twelve-piece rod collection, will inevitably buy hundreds of flies—many, many more than he needs.

Trout flies and salmon flies, especially, are beautiful in their own right, in the same way the fish they are designed to deceive are beautiful. They are delicate and fragile, and their colors mix in unexpected, bold ways. Some are gaudy, like the Royal Coachman, and some are regal, like the Jock Scott. Some are austere, like my favorite, the Adams. There is something about all of them that draws the attention of fishermen and nonfishermen both.

My wife, for example, learned to tie flies before she ever fished. She has wonderful long fingers that can do delicate, precise work easily, and she loves

From the S. Allcock & Co. catalog (1887), England.

color. She found flies and fly tying irresistible.

For the fisherman, there is pleasure in merely owning flies, sometimes thousands of them. You can hold a Joe's Hopper in the palm of your hand and easily visualize a hot late-summer afternoon on the meadow stretches of a river, with hundreds of grasshoppers in the fields, one every now and then misjudging and going into the river, where it floats downstream, kicks once or twice, then disappears in the sudden swirl left by a feeding trout.

Because they can so palpably evoke the sensations of fishing, and because they are designed with such specificity, flies are simply too tempting for the young man who doesn't fish anywhere near as much as he wants to. Selecting and buying flies is a form of vicarious fishing, for one thing. For another, the thought of being on the water when the fish are feeding and *not having the right fly* is almost too much to bear.

That isn't such a likely possibility, but you would have a hard time convincing a fisherman who is a captive of the city and his work of that, especially if he keeps up with the fishing journals. For the past twenty or thirty years the discovery and identification of fly patterns has been a curious analog of the discovery and identification of atomic particles. Every physicist, it sometimes seems, is in a great hurry to discover some new subatomic particle so that he can publish a paper and have the particle named after himself. Likewise, every angling authority scrambles to discover a new fly pattern, write a book or an article about it, then have the thing named for him. If a new pattern doesn't reveal itself, a new way of tying an old pattern will have to do. So we have no-hackle and thorax-tied versions of the standard patterns, as well as parachutes and spent wings, and lately, even stillborns, which are designed to imitate mayflies that perished in childbirth. What is obviously needed, in physics and fly-fishing, is a new Newton or Einstein—or Schwiebert or Flick—to cut through the complexity and give us a new, unifying theory. So far such a giant has not appeared, and the number of patterns continues to expand toward the point of hopelessness.

But the signs are encouraging. The venerable Art Flick (what a great name for a fly fisherman!), whose *Streamside Guide* was probably the original text of the "match-the-hatch movement," has warned in print that things may be getting out of hand. It is time, he wrote in *Gray's Sporting Journal,* to get away from the business of infinite patterns to cover infinite situations and get back to fishing. The finest fisherman he ever knew, Flick writes, used only one pattern, the Leadwing Coachman, which is probably not even among those considered by the present-day entomologist/fisherman. But the man was successful, Flick adds, because he could read water and put the fly where he wanted to put it. Perhaps, if there is no revolution at hand, there is at least the beginning of a neoclassical movement.

I remember a slow trip in the Upper Peninsula of Michigan in a summer when another book enumerating a few dozen absolutely essential flies had just come out. It was full of information about the biology of different mayflies, and it used more Latin than the traditional mass. My two partners and I sat on the bank of an unproductive river drinking Moosehead Ale from bottles we had left to cool in the stream. "You suppose," one of them said, "that there is some fly we haven't tried that would be just the ticket? That maybe one of us should have read that book?"

"Trout didn't read it either."

"Wouldn't have understood it if they had."

"There are times when anything will catch fish and times when nothing will. That covers about ninety-five percent of it. Those guys who write the books are talking about five percent of the time when the fish are selective. Even then you can substitute or trim up a fly that is close. I don't buy all of that exact science. It's fishing."

We watched the river move unhurriedly on and enjoyed our beer and played a time-killing game, much like the one that was popular in the thirties in which you decide what ten books you would take with you if you were exiled to a desert island. What flies would you choose to carry, we asked ourselves, if you

could have only ten? I cannot remember the exact list. It almost certainly included the Adams and the Muddler, the Woolly Worm and the Light Cahill, the Irresistible and the Fox Variant, and the Henryville. Whatever the flies, we all agreed, you could do with only a few patterns in the normal size ranges—do damned well, in fact, though you could not have proved it by any of us that day.

Of course, you don't have to limit yourself to a dozen patterns at one extreme, or fill your vest with a hundred at the other. You can do the sensible thing and buy or tie flies for the river and season in question. If you were going up to the Catskills in May, for instance, you would be fairly safe buying a handful of Hendricksons and Olive Caddises. And you could leave the grasshoppers and the white-winged Blacks at home.

It doesn't work that way, however, to the great relief of the people who tie flies for Orvis and Dan Bailey's. The orders keep coming in from fishermen who are sure that the key to the thing lies in never being caught short when you are out on the stream. Should the *Baetis* hatch appear early, or late, the only thing for it is to be equipped with blue-winged Olives in every size, tied parachute, no hackle, and thorax; also the nymphs in the appropriate sizes, and some polywinged spinners. There is truly no end to it all, and for millions that is the joy of it.

Beside every good trout stream of any size and reputation there is a shop. For the fisherman with equipment fever, this is the first stop on one of his frantic weekend fishing trips. He goes in, he tells himself, just to see what the fish have been taking and to see if he can pick up a useful tip. He leaves twenty dollars or more later. There is always something he needs.

The shops are friendly places that have captured the essence of the material side of the sport. The flies are sorted neatly by pattern and size in symmetrical boxes that are sometimes under glass. There is order here as there never shall be in the fisherman's vest. The rods are racked in soldierly ranks. Waders are clean and unpatched, vests dry and free of stains, lines and leaders coiled perfectly.

In the shop there is no algae underfoot to bring you painfully down on your back and shatter your brand-new Orvis Superfine. The room is cool and free of insects. There is no glare. Tag alders do not grow along the walls in leafy abundance. Order reigns in the conversations as well. Hatches come off the water at precisely predictable times of day. Currents are homogeneous, and flies ride them with no hint of drag. Casts turn over smoothly, and leaders straighten out with Euclidian perfection. Fish rise and fish take. When you leave the shop, you are invincible.

I sat quietly in the Yellow Breeches fly shop for an hour one evening, listening to Vincent Marinaro as he explained to another fisherman just how it was done on the Letort Spring Run about five miles away. He made it sound easy, and by the time I left that night—having bought a couple of dozen flies of the sort he mentioned—I was certain that it would be easy. That night I carefully made up a new leader and dressed my fly line. How many fish, I wondered, could I catch in a morning on the Letort? I fell asleep seeing visions of twenty-inch trout.

I was lucky to take two small rising browns late in the morning when the little olives hatched. At one point I watched a huge brown rooting around in the *Elodea* grass with his nose, stirring up the sow bugs and shrimp on which he then fed. I was near tears with frustration as he passed up my fly on at least six different drifts. I began to curse that trifling little limestone ditch the way a commuter curses the FDR Drive. But Marinaro had made it sound so good in the shop the night before, and he had written books about it . . . so despite my own firsthand evidence to the contrary, I still believe him. Because I very badly want to.

Aside from building your confidence, a visit to the local shop can pay off in advice if you are unfamiliar with the territory. The fishing will never be as good as it sounds in the shop, but what you hear there might be useful. Chuck

Fothergill at his shop in Aspen, Colorado, explained that I would have to fish nymphs and use some weight to get them down if I wanted to catch rainbows in the Roaring Fork. That afternoon when I went to the river, there were blizzards of mayflies hovering above its surface. Without Fothergill's advice I would have started with duns, gone to nymphs in the film, then nymphs rising to the surface. I would never have guessed the bottom and known to put twist weight on my leader. As it was, I caught fish. And spent money.

If the shops are tempting, the catalogs are irresistible. They come in the mail, and once you've sent for one or two of them and actually placed some orders, they never stop coming. Your name is on the master list, and you will never be able to turn the things off.

The merchandise does not vary much from catalog to catalog. The major manufacturers supply everybody. But there is a shading of tone from one mail-order outfit to another—some are handsomely, professionally done and others are strictly mimeograph jobs—and you find yourself deciding to go with this or that one according to such things as prose style. The laconic Maine woods English of L. L. Bean's was for years as much an attraction as the goods it described.

The catalogs pile up, along with the tax records, through the year, and late in the winter, when you should be going through those tax records, the catalogs are a happy distraction. They tend to be studied and thumbed with the kind of love that was once lavished on bedside Bibles. For a time there is no limit to the fishing appetite, and catalogs are a kind of high-starch snack—many calories, but not much solid nutrition.

Eventually all the excess passes. Men do grow old after a while, and in spite of themselves they mature. The fanatical, compulsive, and acquisitive edge softens with time. You cannot catch them all, and every fish cannot be a trophy. Not only is it impossible to fish all the time, it is wrong even to want to.

But fishing is a passion, and it is the nature of passions to run out of control for a while before they stabilize and burn like a hot blue flame. Something happens. Some especially poignant birthday is celebrated. A child grows up. A death hits painfully close to home. A dream is lost irretrievably. Proportion and measure are established.

Owning two dozen rods is seen for the foolish excess that it has always been. You realize that you don't need all those flies and all that other junk. It becomes imperative to cut back and pare down. It becomes almost easy to stay home when a low is hovering over five states and the forecast is nonstop rain for three full days. There was a time when you would have merely thought, *Well, the fish are already wet, so they don't mind*, and put on your specially designed rain gear and gone after them. Now you stay inside and read, not necessarily about fishing.

You learn how to leave a stream before absolute darkness, how to sit on a bank and merely watch when the fishing is slow, how to show someone who has never fished before how it is done, how to release fish that you once would have killed, how to keep a journal of your fishing.

The best way to arrive at this plane is to have been a driven young enthusiast and gotten it out of your system; to have consumed everything you could afford or lay your hands on that might improve your fishing; and to have caught fish. It is most important to have caught fish.

Sooner or later the enthusiast finds himself squarely in the middle of one of those scenes that he has repeatedly dreamed. He is, say, on the Beaverkill River at dusk, his Leonard in his hand and his vest full of Darbee-tied flies. He is wearing Orvis waders and Zeiss glasses. The Hardy reel and Cortland line are in fine shape. He has tied a perfect twelve-foot leader from his Maxima kit. The Green Drakes begin to come off the water, singly at first, in the manner of the tentative raindrops that precede a downpour. The flies begin hatching more abundantly. A few fish begin rising. He searches the various fly boxes for the appropriate size of amber-colored nymph, ties it on, casts upstream, and covers a nice fish that takes. He plays it to the net and releases it. When he looks up, he sees that the huge mayflies are rising in sheets, almost like heat off an asphalt road.

He clips off the nymph and puts on the dun tied perfectly by Harry or Elsie in their shop in Roscoe. He spots another nice fish, flicks a perfect cast with the little blond Leonard, and is quickly hooked up. For a nearly delirious hour it goes like this. When he quits, at dark, he realizes that he has *lost count,* but that he has caught more than a dozen fine browns, one of which was at least eighteen inches long.

Or he is on the Madison during the salmon fly hatch . . . or the Pere Marquette for the giant mayflies (they call them caddises in Michigan) . . . the Letort for the Sulphurs. Whatever the situation, the essential thing is that it all comes together just the way it does in the books.

After all the obvious comparisons, he is left with the awareness that it happened *to* him, and that although it might happen again, there is a limit to what he can do to make it happen. Beyond a certain point he is merely a passenger. The furious expenditure of energy really does not yield much. More than he would like to believe or admit, his role is passive. Wisdom and maturity come with learning to accept that role. And to exploit it.

A 1933 magazine cover that suggests that the eyes are the first to go.

The European Connection

Stylistically, much of the sport's fine writing and fine art was inspired abroad, notably in the British Isles. In the beginning there was Izaak Walton who, in the words of Arnold Gingrich, "is as easy to read as today's paper, but his predecessors are like the meat in the less accessible parts of the lobster. It's there if you want to dig for it, but unless you're practically starved, it's hardly worth the trouble." The sole possible exception was Dame Juliana Berners, who wrote two hundred years *before* Walton. Gingrich observed: "[She] is to angling literature as Chaucer is to English literature." These pages of English art are in commemoration of all that the good Dame started.

Ernest Briggs, *untitled* (ca. 1900)

ETCHINGS BY NORMAN WILKINSON (1878-1971)

A Spey Salmon Pool

Trout Fishing on the Test

Spring Fishing on the Spey

Evening Rise

William Garfit, *Kildonnan, River Helmsdale, Scotland* (1980)

Norman Wilkinson, *Trout Fishing on the River Usk* (ca. 1955)

The readers of *Punch* were treated to a great number of fishing cartoons throughout the second half of the nineteenth century. Examples from the period are shown on these pages.

George Du Maurier, "Encouraging Prospect" (1865)
    Piscator Juvenis: "Any sport, sire?"
    Piscator Senex: "Oh, yes; very good sport."
    Piscator Juvenis: "Bream?"
    Piscator Senex: "No!"

    Piscator Juvenis: "Perch?"
    Piscator Senex: "No!"
    Piscator Juvenis: "What sport, then?"
    Piscator Senex: "Why, keeping clear of the weeds."

John Leech, "Mr. Briggs Practises with His Running Tackle" (ca. 1855)

Charles Keene, "In Flagrante" (1885)
    Keeper (Coming on him unawares):
    "Do you call this Fishing with a Fly, sir?"
    Brigson: "Eh?—I ah—well, I—Look here—have a—
    (diving for his flask)—take a nip? Do!"

Charles Keene, "There's Many a Slip" (1885)
    Waggles saw a splendid three-pound trout in a quiet place
    on the Thames one evening last week. Down he comes
    the next night, making sure of him! But some other people
    had seen him too!"

Frank E. Schoonover, *The Picarel* [*sic*] (1917).

FINDERS, WEEPERS:
Welcome to Muskie Country
By Robert F. Jones

N THOSE DAYS we would leave at dawn and drive north through Green Bay, hoping for a glimpse of Don Hutson or Tony Canadeo or maybe Johnny Blood (perhaps they'd be coming out of a drugstore; who knew?), then angle northwest through dairy country to Shawano, turn north again through the Menominee Indian reservation (tar-paper shacks; the big, bleak, yellow brick orphanage and comfortless church at Keshena; roadside stands that sold flimsy toy birchbark canoes and headdresses of dyed turkey feathers and moccasins that fell apart in the first rain; a few fat young Indians in dirty Levi's and gray shirts sitting and staring into the gloomy pinewoods—so much for the Romance of the Red Man), emerging once more into the cutover country around Langlade and Lily and Pickerel—country that only half a century earlier had stood sky-high in white pine, the Paul Bunyan country from which our schoolboy legends grew, now laid flat, stumpy, regrown in weak popple, birch, and alder, like a woman with lovely hair who has lain with the enemy and then had her head shaved—on up through Rhinelander, where the townsfolk, largely of Baltic blood, all looked pale and misshapen, with bulging foreheads and washed-out eyes, as if they had sprouted from the potato bin, and the sour stink of the pulp mills invaded the car through the floorboards; then more cutover country, and then we would emerge—abruptly, marvelously, rolling down all the windows—into what we really meant by Up North: the road shooting straight and dusty through dense stands of spruce and tamarack, with muskegs sprawling right and left, stippled with crooked, wind-silvered snags on some of which perched eagles and ospreys, erect and wild-eyed, and always more frequently the crooked lakes and flowages glinting hard blue and brown in the sunlight that—Up North—seemed cleaner and harsher than anywhere else, a sharp wind out of the northwest kicking up whitecaps on the open reaches, and wooden rowboats painted dark green tied up to cockeyed piers, with cabins of peeled spruce logs squatting, smoking, back in the woods, and always a lone man in a red-and-black-checked lumberjack shirt fishing from the shore—casting and reeling, casting and reeling, again and again and again. . . .

Muskie Country.

Certain fish seem emblematic of their surroundings. Trout, though they abound in certain streams and lakes Up North, seem out of place there: that quicksilver beauty, those finicky feeding habits, don't set right with the burnt-over hunger of the place. The muskellunge and his lesser but even more voracious brother, the great northern pike, are by contrast built for the country: lean, snaggle-toothed, slimy, foul-smelling, hard-eyed backshooters. The Pitiless Pike. It seems fitting, in a way, that when John Dillinger and Baby-Face Nelson were on the lam in early 1934, they hid out at the Little Bohemia Lodge near Rhinelander, Wisconsin, in the heart of Muskie Country. During a shoot-out after the FBI was tipped, Nelson killed one agent, wounded another and a local cop, and made his getaway. Residents of the region are as proud of that bloody bit of history as they are of their pike fishing.

"Look at this," my father said. We were cleaning a string of fish we'd taken that afternoon, plugging on Four-Mile Lake. There were rock bass, crappie, yellow perch, a couple of walleyes, and a big northern, about ten pounds, that he'd hooked out of a weed bed across the lake on a silver spoon. He had just unzipped the pike and he pointed with the bloody tip of the knife. Inside the big northern was a smaller one, nearly as long but skinnier. He slit the smaller fish and groped in the stomach cavity. Then he pulled out something longer and skinnier and even slimier. It was a half-digested pine snake.

"Two for the price of one." He laughed. "Three if you don't mind eating snake."

My father was a tall, slim man—pike-slim, I'm tempted to say—who worked in a bank in Milwaukee. When he went to work he wore a suit and tie and a snap-brim fedora, dove gray, and nicely shined, low-cut shoes. Up North he wore moccasins and faded cords worn thin at butt and knees from rowing in a boat, and of course a red-and-black-checked lumberjack shirt. He had a mustache and looked a lot like Henry Fonda as Frank James, in *The Return of Frank James,* when Frank comes back to take his revenge on Bob Ford. He was a good fisherman—I never heard the word *angler* used seriously until I went east, much later, and I still wince a bit when I hear it or see it in print—with no pretensions that fishing was anything more than what men do Up North, along with playing poker at night, and drinking boilermakers, and in the morning shaving out-of-doors from a soapy basin of water heated over the stove and a cracked mirror nailed to a pine trunk. He taught me a lot about fishing and nearly everything I know about pike.

The genus *Esox,* of which the muskellunge (*E. masquinongy*) and the northern pike (*E. lucius*) are the largest representatives, is notorious for its appetite. A checklist of pikey comestibles would include not only one another and snakes, but every other kind of fish from dace to black bass, as well as ducks, loons, redwing blackbirds, chipmunks, red squirrels, and muskrats. Frogs and salamanders rank right up there in the table of stomach contents. My uncle was once drifting the Wolf River in central Wisconsin after a day of trout fishing, lying back in the stern of the canoe, sipping a beer, and smoking a cigar, and when he flicked the cigar ash over the side, a northern grabbed him by the hand. Northerns have long, sharp teeth, and this one locked on tight. My uncle flipped it into the canoe and beat it to death with an empty bottle of Blatz. The pike must have mistaken the glowing ash of his cigar for a firefly. It took weeks for the wounds to heal. (One could almost make a case for an affinity between fish and tobacco: I once cleaned a rainbow trout I'd caught in Costa Rica and found two cigarette butts in its stomach, along with some garbanzo beans, bits of boiled potato, and shreds of lettuce. Some workmen at a dam up above me must have dumped the remains of their lunch into the river.)

Because of their voracity, pike grow to enormous size very quickly. I've always been as interested in the legend surrounding a fish as in its value for sport, meat, or trophy, and the pike has plenty of all of the above. One of my favorite bits of lore concerns the Mannheim Pike of Germany, a fish reputed to have been 267 years old and capable of eating horses. Another German pike (the European and American pike are the same species, *E. lucius*) taken from Lake Kaiserweg measured nineteen feet long and weighed 350 pounds but proved to be a fake constructed of sections cut from other, smaller pike. Of course pike don't live that long or grow that big, but even so the records are impressive. The world all-tackle record on northerns is 46 pounds 2 ounces, a fish taken in September 1940 from the Sacandaga Reservoir in New York's Adirondack foothills. Bigger northerns are taken in Ireland—fish up to 50 and 60 pounds—but none has yet been accepted in the books because of lack of proper authentication. As for muskies, the world record also comes from New York—a 69-pound

15-ounce brute taken from the St. Lawrence River in September 1957. There is a photograph extant of a 100-pound muskie landed by hook and line on Intermediate Lake, in Michigan's Antrim County, back in 1919. The fish measured seven feet four inches long. I have seen photographs taken during the logging boom in northern Wisconsin back in the 1890s showing heaps of muskies nearly that size. Lumberjacks trolled deadly metal spoons behind their boats whenever they rowed across the lakes. Most of the fish they killed were left to rot after the photo was taken. Ah, well, they just didn't know.

"Drop it by the edge of the lily pads," my father said. It was one of those dead calm mornings when the water looks like cooking oil. A loon was into a laughing jag across the lake and his chortling echoed back from the tangle of spruce snags that lined the shoal shore. We had had no luck at all that morning so far, and I would rather have been swimming back at the cottage than sweating my T-shirt sodden out there. But I cocked the five-foot bait-casting rod like a dutiful son and laid the plug—a heavy wooden red-and-white Bass Oreno already scarred by pike teeth—into a salient that the lake made on the right side of the weed bed. No backlash, thank God. I waited for the ripples to fade a bit and then began a medium-fast retrieve, watching the plug wriggle its way back along the edge of the pads toward the boat.

"You've got a follow."

I stopped the plug for just a single beat, then speeded up my retrieve. There was a swirl and a flurry and I saw the fish roll as it took the plug, and flexing my wrist, I popped it once, twice, setting the hooks, my thumb tight on the spooled ten-pound-test linen line. The fish yanked back and my thumb caught fire, or at least it felt that way. The drag screamed the way I wanted to.

"Get the rod tip up. Up!"

That lessened the burning.

"OK, no rush now. Just let him work himself out. Easy, easy. Try to keep him out of the weeds. That's the way."

My father worked the oars easily and brought the stern of the rowboat around so that I was facing the fish. I kept the rod tip up and put pressure on with the reel handle. The fish shook its head and made a run parallel to the weed bed.

"It's a nice northern. A regular ax handle."

I could make out the pale lozenges that marked its dark green sides and see the flat alligator jaws clamped on the plug, and the fish looked, to me, enormous. There were three classes of northern pike, the way we looked at it. Snakes were the scrawny little guys that usually hit your plug, never much more than a foot long and weighing less than a pound. Then came hatchet handles, eighteen or twenty inches and maybe two pounds tops. This

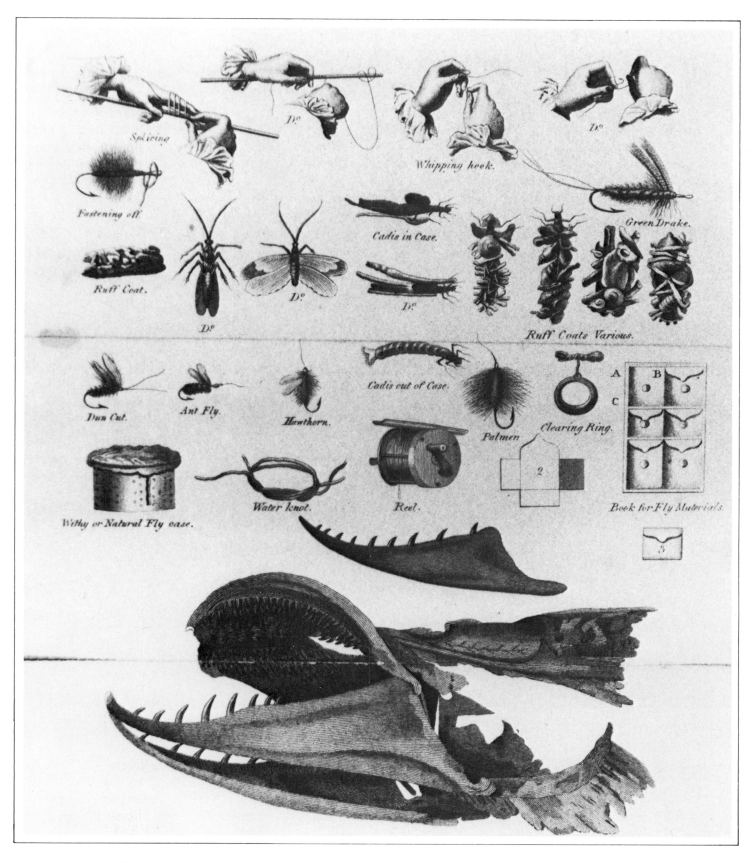

An early-nineteenth-century engraving from *Rural Sports,* Part I,
Volume II, by the Rev. Wm. B. Daniel (1803).

Oliver Kemp, *Pickerel Fishing* (ca. 1930).

Winslow Homer, *Pike, Lake St. John* (1897).

was a proper ax handle, though, a good thirty inches long and maybe six or eight pounds in weight. But like most northerns it played out fast. After the first few surges and flurries it seemed to lose heart, and then it was merely a matter of cranking it in. Still, it was the first decent-sized northern I had ever caught. I was ten years old and, despite my seared and line-split thumb, I was very proud.

My father netted the fish and held it up to let the light glint off the spotted body. The fish glared back at us through the webbing, its eye a hard, malevolent amber. We put it on the live stringer—I held it down as my father punched the metal clasp through the fanged jaw—and trailed it behind the boat as we rowed on.

"He didn't put up much of a fight," I said.

"No. They don't, as a rule. But wait until you get into a muskie. All of this is just training, and I think later this summer, when the water cools down, you'll be ready for muskies."

Since then I've caught northerns twice the size of that fish, and ten times scrappier, but of course the first decent fish of any species a kid catches is the Big One and you don't forget it any more than you forget the first girl in your life. I later learned a way to prevent the loginess that most northerns exhibit soon after they're hooked. I was fishing a trout lake in northern Saskatchewan and the trout action one day was very slow, so my partner, George Reiger, and I decided to plug for the huge northerns that inhabit the shallows of that rocky shoreline. We were casting with ultra-light spinning gear, whippy little rods that made every hookup feel like a potential tarpon. But again, each fish went doggo after the first surge.

"Take a gander at this," George said, holding a five-pounder in his hand. The flat, toothy mouth gauped and twitched on the treble hook of the spoon George had caught it on. "One of the hooks is in his lower jaw and the other two are in the palate. I'll bet that paralyzes him in damn short order." We altered a couple of spoons by removing the treble hooks and replacing them in the split ring with singles from George's amply stocked tackle box. The next northerns that hooked up—and we were taking fish on nearly every cast, speedy water wolves that lanced out of the shadows to smack our lures at flank speed—really kicked up a fuss. Some of them actually jumped, the first time I ever saw such acrobatics from the species. All were hooked as a fish should be—cleanly through the side of the mouth. Hooked that way, the fish were easier to release as well, although we killed many of them for our Cree Indian guide, Walter, who wanted some to feed to his sled dogs.

As the afternoon wore along, George and I began keeping count and competing to see who could catch more northerns. The count had risen to some twenty-five apiece when we entered a shallow bay on the east side of an island. We could see the fish lying like logs in the icy clear water near the shore, and in the fever of competition we both cocked and cast as soon as we felt we were within range. As my cast hand snapped forward, I felt a sharp clunk on the back of my head and the fiery bite of the hook in my scalp. I had left too much line dangling from the tip-top and had cast the spoon into my own head. I damn near cast myself out of the boat. George's lure, on the other hand, had sailed out neat as could be, and on the first couple of cranks on the reel he was hooked up.

"George," I bleated, "I'm hooked!"

"Just a minute," he said. "Wait till I boat this sonofabitch and then I'll unhook you."

I gritted my teeth and yanked the barb loose on my own. Walter was laughing. I could feel the blood running down my neck, but I cast anyway. A fish darted out, followed by two smaller northerns, and one of the little guys won the race. I can't remember who won the contest, but it was certainly the most productive day of pike fishing I've ever enjoyed. I know now how those Wisconsin lumberjacks must have felt back in the 1890s when muskies were as thick as the northerns that day in Saskatchewan.

It is said (God knows how they compute these statistics) that a fisherman must be willing to deliver at least 1,500 casts into muskie waters, and perhaps as many as 5,000, before he can hope to catch one. I knew I had to be up around 4,999. All that summer I had been plugging for muskies—from the boat, from the rocks that lined the shore of the lake, from rocks in the lake itself. I had developed an uncanny accuracy with the plug—usually a jointed, two-ounce pikey-minnow, mottled green and very splashy on the retrieve—and I could hit a lily pad, or just miss it, which was more to the point, at twenty-five yards. I could have snagged an El Corona out of my father's mouth at a somewhat lesser distance, but he didn't smoke. Sometimes I wish he did. No muskie.

Where I grew up, there were two criteria for the achievement of manhood. You heard them all the time in the barbershop. In the fall the barber would ask: "Got your buck yet?" In the summer: "Got your muskie?" Actually, the getting of the buck was by far the easier of the tasks. I knew boys of twelve who had already killed ten-pointers. I knew only one under the age of sixteen who had taken a muskie, and that lad was suddenly a foot taller and all covered with hair on the day he brought it home.

There were a couple of easy ways to get muskies, of course. Just as there are to get a million dollars. If you knew the guides, and sent them cases of Granddad every Christmas, and set them up with the gal who sang at the Blue Pike Inn at Manitowish (her name was Jeanne and my mother always suspected, from Jeanne's suntan which seemed to descend well down her low-cut chantoozie's dress, that she was a woman of low moral character) at least once a summer, the guide whom you had thus greased might very well "stake out" a muskie for you. *Esox masquinongy* is a solitary. One muskie, male or female, occupies the same "hole" all summer long. If you happened to be there on a day when the water temperature was precisely sixty-eight degrees Fahrenheit, and the barometer was rising on a northwest wind following a three-day blow, and the chop on the water was just high enough, say, to trip the foulmouthed little dwarf who bummed drinks in the bar down by the hotel in Eagle River and would bite you on the knee if you didn't come through, and if you cast the right plug and brought it in fast enough, you might very well hook a muskie. Then it was up to you to fight him.

The other way was live bait. One popular and productive bait was the mud puppy, a slimy, smooth-skinned critter about nine inches long that looked like a catfish but was actually the larval form of the tiger salamander (*Ambystoma tigrinum*), which I have since discovered is called the water dog down South and out West. Hooking up a mud puppy was a slippery, bloody business, but the other, and more surefire, bait tactic was even worse. What you needed was a live chipmunk and the lid from a cigar box. You fitted the chipmunk out in a girdle of hooks (don't ask me how this was done without suffering the loss of a thumb ball—I never tried it) and then set him adrift on the cigar-box lid over a muskie's lair. When you were well clear, and the chipmunk teetered like some rodential Ulysses on his raft over the target, you twitched him off the lid with your fishing line. The chipmunk, of course, would splash frantically toward the shore—never too far off, since muskies tend to hang out in water no more than fifteen or twenty feet deep. The muskie would respond in his usual cautious way: shadow the chipmunk toward the shore, size it up, verify its edibility; then he would cock himself into an S-shape and strike, quick as a timber rattler. Gulp. Turn. You waited until he had returned to his lie, then snapped the reel out of free spool and socked the hooks home—once, twice, three or four times—then held on tight. . . .

And if you did finally manage to bring your muskie to the side of the boat, so popular opinion held, you had better have a .22-caliber pistol loaded with soft-point bullets at hand to finish him off before netting the rascal. A twenty- or thirty-pound muskie thrashing around in the boat with his choppers flailing is no joke. Seasoned and sober fisherman have been known to abandon ship in the presence of those jaws. A mere gaff hook was no insurance against Stitch City. (Handguns are illegal now in boats, at least in the state of Wisconsin, but a guide told me a story about the old days when the .22 Colt Woodsman was *de rigueur* in any muskie boat. His client on this particular day had never fished for muskies before—he was from Chicago—and knew nothing about pistols. He asked for instructions on how to shoot the gun if it came to that, and the guide showed him how to jack a round into the chamber, the sight picture, trigger squeeze, the lot. "Damn if he didn't hook up, just about sunset," the guide said. "He fought the fish well, listening carefully to my instructions, and then, when he had him within twenty, twenty-five yards of the boat, rolling on the surface the way they will, he grabbed for the pistol. I started to holler, but he flat upped and shot—a quick, offhand snap shot. The muskie rolled belly up. Popped him square between the eyes.")

Well, we had neither a .22 pistol nor the inclination to fish with live bait, so we cast and carried a landing net. One hot late August afternoon on Sand Lake, with me plugging the shoreline from the bow while my father magnanimously rowed, we witnessed a little tragicomedy that for me remains the essence of muskie fishing. There was only one other boat out, with a man and a woman in it (probably husband and wife) trolling the holes and shelves in the middle of the lake. Shortly after noon the man got a hookup, and for the best part of an hour we watched him fighting the fish. While I cast and reeled, my father kept an eye on the fight and filled me in on what was happening.

"It just rolled about a hundred yards off his bow. Now it's taking line . . .

"He's gaining on it now, bringing it in . . .

"Oops, ran again. He lost all that line he'd picked up . . .

"Now it's around the other side of the boat and he's scrambling up to the bow. I think he stepped on his wife's hand. She's saying something to him . . .

"Now it's come around the bow and stripping line . . ."

Though my arm had long since transmuted to lead, I kept casting. The thing about muskies that is most frustrating is their total unpredictability. They hit when the plug strikes the water, or they hit when it's nearly back in the boat. Or anywhere in between. Sometimes they ignore a lure five times straight and then gobble it like the proverbial starving Armenian on the sixth go-around. More than any other sort of fishing (and I have fished from New Zealand to East Africa, from Alaska to Central America), muskie fishing demands utter patience and total attention. It's like dialing every number in the Manhattan phone book and knowing that only one phone will answer, but when it does, the voice on the other end will say: "Congratulations. Now we're going to cramp your hands, break your wrist, and stretch the muscles in your arm to half again their length."

Ted Williams – the Hall of Famer, not the essayist in this book – with a twenty-one-pound muskie (late 1940s).

The guy in the boat was enjoying that part now.

"I think he's got it whipped," my father said. I reeled in and hooked the plug to the butt guide, then sat down in the stern to watch. The fish was splashing about ten yards off the bow of the other rowboat. We saw the man turn his head and say something to his wife. She reached down and came up with a big landing net. Then she made her way forward. He brought the fish in on the far side of the boat, so we couldn't see it, nor at that distance could we hear their voices, though we could see them talking to each other excitedly. The woman pushed tentatively over the side with the long-handled net.

"Oh-oh," my father said.

The man yelled something at her, and she poked hard with the mouth of the net, then poked again. There was a flurry of white water. The man's rod tip, which had been bent by the weight of the fish into a half circle, suddenly snapped straight.

The woman's shoulders slumped.

The man sat down in the bow and the woman stood up with the net and walked back to the stern sheets. They didn't look at each other, and they didn't talk.

"I wouldn't want to be in that boat right now," my father said.

I didn't catch a muskie that summer, or the summer after that, or the summer after *that*. Indeed, it wasn't until I was fourteen years old that I even had a follow-up, and as the saying goes, a follow-up makes mighty thin soup. But it was enough to rekindle my waning enthusiasm for the agonizing frustration that is muskie fishing. It was a cool afternoon in late August, and I was out alone at the north end of Sand Lake, letting the breeze push me and the boat down along the shoreline. The breeze had kicked up a bit of a chop. I could get off maybe four or five casts and then had to sit down at the oars and straighten the boat out, and then I could cast a few times more. I was casting in toward the tangle of sunken logs that line the shore, to no avail as usual, and I was just about ready to call it quits for the day when it happened.

The lure—a Darter type that I was twitching back to the boat in jerks and stops—was halfway home when I saw a black streak emerge from the shadow of the logs and shoot straight as an arrow for my lure. I instinctively quickened my retrieve and then stopped it for a moment. The black streak stopped too, and I saw him out there, the long, mottled tan body seeming to quiver even at rest, the flat, long snout and those hard, unblinking eyes locked on the sinking lure. I picked the lure up again with a few turns of the reel handle and brought it at medium speed back in to the boat. The muskie followed without seeming to move his tail. He followed clean on in to the side of the boat. I was running out of line, not the usual way you do with a fish when he strips it off the reel when hooked, but the reverse of that: I'd reeled in all that I'd cast, and though the muskie was interested, he hadn't hit yet. I remembered my father saying that when this happened you had to work the lure from the end of the rod in a figure eight through the water. The muskie watched me do this for what felt like half an hour but was probably no more than a minute. His eyes were fixed hypnotically on the lure as it danced not a foot from his snout. Then he began to sink, slowly, almost imperceptibly, deeper and deeper, until he faded against the sandy bottom.

For the next half hour I cast back to the shoreline, trying to duplicate the retrieve that had provoked the follow-up, then varying it until I had tried everything that the tackle was capable of. No go. I nearly screamed with frustration, but the wind was kicking up stronger now, and I knew I had to get back or risk swamping the boat and having to hoof it home through the muskegs.

I had just started the long row home when it

occurred to me that there was one angle I hadn't tried—casting from the shore out over the muskie and bringing the lure in to him, like a scared frog, say, that had gotten carried offshore and was high-tailing it back in to safety. I could see storm clouds rearing blue black to the northwest, their bulbous heads fringed with streamers of silver and dirty white. A dim rumble of thunder from over the horizon rolled down the lake. White horses galloped the deeper water, flattened in spots by the push of the wind into glinting smears. I nosed the bow of the boat into the timber tangle, well to the right of where the muskie had first appeared, and secured the painter to a barkless limb. Then I took the rod, changed the Darter for a single-hooked rubber frog, and began picking my way across the pile of jumbled logs. The single hook would put me at a disadvantage, I knew, but on the other hand it was my only frog lure, and it had worked wonderfully on northerns. They had chewed up three of them the previous summer.

I stayed well back in the timber tangle as I neared the spot where I figured the fish would be lying, then bellied cautiously out into the clear where I could cast from a crouch behind a weathered tamarack stump whose roots groped toward the gunmetal sky like an octopus pleading for mercy. Before I cast I checked over my gear. I knew that the green twenty-pound-test linen line was sound because I had spooled it only the previous afternoon and I'd caught no fish on it yet. The eight-inch wire leader was unkinked, and the snap swivel that held the lure to the leader was snapped tight and looked sound as well. I took the file from my hip pocket and touched up the point and barb of the hook even though they felt needle-sharp to my thumb. Then I looked out over the water. The wind was gusting sharper now, and there was an icy edge to it. While I waited for a gust to die down I said a quick Hail Mary. I had just gotten to the "pray for us sinners" part when the wind temporarily abated. I cocked my right arm and cast.

The frog arched high and slow against the angry sky and then plopped almost without a splash into the rising waves fifty feet offshore. I could see it bobbing on the crests of the short, slate-gray chop. I began my retrieve, twitching the rod tip in small beats to get the frog's legs working, stopping every three or four beats to let the frog float—legs bent and trailing behind it—on the tossing surface. About halfway in, the frog disappeared in mid-kick and I saw the swirl, faint and almost invisible against the wind's roil. The line tautened. I thumbed the spool and hit, then hit again, three, four, five times. It was like yanking against a boulder, and for just the flicker of an instant I was afraid that I'd fouled a sunken log or an invisible rock.

Then the rod hummed and I felt movement—no, not movement, but rather the whole electric shock of the fish becoming aware of the hook, a gathering of force at the far end of the thin line that connected us, and then a surge of raw power. The drag yapped and then screeched, and I leaped out from behind the tamarack root to stand clear for the fight. At that moment the muskie emerged, in a head-shaking, long, corkscrew leap that rivaled the very storm for spray. He was long, long and thick around as a sawn beach log, and his jump nearly pulled me off the log I was standing on. He jumped again and headed out into the lake, peeling line off the drag as he went. I skipped gingerly down the log tangle to a spot where my line wasn't likely to get tangled in the dead branches that groped all around me. It began to rain, a few fat drops at first, warmer than the wind, then a gray-white sheet of rain moving in across the water, peening it white where it hit, then the wind whipping it horizontally into my face so that for a minute I couldn't see the line or the lake, much less the spot where the fish was running.

I could feel him turn and head to my right, along the shore, and I went with him, skipping from log to log, ducking under big sawyers and snags, passing the bent, thumping rod from hand to hand.

Then the rain stopped as suddenly as it had started, and the wind died to a flat calm. Waves were breaking, dirty brown and laden with weeds, over my sneakers and up to my knees. I looked back for a flash and saw the rowboat belly up on the logs. One oar was drifting out into the lake. Shit! Then the muskie ran again, farther up the shore. I looked ahead and saw that I was running out of logs to run on and, looking down, that I was also running short of line on the spool. I tightened the drag just a touch, just as far as I dared. Beyond the log tangle was a shallow bay, weedy and muck-bottomed. I doubted that I could wade it. I knew I didn't want to wade it. I shivered remembering why.

Two summers earlier I had waded the weedy bay, casting a popper for crappie and bass. When I came out of the water, my legs were covered with bloodsuckers—flat, black, slippery leeches that I couldn't pull loose without taking skin with them. They didn't come off until I'd gotten back to the cottage and sprinkled salt on them. I didn't want to go back in with the leeches.

But I had to. The muskie moved slowly across the bay, shaking his head from time to time. Maybe he's working a hole in his jaw where the hook had him, I thought hopefully. Maybe he'll work it loose and I won't have to wade. If I give him a bit of slack, maybe the hook will just fall out of its own accord. It wouldn't be my fault, not really. I'm just a kid. Grown men have fished all their lives and never hooked one of these bastards, and even those that hook them don't always hang onto them. Hell, they don't land them half the time. Maybe less. Remember that guy in that boat when his wife went for the muskie with the net. Maybe it wasn't her fault. Maybe the hook just fell out. You've seen that happen often enough when a fish has been fighting a long time. Like on that black bass last summer on Pine Lake. Just give him a touch of slack now. . . .

But I couldn't do it. I slid off the last log down into the water, which felt warm and greasy after I had been standing in the wind and the rain, and I felt the mud ooze into my sneakers and up over my ankles, greasier and warmer than the water. I began to wade across the bay. Weeds slithered across my bare legs and reached up my shorts, and I winced and shuddered. God, you're a chicken bastard, I cursed myself. What kind of baby are you? They're just weeds. And at worst just leeches. In the old days doctors prescribed leeches to bleed people. They're good medicine. But I shuddered and winced anyway.

The fish took me to the middle of the bay. The water was armpit-deep. Please, God, turn him now. Please, Holy Mary, let him go back to his lie. I could see the steel of the spool through the last bends of line. The muskie kept moving. OK, you've got to swim now. You can do it. You learned to swim in these waters when you were five years old, and you're on the swimming team, and you're a state champion. Next year you'll be a lifeguard. Make like it's a rescue. I sidestroked into the channel, holding the rod high over my head, angling to my right to keep tension on the line, not to give him that slack he wanted, and the waves crashed over my face. Then I felt the mud underfoot again. The bottom shelved up to a wooded shoreline and I made good time up there. I looked down at my legs. There were only three or four leeches. I snapped them off as fast as I could with my free hand, leaving a few red spots where they'd sucked on.

I found I could gain on him now. I began pumping and reeling, holding the cork butt of the rod against my belly. He came slowly, shaking his head, running from side to side in short bursts. But he came. Then I could see him flash through the dirty water as he rolled on his side for a moment. He looked like a sunken log there in the moil, but then he flashed silvery white again, and I saw his tail break water and the blunt red brown of his dorsal just ahead of it, and then his jaw full of teeth with the tattered green of the frog in the angle of it, and then I remembered.

The landing net was back in the boat.

For a long, loud moment I stood there, stunned. I'd planned, naively, on leading the muskie back toward the boat after I'd hooked him and then, when he was played out, netting him as I had many a northern in years past. But the muskie had taken *me* for a walk instead. There was no way I could now lead him back to the boat, across that channel, back over the logs. I was too tired. My arm felt as

if someone had used it for the bat in batting practice. Lightning was flashing from across the lake and moving my way. Standing there with a steel fishing rod, I was asking for it. I waded reluctantly out, reeling as I walked, toward where the muskie lay, rolling sluggishly and shaking his head. When the water was knee-deep, I brought him the rest of the way to me. He stared up at me with a blank yellow eye, his jaws working slowly. The hook, I could see, had indeed worked a big hole in his jaw. The frog was chewed to green ribbons. The hook itself looked bent and scarred. I reached down and turned it by the eye, and it fell to the sandy bottom. The fish just lay there, finning. He looked as long as my leg. But there was no way now that I would know his true length or his weight. He would not ride back to Milwaukee with me, wrapped in burlap and packed in dry ice in a crate in the trunk of the car. He would not earn me the envious stares of my friends or the backslaps of their fathers. He would not visit the taxidermist and return to hang on my bedroom wall, glaring down at me with his wide, toothy jaws spread and his powerful body arched in mid-jump forever.

I placed the sole of my sneaker against his side just aft of the pectoral fin and pushed him gently so that he was headed out into the lake. Slowly, imperceptibly at first, he sloped off into deeper water, upright and finning still so that I knew he would make it and not go belly up later. He faded back into the tan, cold deep as slowly as a fading dream, back to where he had come from, back where he belonged.

Fresh thunder boomed and grumbled down the lake.

That was the summer of 1950, when the muskie was still a rare fish even in its already limited area of distribution along the U.S.-Canadian border. Today, thanks to stocking programs, the fish is found much more abundantly everywhere it once existed, and even as far south as North Carolina, Tennessee, and Georgia. Fishing has become Big Recreation. Men go after muskies in powerful, specially designed boats, using tackle much stronger and more sophisticated than what we used in the old Muskie Country, tackle that even extends to electronic fish-finding sonar. At the same time, the old Muskie Country, which was scruffy and dirt-poor, has grown up with fancy new lodges and fast-food joints and chamber-of-commerce slickness. Water-skiers churn the lakes where once we rowed in heavy wooden boats. Even Dillinger and Baby-Face have undergone a transition to made-for-TV movies. The only outlaws left are the credit-card variety.

But the wild muskellunge, at least, remains the same: an emblem, a talisman, from which each fisherman who hunts him can draw his own store of memories. For me, then, of people and places dead and gone. Old Crazy Joe, who had been stomped by a pasture bull and smiled all the time, even on that afternoon in the haymow when I saw him skewer three king snakes on a pitchfork and then bring them out into the sunlight, still squirming, with blood running thick through the chaff and dust on their brilliant skins. Of the cellar pool hall in Rhinelander, with its floor pocked by the spikes of long-ago lumberjacks and the tables warped, where I learned to shoot eight-ball and had a fistfight with a kid who said I held my cue the way he held his dick. And of the dark, cool tackle shops, with their gurgling galvanized tubs full of live bait—shoals of shiners and olive-drab mud puppies circling slowly and glinting in the dark, and the clusters of oiled steel traps dangling from the roof beams so that my father had to duck under them, and rows of Red Ball gum boots along the wall, and racked bamboo rods gleaming with lacquer, and whole walls of dully gleaming walnut-stocked and blue-barreled deer rifles.

Of the cemetery outside Peshtigo, where the victims of the Great Fire are buried, people who died more horribly and in greater numbers than the victims of the Chicago Fire, which happened the same day but closer to the newspapers. Of the roadside restaurant near Thorp, where you could gobble roast chicken with stuffing and gravy and mashed potatoes and fresh green peas with home-made apple pie or cherry pie *à la mode* for dessert as long as you wanted to keep shoveling for $1.25 a head.

Of the pretzels we got up there, crisp, thick rye pretzels crusted with rock salt that they don't make anymore, and the local beer in brown bottles of thick glass, the beer itself thicker and darker than the fizzy piss they call beer today, bitter and cold, which we drank while we listened to the Cubs play over the radio full of static. And of the old trapper's cabin we found rotting back in the woods, mossy logs melting back into the soil they grew from, in the last lone stand of virgin white pine left in the Four-Mile Lake country, the pines soaring into the sky like clipper-ship masts and the ground so thick with old needles that you bounced when you walked. And of the old man, a friend of my father's, who owned that stand of pine and had as well a collection of walking sticks from all over the world, one of which, my father told me in a whisper later, was made from "a bull's pizzle."

And of fish fries at the cottage, with my mother's sweet-sour coleslaw chopped from red cabbages and the slabs of golden fried walleye flaking to the fork, and coffee perking on the wood stove, and then later all of us walking down to the lake to watch the Northern Lights arching overhead and reflecting upside down on the mirror of the night-still lake, rainbow charges pulsing from black horizon to horizon like a giant, universal Wurlitzer jukebox, the far-off splash of a leaping fish the only other sound in the humming night.

All of that.

Yeah. Muskie Country.

MASKALONGE. GREAT LAKES.

ESOX ESTOR.

FROM NATURE, ON WOOD, BY H.W. HERBERT.

Etching by Sandy Scott (1979).

PRIVATE WATERS:
Rolling Your Own Farm Pond
By Vance Bourjaily

HE MOST EXCITING fish I ever brought out of the water took me two years to catch.

I finally got it on a lusterless, old, machine-tied, Japanese white streamer fly, using a workaday eight-foot fly rod, the maker's name of which has long since worn away. It was equipped with one of those small-boy, skeleton fly reels, without click or drag, a frayed silk line that didn't float anymore, and, for leader, about twenty inches of undifferentiated monofilament snipped off the end of the supply on an abandoned spin-cast reel.

My cast, if that's the word, was a fifteen-footer. I let the old fly sink away, started to retrieve slowly, overhand, and the fish appeared, drifting upward toward the lure, opening its mouth just under the surface, sucking in, and hooking itself.

There were a couple of bullfrogs watching. They didn't move. It was three o'clock of a hot afternoon.

My fish, as I eased it in, was seven, well, six, inches long. It fought with all the ferocity of a ladyfinger being slid out from among the whipped cream and strawberries of a charlotte russe. It looked up at me from the shallow water at my feet, goggling at, I think, the sheer incomprehensibility of what was happening.

I looked back, grinning in absolute joy. I knelt, wet my left hand, took the little thing off the hook, and sent it swimming away with a whispered word of benediction. Then I whooped like a drunk cowboy, dropped the rod, jumped up in the air, turned, and ran all the way down to our farmhouse, half a mile away, to tell the family:

"They survived. We've got a walleye population."

This was in the fourth of the five ponds we've built and stocked with fish on our Iowa farm, and if the fishing memories, some a little more conventionally dramatic, mostly belong to spring and summer evenings, the story of each pond would start with winter dreaming.

The first was conceived on a February afternoon, and not by me. I would have to admit, as a matter of fact, that I found it inconceivable, to begin with.

It came into the conversation as my wife and I were being shown the land by a real estate man, but the seller was along, too. The seller was anxious. In his view the place was hilly and farmed out. It had a muddy creek flowing through the best field, a branch of the same creek flowing through another. It had a lot of timberland he hadn't been able to afford to clear, some places that were too steep to fence off, and even several patches inaccessible except on foot. I'm not sure if he realized that some of these drawbacks were assets in our eyes; he kept pointing out commercial virtues he thought we might miss.

"Had corn right here, three good, hundred-bushel years," he was saying, as we climbed toward the highest land on the farm. "You could put it in beans now, and get a heck of a crop."

I wasn't much of a farmer, but even I knew, looking at the eroded soil, that those hillsides needed to be put in pasture and would be, even so, a long time healing. And that a crop of soybeans would only loosen the dirt more, and turn the ruts and washes into gullies. I replied with an unfriendly grunt, and the man changed the subject.

"Me and my brother was going to build a big pond here," he said. "Raise catfish. Now pond-raised catfish, that's the new thing. Sell 'em to restaurants and supermarkets, they'll take all they can get."

"Weren't you telling me the creeks flood all over the bottom fields in the spring?" I asked.

"Well, not every spring. And like I say, when the water goes down, that silt's left with a world of fertilizer in it. Washes off the other fellow's field, right onto yours."

"How could you dam one of those creeks to make a pond? It would cost a million dollars."

"Couldn't do her for a million," he agreed.

"Then where were you and your brother going to hold the water for your catfish?" I asked. "Or were those cornfield catfish?"

"Right here, like I told you." He was pointing across about as dry-looking a gulch as I'd ever seen. Furthermore, it was a gulch full of trees, some of them quite large. The gulch was about ninety feet across and twenty deep, and it cut back between the hill we were standing on and the next hill over, its floor sloping up between them for a hundred yards or so until it split into two smaller gulches and disappeared into deep woods.

Before I could ask my man what sort of fool he took me for, he told me: "Why, you just can't understand at all, can you?" He slowed his speech and separated each word distinctly. "Now: this here we are looking into, it is a main waterway. This here drains about forty acres up above. What you have to do is clear the sides and bottom. Then you block it off with a clay dam, right across, from one sidehill to the other. See? You drop in a tube for the overflow, and you got her."

"Sure," I said. "And what do you do for water? Haul it up in buckets?"

"Didn't I just get done telling you?"

"Are you trying to say there's springs, or what?"

"Runoff. Runoff." He shook his head at my dimness. "Melt of snow and fall of rain. Drainin' down through the grassy roots, and all the weedy waterways, and down between the trees in the timbers . . ."

I swear I could smell it, when he said that, all that lovely soft rainwater, sifting through leaf mold and around wild-flower stems, dripping off limbs and seed heads, gathering, and I almost missed the wonderful thing he said next:

"Believe you could get cost-sharing."

That was when I learned that the state and especially the federal governments are more than casually interested in having farm ponds built, and that the Department of Agriculture may, if certain requirements can be met, help pay for the building. Equally important, the department will send along government engineers, my favorite public servants, to look at locations and do survey and design.

Nor is it inconsistent with my present purpose to add that, although getting its citizens to go fishing is not the government's goal—its interest is in the soil conservation that results from water control—nevertheless, it will good-naturedly send along some fish when things get ready.

By our first summer on the farm, we had our application in for help. The engineers had come out and agreed, to my slight chagrin, that the seller's spot was a fine one for a two-acre pond. We were approved; we solicited bids; we picked a contractor.

Daniel Keith Yoder was and is the contractor's name; he has built four of our five ponds, and I celebrate him here as a Michelangelo of the bulldozer. Daniel Keith has an eye for dirt, for where to dig it, how to shape it, finish it, and dress the job. His work delights not only his customers but even the engineers whose designs he accomplishes. Other contractors they grumble at; Daniel Keith is their pet. It was after I had watched him through our first project that I began to hear myself, sworn enemy of all machines with blades, say: "Perhaps, after all, man was born to move dirt."

It began sadly, though, and there were unexpected sorrows down the road. Argue, if you wish,

Drawing by Ernest Lussier (1979).

that they make the joys keener; still, I recall my hackberry tree.

Most of what had to be cleared from the pond site was brush, box elder, willow, cottonwood, and aspen—nice things, but fast-growing, and plenty more like them were around the farm. There were, on the other hand, half a dozen decent white oaks and a fine black cherry; but those I could take out with a chain saw, and would be glad to have the lumber. There were some straight young hickories, hardly more than poles, which I didn't like to lose, and there was the hackberry. It was the biggest one of its kind on the farm, a beautifully shaped shade tree of no great value as lumber, a relative of the dying elms but immune to the beetles that were killing them, a corky-barked, silvery, big tree.

"Anything you don't want to salvage, we'll grub out and push into a pile. You can burn it or not," Daniel Keith said.

"Or leave it for a rabbit house," said my friend Tom, who was thinking of getting a beagle.

Daniel Keith walked off, to set engineer flags around the projected waterline.

"It's that hackberry, Tom," I said. "It must be a hundred years old."

"You never get anything without giving up something else," Tom said, but I'm pretty sure his mind was sorting through the half-dozen Orvis bamboo rods he owns, as his eyes followed Daniel Keith's journey around the waterline. I decided Tom was watching for places with room for a decent back cast. Thinking so cheered me up, anyway.

Our chief entertainment that August was walking up to watch Daniel Keith on his dozer, directing, as he drove it, the work of two other such machines and a couple of big scrapers that moved most of the dirt.

Once the clearing was done, they rolled back and piled all the topsoil, to use for dressing later. Then, just past the line which the dam was to follow and down at what would be the base, Daniel Keith began, to my astonishment, to dig. What he dug was a trench, eight feet deep and ten feet wide, straight across the bottom of the gulch. This was to be packed with the best clay they could find, he explained, so that water couldn't work through the ground under the dam.

On the day he was to start packing the trench, my wife and I were walking up to watch when we heard the motors stop. All of them.

"That's ominous," Tina said, and we hurried. At the site, we saw that Daniel Keith was off his machine and down inside the trench. He looked up, saw us, and waited till we had slid down to a place just above him.

"Sand," he said, in about the same tone of voice one might use in saying *scorpion* or *rattlesnake*. Sometime in the recent geological past, there'd been a watercourse down there, with a sandy bottom, just the sort of thing the trench was supposed to intercept but deeper, more extensive. "We'll need to get a dragline now," Daniel Keith said, "and see can he get through the sand, dig it out. It'll cost you. If he can't get it all, we'll have to give up on this pond. The other thing we can do, now, is save the cost. Just fill in and go away, not take the chance. It's up to you."

I'm not sure I said anything.

"Depends on how much a fellow wants a pond, I guess," said Daniel Keith, sympathetically.

I looked over at the pile where my hackberry tree lay on its side, roots and all, with brush and young hickories piled against it. There was no thought involved. I just felt like a fellow who wanted a pond pretty much, but I glanced at Tina next. She seemed to be the same kind of fellow, because she nodded without any hesitation at all.

"Let's get that dragline, Daniel Keith," I said, and he grinned, and I'm happy to report that it all worked out. The added cost wasn't more than a couple of hundred dollars. Daniel Keith supposed I knew—but I didn't until later, or I wouldn't have been so firm and cool—that it could more easily have been a couple of thousand.

That first pond, in those uninflated days, cost $2,500. The government paid a little over half.

What we had, when the machines rumbled off, was a deep, raw, two-and-a-half-acre basin, steepest and deepest where the dam blocked off the lower end. I think it was twenty-one feet down, from the brave little flags that marked the someday-water-line, and the question now was *how soon?* In late September we had a half-day's rain. I hurried up to the pond as soon as it ended, and saw that the sides of the basin were scarred from little rivulets of water now collected at the bottom in a lot of mud and perhaps a 50-gallon puddle. At 326,000 gallons of water per acre foot, times 2½ acres, and an average depth of 8 feet, we didn't have much more than 5 million gallons to go. I thought it might take two or three years; it didn't. By the end of April there was water trickling out the overflow tube. By the middle of May it was roaring.

By June, though the pond was a mile away from our creeks, the nearest source of aquatic life, we'd begun to have an environment. Frogs and muskrats had found the pond, an aquatic plant with arrowhead-shaped leaves, and some marsh grass. There were water bugs and dragonflies. A flock of lesser scaup had rested over one night, on their way north. And the next morning I was on my way in the pickup truck, answering a call from the Soil Conservation Service to pick up fish.

These were to be largemouth bass fry. Later I'd get some catfish, but for now it was eight hundred little bass, and I had, in the back, a clean, new, thirty-gallon garbage can, two-thirds full of pond water and held fast with log chains. I went slowly, so as not to lose water, and worried all the way about whether the can was big enough. If I'd had

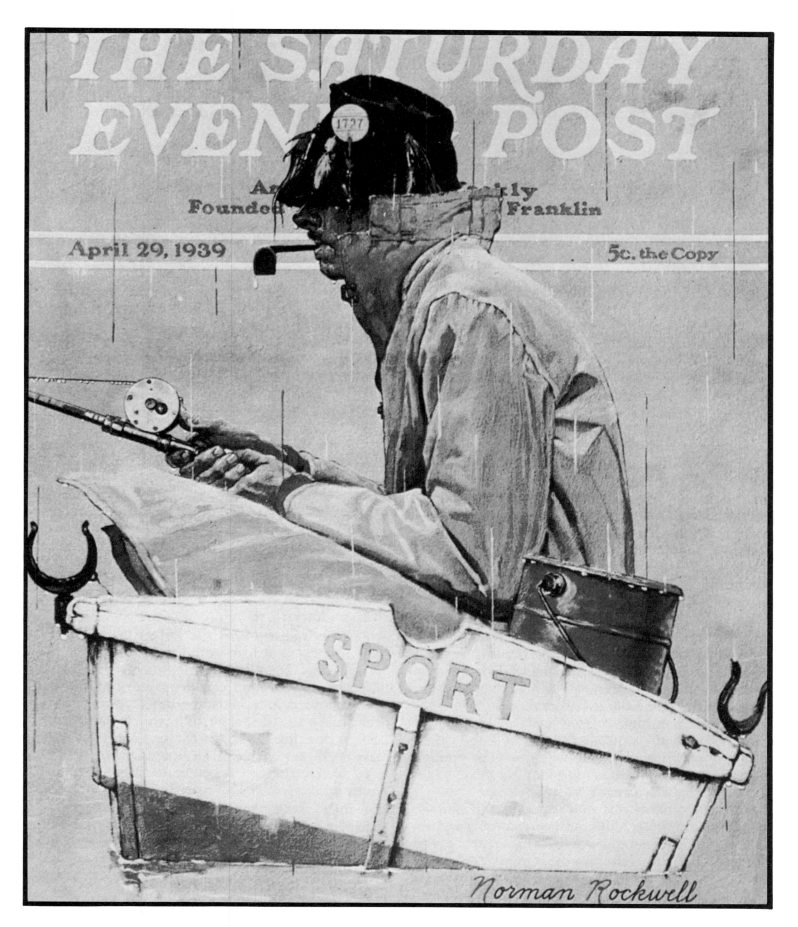

Cover illustration by Norman Rockwell (1939).

time, I'd have stopped at the hardware store, bought a second can, and gone home for more water. Eight hundred sounded like a lot of fish.

In front of the SCS office when I arrived, and already surrounded by others on the same errand, was a federal-green truck with built-in tanks and the name of a fish hatchery lettered on the door. A couple of men in olive-drab jackets and whipcord pants stood by, one of them with a list. I got out and approached just in time to hear my own name read out:

"Vance Boo—Booj—well, Vance. Is Vance here?"

"Here." I figured I knew whom he meant.

"Eight hundred bass, no bluegills," said the man with the list, and the other one dipped into a tank with a graduated beaker that looked a good deal like my wife's one-pint Pyrex measuring cup. He poured the water out, looked at the graduations, and poured back about half of what seemed to be a seething black mass of tiny organisms. Then he added water back, and asked if I had a bucket.

"Is that all of them?" I dipped a bucket of water from my garbage can and handed it up. What he held was three jiggers of fish.

"Probably a few extra," he said. He emptied his beaker into my bucket, and his partner called the next name. I drove slowly back to the farm. I remember pouring three jiggers of fish into five million gallons of water with a sense of total disbelief that I would ever see any of those bass again. But a year later they were five inches long, and we could see them clearly, swimming by in schools of fifteen and twenty. We'd added channel catfish, too, by then, but those we didn't see; they stayed deep.

In their second summer, when the bass were eight and ten inches long, there came an extraordinary day when, wading into the pond to swim, I became aware that there was a cloud of new fry scattering away from my legs. I walked around the edge. There were hatches everywhere.

"They've reproduced," we said, in some awe. "There's a supply of fish now, for food and recreation, that will renew itself as long as the pond is there." We were wrong about that, but meanwhile, and finally, it was time to go fishing.

It was fairly slow that first summer, and the fish were still small. We did so much catching and releasing that my son still won't keep a fish (he eats the ones I catch). On calm evenings they would take surface lures—poppers and flies and things like fly-rod Flatfish—and that same son bought me a gorgeous deer-hair frog for my birthday, having sent off to Orvis for it, which probably did the best of anything we used.

It will not surprise bass fishermen to hear that in the third spring, when the fish were a foot long and more, and the bulls guarding the nests, they would fight anything that came along, never mind how bright, how big, how noisy. They were so easy to catch, in fact, that we stopped fishing for a time—the fish were also full of milt and roe, many of them, and it didn't seem proper to mess up their spawning.

The fishing was nice, now, on summer evenings, particularly from a canoe with one paddling and the other casting in toward shore. That hair frog and other lures of its size would tease the fish out of their feeding stations in the undercut places along the bank, and though they certainly weren't as wary as trout, it took a nice presentation to get one. Nor could we count on them; "How about fish for supper?" became a clear signal to Tina to defrost some hamburger.

It was fun. It was soothing. We built a second pond, the same size, this one without cost-sharing. We left the timber standing in the upper end of the second one, something the engineers wouldn't have sanctioned, in order to create snags as the trees died naturally. This pond became the one in which snapping turtles congregated and wood ducks nested. It produced, after a couple of years and having been stocked from the first pond, larger bass—I couldn't understand why the snags would have that effect, and didn't learn how little they had to do with it until a really big fish came out of that second pond.

Now I am, of course, like anyone with a strong preference for the fly rod, totally indifferent to how large a fish I catch by comparison with other fishermen. So when a fifteen-year-old called Fred, fishing deep in midsummer with a hideous plastic worm, caught a four-and-a-half-pounder—still our homeplace record, and a sizable largemouth for Iowa waters—I naturally felt no resentment beyond wanting to break the kid's thumbs. It really was a heck of a fish, and I have to admit that a good many lavender plastic worms got bumped along the bottom in the deep parts in the week that followed, and that some other pretty fair-sized bass came up. But it wasn't until I went back to my fly rod that I caught the explanation for why this pond had bigger fish. I was using the hair frog, and what I got first was a remarkably hard strike from what looked, as it swirled, like an eight- or ten-inch bass. I managed to hook it. I'd filed the barb off my hook, and so brought the fish in rather quickly, expecting it to do some tail-dancing. Instead, it plunged and fought all the way and, when I got it to hand, wasn't a bass at all. It wasn't a catfish, either, the only other species we'd stocked. Instead, it was the fattest, brightest, healthiest-looking young bluegill I've ever seen.

How it got into the pond—along with quite a few more like it, as we soon learned—is anybody's guess. The most persuasive explanation I've heard is that they came air mail. It's said that fish eggs stick to the legs of waterfowl, sometimes, and are

Illustration by Luther Schelling (1979).

transported that way from pond to pond. Whatever the explanation, it's confirmation of the current attitude of fishery technicians: put in a bluegill population for forage fish, they say, if you want large bass. So it was my intention, as winter approached, to get the bluegills established in the first pond as well, just as soon as spring arrived.

Spring never came for our bass and bluegills, or for our generally forgotten catfish, either. We went off traveling that winter, not that our presence on the farm would have prevented what happened. It's called winterkill. The ponds froze, as they always do, but the weather was more severe than usual, the ice thicker, the snow heavier and longer-lasting. As I understand it, the plants in a pond generally continue growing in the winter. Enough light filters down through the ice to keep the photosynthesis going. Growing plants consume carbon dioxide and excrete oxygen; that keeps the fish alive. But if light is totally blocked off, the process

reverses. The plants die, the oxygen is consumed by decay, the carbon dioxide excreted. The fish smother.

We returned from our journey in March, as the thaw was starting, and on the first day back I visited both ponds. There were dead catfish, two and three feet long, all around the margins of the ice, and hundreds of raccoon tracks. The coons were cleaning up the carcasses as fast as they could, contesting for them with a good number of crows.

I was sad, of course, and yet we wouldn't miss the catfish; we'd stopped fishing for them, because the pond-raised kind were muddy-tasting, and seen them only when, occasionally, one would hit some sort of bass lure—they liked one called a Johnson Silver Minnow. In any case, whatever hope I'd had that the bass might have survived disappeared in the next few days. It took the bass bodies, for some reason, a little longer than the catfish to start floating to the surface.

I asked around, looking for consolation, and found people willing to declare that the winterkill phenomenon was exceptional, unlikely to happen again. Impatient to restore our pleasure, one that friends and neighbors enjoyed as much as we did, I restocked with catchables—foot-long bass from a commercial hatchery, one hundred of them, I think, at a dollar each. I saved two years that way, because the new fish reproduced the following spring. We had a pleasant summer of fishing. It was a picnic summer. The bass were just large enough to fillet—we'd make a fire; heat butter in a skillet; shake the fillets, a minute after catching, in a bag of seasoned flour; and sauté them. Ah, they were good.

My friend Tom tried all his bamboo rods in turn that summer at the ponds. The kid, Fred, came back, seventeen now, and couldn't catch anything bigger than anyone else could. My daughter was old enough to learn to cast with ultra-light spinning gear, and caught her first fish. Not to mention her second, third, fourth . . . I got a deer-hair crayfish for my birthday this time. . . . Winter came, the second after the winterkill, and I learned that we were in a cycle of hard winters. We lost our fish again.

We had built, meanwhile, a really large pond—an eight-acre affair—at the west end of our farm, in connection with selling off some of the land up there. Because of its size, this pond is winterproof, and we had stocked it, like the very first, with government-donated bass and catfish fry. After the second winterkill, I went to the big west pond, just before spawning time, and caught mature, gravid bass to restock with. They took. They reproduced. After another summer's wait, we had fishing again in the original ponds. I learned about a device that might prevent winterkill, and began to yearn— windmill-driven propellers is what they are, floated in rubber rings. They are said to keep an area of water open, thus admitting light and oxygen. They cost, well, not as much as a fishing vacation in Argentina, but, for me anyway, close: they cost $350 each, and I now had three ponds to worry about, the first, the second, and a new one, the most beautiful of all. We had felt flush and built the woods pond just a year before, along with still another—a half-acre, very deep pond with steep sides—near the buildings. A swimming pond. This swimming pond, in which few plants grow, had no fish, either, and so was not a worry. But in the new woods pond, and contrary to all reasonable advice, I'd stocked walleyed pike. Not a pond fish, they said.

It was a deep, well-shaded pond, about an acre, and the prettiest of all. Wood ducks loved it, and so did we. Stubbornly, I bought 250 little walleyes; I knew they wouldn't reproduce, but I thought that, with luck, they might survive. I got them in during August 1978, a year that must be specified because the winter of 1978–79 was the worst in the Midwest since 1935.

And I was out of money, and had not been able to spend $1,000 for floating, windmill-driven propellers, one for each of the three fishing ponds.

As that winter got worse and worse, as the ice thickened and the snow deepened, I thought a lot about fish. I thought about them as creatures for which I'd created certain worlds, in which I had put them to grow. I did not think of them as having minds or feelings, but as a form of life I'd fostered which would now, individual by individual, die— not in pain, I thought, or despair, but as victims, nevertheless, of a kind of wantonness, and the wanton was myself. I assumed, as Tina and I brought our flocks and herds through the bitter weather, my third fishkill, and did not suppose I would want to restock a fourth time—not until the windmills could be bought, anyway, and perhaps I was too discouraged by now even to believe in windmills.

There came the spring of '79, and yes, coon tracks around the ponds. And yes, I found a small, dead walleye by the woods pond one morning, and after that stopped looking. I didn't want to see dead fish again. Let the coons and the crows have them. 'Bye, fish.

But we still loved our ponds. If fish couldn't survive in this cycle of hard winters, nevertheless, the ponds were beautiful; the waterfowl and deer and all the other wildlife used them. Windmills might be afforded sometime, or some new technology come along. The snapping turtles had delicious meat in them, and we all loved frog legs.

It was August 1979. About frogs: I don't think of gathering them as a sport, only a harvesting operation. Gigging them at night has no appeal for me. What I've settled on for frogging is a .22 rifle with long-rifle cartridges. These knock a frog out instantly and completely, if they hit at all. So I was slipping along the bank of the second pond, rifle in hand, looking carefully for the next OK bullfrog, when, glancing into shallow water, I saw fish. I took another step, and checked myself. Fish? I crouched, and looked back, and there they were. Bass. Survivors. Reproducers. That was my first yell of the day. I may even have done a little dance. The next yell, I've described. It came after I'd run back, put the frogs in the refrigerator, swapped the rifle for my nondescript bugging rod, and run to the woods pond. That was the day I caught the little walleye, and learned that most of them, too, seemed to have survived. And now I am waiting for another summer, fairly certain that the walleyes have come through the winter passing as I write.

Even before summer, though, there are instructions to follow:

"For two years," said the hatchery man who brought my walleyes, "they'll do fine on larvae and tadpoles. The third year, you ought to add some forage fish. . . ."

Casting the Fly for Black Bass from *The Basses* by Louis Rhead (1905).

From Eugene McCarthy's *Familiar Fish* (1900).

From Thomas Chubb catalog (1888).

And so my fishing fantasy is much in mind, as the ground thaws. It has no trout in it, or muskies or landlocked salmon, no tuna, marlin, swordfish. It takes place in just a few weeks, now, in a small pond to which I may have access—Knowling's or Zach's or perhaps a certain quarry. The fish, of course, are bluegills, fifteen or twenty pairs, mature, ready to spawn. I'll get them, keep them alive, put them in, and some for the bass ponds, too.

Then in August, it will be another white streamer fly, a hushed moment, and, as the fantasy goes, another walleye, a year older than the last. Even so it will not be eating size. It will be, I think, what walleye fishermen call a "hammer handle"—twelve to fourteen inches long, two inches thick, and full of bones.

Next summer? Maybe there'll be one or two to eat, and the summer after that . . . and, of course, bass to catch, all along. The catfish in the big west pond must be monstrous now. Windmills to shop for. And a new winter dream.

I wrote about a fifth pond, small and deep, near the buildings, which we use for swimming. It's unusually clear for a farm pond, because of the steep sides, and the water, twenty-eight feet down, must be really cold.

No one is going to encourage me to carry out this plan, and it will take another $500 which I may or may not ever feel I can cut loose, but before I'm done with pond-making, I've got to try trout again. Once, long ago, I answered an ad for "farm pond adapted trout fingerlings," bought a couple of hundred, put them in a pond, never saw one again. But I don't think the problem was temperature so much as oxygen.

So: what I think of now, more often than I ought, is a device called a GenAIRator, made by some people in Wisconsin, which is designed to aerate lakes and ponds. It consists of an electric air pump which you're supposed to fasten to a tree or post on the shore. It feeds air through plastic pipe to a venturi tube, down at the bottom of the pond. The function of the venturi is to send a stream of air bubbling up to the surface, and I assume that this will both give oxygen and, as that cold bottom layer of water is raised up, lower the temperature at the surface.

I don't know for certain that this will enable me to raise trout. I don't know if the windmills would work. I don't know, for that matter, that my walleyes will go on living through hot Augusts as they grow large, or that my bass won't winter-kill again. But fish are like other crops, it seems to me by now. You fix up an environment, you plant, cultivate, protect as best you can, and with luck—and a white streamer, or a deer-hair frog, or even a lavender plastic worm—you harvest. For food, sometimes. For fun, more often. For the feeling of putting into the world a good thing that wasn't there before.

Drawing by Ernest Lussier (1979).

FALL

*The light fades early; the angler is pinched for time.
At sunset he considers how he might best use the
remaining hour, which reminds him—in a flash
—of mistakes and misconceptions of hours, weeks,
and years gone by. Don't try to be fancy now,
he tells himself; go with what works.*

When you reach the period of your life that is the equivalent of fall, you do not have time for nonessentials. You want to pare down and take full advantage of what you have left. You do not want to waste time.

If you are a fisherman, you probably find yourself concentrating on the kinds of fishing you love and passing up opportunities when you will likely find yourself merely going through the motions. Tackle loses some of its a priori fascination; you are quicker to see gimmicks for what they are. The big numbers are not necessarily so impressive, and you find yourself measuring your success against wholly private criteria.

I remember watching a man on the Beaverkill several years ago. I was standing on an iron bridge drying out from a fall in the river. I had been watching a fish and not my step. There had been some fairly good hatches up and down the river, and there were dozens of well-equipped fishermen working all the larger pools. There were some elegantly outfitted dudes among them and several men who could surely handle a fly rod. There was a lot of posing and outright showing off on the Beaverkill that weekend.

But this man was different. He was no hick; his clothes were clean and his waders were not patched. He wore a simple vest and a hat that was jaunty without being outrageous. His picture could have run in any of the outdoor magazines.

But he was not out to impress anyone, either. He had taken a spot just below the bridge and was casting back upstream, across the current, with some sort of dry fly. He was using a cane rod that look weathered and well loved, and he wasted no motion and squandered no energy. He fished as efficiently as any man I have ever seen, and he looked like a man who believed that he was all alone, even though he must have known I was on the bridge watching. His fishing seemed as private as devotionals.

I watched him catch four fat browns, admire them, and return them to the water. After releasing each fish he patiently checked his fly and dabbed a little Mucilin on the body to refloat it, then false cast a few times and was back at his fishing. It was as though not even catching a fish would be allowed to disturb his serenity.

After thirty or forty minutes he left the stream. It seemed odd. There was another hour or so of daylight, and trout fishermen don't ordinarily leave the stream when the fish are still taking.

He joined me on the bridge. "You look," he said, "like a man who fell into the river and could use a drink."

"I did," I said, "and I could."

He had a very old silver flask with initials engraved on the side in one pocket of his vest. He poured a capful of something brown and offered it to me. "You first," he said.

I thanked him and took the drink, which was very smooth cognac.

"Warms you right up," he said, and took a drink himself. He was very delicate and poised about it, almost ceremonial. He looked to be about forty-five or so, but was frail in the manner of a man who is still recovering from a nearly fatal accident.

"You were doing all right down there," I said.

"Good day. Plenty of flies. And there are always a lot of fish in this stretch."

We talked some more and watched the river. He told me that the Beaverkill was the first river he had ever fly-fished. "Not long after the war. My father came back from Europe with a lot of English tackle, and we came up here from Manhattan to fish together. It was wonderful the first few years. Then I quit fishing it."

I asked him why.

"Too many fishermen. Too easy for them to get here. The river was full of stocked trout that weren't worth the trouble it took to catch them. If I fished at all, I traveled."

He told me about fishing in New Zealand, where rainbow trout of five pounds were the rule on dry flies. He had also fished in Alaska and Iceland, where he had caught Atlantic salmon, the prince of all game fish.

A page of trout flies from *Favorite Flies* by Mary Orvis Marbury (1896).

Eldridge Hardie, watercolor (1981).

Robert K. Abbett, *Bridge Pool, the Beaverkill* (1981).

"I've got arthritis now," he said. "I can't take the cold water and the standing straight up for more than an hour at a time. Couldn't believe it when the doctors first told me. Thought you got that sort of thing when you were really old, not just running down a little. But I can't travel that far anymore, certainly not to hobble out of the water after an hour."

He still worked in New York City, he said. "I can drive up here from my office in two and a half hours. Now that I can't go on those lavish expeditions anymore, this is the only river I ever fish. And you know what? Almost the whole story of American fishing could be written on this river."

I did not know it then. I was working in Manhattan too, and when I had a little spare time, I used it to fish, not to bone up on river lore. To me the Beaverkill was a river that had a fly named after it. I'd had some success with the wet, never the dry. That was the extent of my interest; but then I was still young and rude.

The Beaverkill, the arthritic man said, was probably the queen of American trout streams. Theodore Gordon himself had fished the stream, and it is mentioned often in his writing (though he is properly associated with the nearby Neversink). The river figured in the early experience of numerous other celebrated American anglers, including Ray Bergman and Sparse Grey Hackle. Most of its upper reaches are leased to private clubs that have their own long traditions.

"Back when I was a boy," the arthritic man said, "you could come up here and catch just worlds of trout. This stream had some of the finest mayfly hatches in the East. The Hendrickson fly was created just downstream from here. It was a streamside operation to match the hatch.

"What a lot of people don't realize is that pollution and stream damage are tougher on the mayflies than they are on the fish. So you can experience the depressing phenomenon these days of coming up to the Beaverkill in May when the Hendricksons should be hatching and not seeing any bugs." He shrugged and we had another drink of his brandy.

"What's worse is that after the war, the river was pounded so hard, particularly by people who bought those newfangled spinning rigs and figured that they were to fly rods what the machine gun was to the muzzle loader, that this stream was just about fished out, especially of those mature, middle-sized fish that you catch on a good mayfly hatch. They had to stock the river, and you saw these horrible Opening Day extravaganzas: fishermen lined up elbow to elbow in a little pool, casting worms and hardware for seven-inch fish that were just out of the hatchery.

"But you know, the world is a pretty tough place, and you can't just write something off. A couple of things happened on this river that were like a rebirth, a second chance for trout fishing in the East. The fishermen pressured the state to put in some special regulations on the stream. This was the no-kill experiment, which they started in about 1965. Now we've got a good strong population of reproducing brown trout and even some decent brookies. When you come here, you know this stream is not fished out.

"It's not wild, natural fishing . . . but we got chased out of Eden a long time ago and whining doesn't help. This is the fishing we've got now. It's hard on the trout too, but you don't hear them complaining. When the mayfly hatches started falling off, the fish moved on to other things, but the fishermen kept fishing the classic mayflies with upright wings. Then somebody discovered that the fish were eating caddis flies. They weren't going to starve just to keep the purists happy. Now we fish caddis imitations and move the fly around on the water, and we catch fish. I caught four just now on an Olive Caddis. They call it a Shad Fly around here for some reason. But it is a dry fly and it takes fish."

We watched another fisherman make his way into the pool below us, strip some line off his reel, and begin false casting somewhat sloppily but with enthusiasm. There was only a quarter-hour of daylight left. The nighthawks were sailing over the corridor of the river, swooping low to take insects and then banking effortlessly to avoid the overhanging limbs of streamside trees. The water had changed color, to a kind of shimmering violet.

Casting in the Shallows from *The Speckled Brook Trout* by Louis Rhead (1902).

Thomas Aquinas Daly, *Brown Trout* (1978).

Thomas Aquinas Daly, *Bruce's Backwater* (1978).

"It's a beautiful river," my companion said, "and I had almost written it off. But I think this river is going to show us the way for public fishing in this country. We don't have a wilderness anymore, and we're going to have to learn to live with that instead of just lamenting it. In a way, this stream gives me faith. It has survived, even prospered in a fashion. There's a lesson in that for me. Being crippled doesn't finish you; it just changes the terms. I've gotten used to it, adjusted and made my peace. Just like this river did. Just like we all have to do, sooner or later. I suppose that's why I like to fish here if I have an hour to fish."

Cutting out the nonessentials strengthens your loyalties to what remains. You are left with what you love: the rods you love, the rivers you love, the fish you love.

Judge John Voelker (Robert Traver to his readers, as we've explained earlier) lives among a superabundance of fine fly-fishing on the Upper Peninsula of Michigan. When the Great Lakes were ravaged by lamprey eels that swam in through the newly opened St. Lawrence Seaway, and by pollution from the heavy industry along their banks, fishery experts looked around for some means of rejuvenation. They settled on salmon, cohos and chinooks which would eat the alewives that had multiplied unchecked since the lampreys devastated the natural population of lake trout. The program worked wonderfully, beyond anything even its strongest advocates had anticipated. The salmon thrived. The lake trout returned. And a vast new recreational industry sprang up around these new fish—charter boats, guides, tackle stores, marinas, and so forth. Brown trout and large rainbows were also introduced, and with the abundant alewives to feed on, they were soon growing to nearly record size. Experts expect a brown trout in excess of thirty pounds to be taken in Lake Michigan one day soon. There are also river populations of brown trout, and bass in the lakes and ponds. Altogether it makes for a great choice in fishing, much of it excellent and some of it for trophies and world records—to which Judge Voelker thumbs his nose. He fishes strictly for native brook trout, which he calls his "speckled darlings" and which seldom grow to more than a foot in length. A fourteen-incher is grounds for a parade through town.

The brook trout was the native American salmonid for which the first fly fishermen on this continent fished. It is a lovely fish, colored more resonantly than any other fish in the world. It is also, sadly, somewhat stupid and very delicate. The early fly fishermen had an easy time with brook trout, and what they were unable to catch the logging industry destroyed when it ruined the watersheds. It is cold comfort to know that the first hatchery for trout in this country was established in 1864 to resupply the dwindling stocks of brook trout. The fish has been engaged in a losing rearguard action ever since. Today in the Adirondacks, Art Flick, Jr., is conducting a program to develop a hybrid brook trout that will be both tougher and smarter than the little char that was here when the first white man arrived. But Flick seems to be losing a race with the latest enemy of the brook trout: acid rain. The rain changes the pH of the water and makes it an unsuitable habitat for brook trout and for most other fish as well. Already there are some dead lakes in the high mountains of the Adirondacks.

But there are still some brook trout left. And John Voelker passes up the larger fish and the Escanaba, Ontonagon, and Yellow Dog rivers to fish for them in the little bushy streams and random beaver ponds in northern Michigan. He has caught big fish, particularly one very large brown trout which he took on a very small Adams. He describes the experience in a tone of amusement and befuddlement, as if to say, "Damnedest thing happened to me the other day. Caught this trout. Enormous thing. Can't imagine how I did it."

But when he talks of his "speckled darlings," there is love and reverence in his voice. He uses fine leaders—I once sent him some tippet material of 7X and 8X diameter because he couldn't find anything that small where he lives. I think he uses such wispy leaders to give the fish a better chance, not because his flies are especially small or the water he fishes is terribly clear. Those fish

1919 catalog cover from Abercrombie & Fitch Co.

N. C. Wyeth, *September Afternoon* (1916).

George Inness, *Sunset with Boy Fishing* (1866).

are precious to him, and he honors them by using the most delicate tackle. Voelker is a curmudgeon who flirts with outright misanthropy. His taste for things modern is limited to nylon leaders and perhaps graphite rods. He prefers the older, simpler days and the brook trout that were abundant then. Fishing for them, he enters a world that he finds better and cleaner than the one we are all forced to live in. And that's fine. I've never been fishing with anyone who loved the sport more.

When the brook trout began to suffer from overfishing and pollution, in the latter part of the nineteenth century, the brown trout was introduced to America. Browns were native to Europe, especially Germany and Scotland, and you can still find some old-timers who call the thoroughly Americanized fish German browns or Loch Leven trout. But no other transplant has taken so well to North America, unless it is the ring-necked pheasant, which is native to China. It is hard for most American trout fishermen to imagine a world without brown trout.

For one thing, of the salmonids, the brown trout seems the most American in character and temperament. Browns are tough and resourceful, not excessively fancy about the things they eat or the places where they hang out. They can tolerate water temperatures and pollution levels that would turn a brook trout belly up. They forage successfully enough to grow and thrive in streams where rainbow trout five and six years old are less than twelve inches long because they cannot find enough to eat. Given sufficient food and cover, brown trout can maintain an adequate reproducing population despite heavy fishing pressure. And, best of all for the fisherman, brown trout grow big and very wary. A modest cut bank in a small stream may be the home of a four- or five-pound brown trout. On big streams they grow much larger.

A fisherman can learn a lesson in humility and respect for his quarry by watching a shocking operation on a trout stream. The fishery experts throw a current into a pool or cut bank or any stretch of good holding water, then count the stunned fish that come to the surface. I remember watching once when a little stream I fished was surveyed in this fashion. Trout came out of places that I would never have expected to hold them. And from one old undercut stump the wardens stunned a brown that must have weighed four pounds. The stream was so narrow at that point that you could jump across it.

When most fishermen think of individual trophy fish, they think of brown trout, in many cases a particular fish that lives in a particular place in the fisherman's favorite river. But a big brown trout did not get that way by being stupid, as any fisherman will be happy to remind you. Also, he is not going to be interested, ordinarily, in feeding on small hatching mayflies. To feed on Hendricksons, say, he must leave his cover—and big fish have the best cover in the river—for an exposed position in a pool. He must remain there long enough to eat sufficient insects to make the trip worthwhile, and in his case that's a long time, since he is a big fish with a big appetite. All fish are acutely sensitive to overhead danger. Perhaps this is a genetic throwback to the days when there were large populations of predatory birds that fed on fish. Or perhaps fish know that movement above them could come from a stalking human. Whatever the reasons, no fish likes to leave overhead cover for very long. Old smart fish like to leave overhead cover even less. So the dry-fly fisherman who casts mayfly imitations to rising trout is not likely to catch a large brown no matter how carefully he ties and presents his flies.

Big brown trout feed on anything that fills them up. The very biggest fish were routinely called cannibals until a few years ago because they were known to eat smaller brown trout. Such a fish should be removed from a stream, the thinking went, to make it safe for smaller breeding fish. We now know that although a big brown trout does eat smaller ones, he is not exclusively a cannibal. He also eats small rainbow trout, brook trout, chubs, sculpin, and dace. Nor is he exclusively a fish eater. He eats mice and birds if they fall into the water; moths, grasshoppers, and dragonflies; as well as all the things that trout are known to eat—nymphs of all sorts and occasionally a hatching mayfly or caddis fly.

On the Pere Marquette River in Michigan one afternoon, I fished to a sporadic hatch in a good-looking pool that was defined on one bank by deep water and a logjam. Half a dozen fish were rising in the pool. I hooked a small brown trout—so small, in fact, that I considered the fish a nuisance and began stripping line in with my left hand, eager to release the fish, refloat the fly, and begin casting again for one of the better risers. As I stripped line, the little brown skipped helplessly across the river's surface on his side. When the leader reached my top guide, I bent over to free the hook. My face was about two feet from the little trout. As I reached for him, I saw a sudden, startling swirl that sucked him under the surface. He reappeared, and a few inches beneath him, in clear silhouette, was the largest brown trout I have ever seen. The spots on his side looked as big as dimes. His underslung jaw looked wickedly prehistoric. There was a cold and distinct aspect to his eyes. He made another lunge at the little trout, had it briefly, then felt the resistance (I suppose) of my fly line, dropped his prey, and was gone, probably back to the protection of the logjam. From there he ruled the pool, and anything that appeared and could not evade him became a meal.

I released the little trout and stood there breathing deeply and trying to calm myself. That was an awesome fish, perhaps a ten-pounder, I told an old Pere Marquette hand that evening. "Could be," he said. "They're in here that big. I've fished this river twenty years now and never caught one that size. Got a couple that went five pounds. And I've seen one or two like the one that went after your little fish."

"I want to catch that fish," I said. I had made one or two casts to the logjam after I settled down, tied on a Muddler or something big in the forlorn hope of moving him. But the largest Muddler in my vest was not a third the size of the fish that trout had tried to eat. I knew that it was useless.

If you want to prospect for large trout, you must first study their methods, which are not the same as those of the smaller fish. You can forget about duns and spinners and midges and learn to expect barren days. Fishing for those fish becomes something of a quest, and it is entirely proper that William Humphrey's delightful little tale about one man's pursuit of a giant brown trout is called *My Moby Dick*.

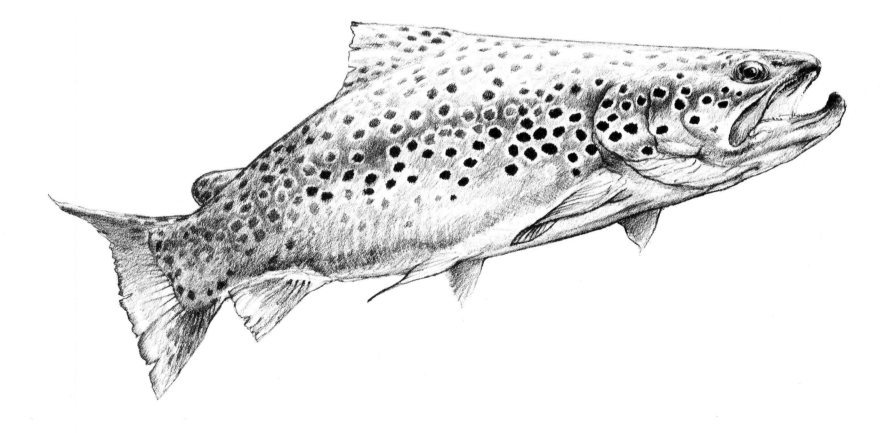

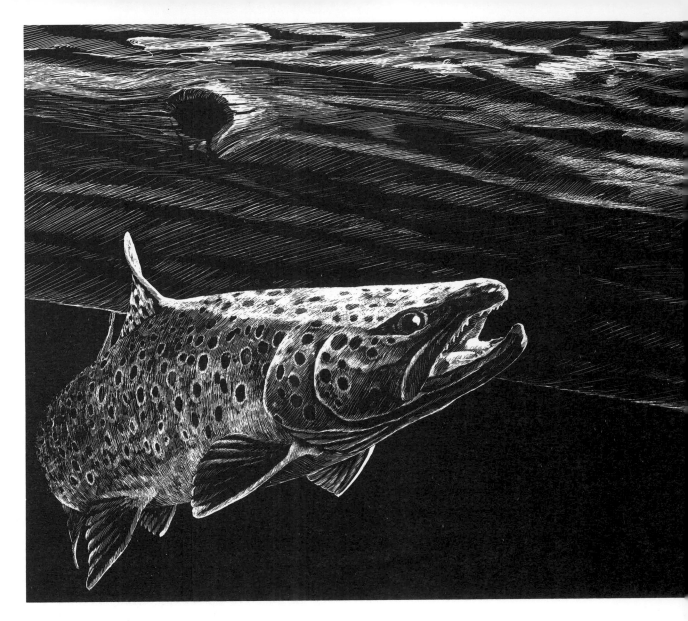

The best tactic for large brown trout, especially in the heavily fished streams of the East, is to fish at night. That is when the larger fish do most of their feeding. It is safer then for them to move out of their protective lies, and there are more large things for them to eat in and on the water. But so many of the pleasurable sensations associated with fishing are visual that most fishermen do not even try fishing at night unless something gives them a good reason.

What seems best about fly-fishing is that you see almost everything. Often you see the individual fish that you are trying to entice. You watch him holding in the water, waiting for an insect to drift into his feeding area. And if you are casting to a visible fish like that, you can watch your fly drift down over him, and you tense while he decides whether or not to take it. Even if you do not see the fish you are after and stalk it, you might see the sign of a fish—the rise form it leaves when feeding on the surface insects, the bulge it makes when nymphing. You watch the water for signs and try to decipher the stream and pick out the good lies. You watch for the wink of white that is the inside of a feeding trout's mouth. In night fishing all this is lost.

Once I had seen the big fish that held in the pool with the logjam, I was ready to try anything to hook him. I consulted Ivan, a fine fisherman and guide who had lived on the river for years and who had sold me a gross or two of flies in the time that I had been fishing there.

"You won't catch him in the daylight," he said. "Not unless it's some kind of freak. The best way to catch a big one like that is fish for him at night." Then he explained how it was done right, so that you caught fish and did not step into a deep hole, fill your waders, and drown in the dark, cedar-stained water.

First, Ivan said, you scout your fishing places in the daylight. You find a good place to stand and cover the whole pool you intend to fish without fouling your back casts on a vagrant alder branch. Once you are in position, it is best not to wade any more than you have to. You check your fly and leader by touch as much as possible but carry a small light for those times when you'll need it, but only one with a very small beam, and you try not to put any light

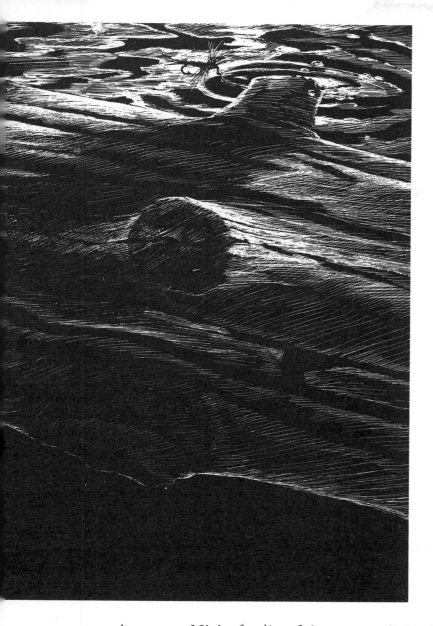

Drawing by Russell Buzzell (1979).

on the water. Night-feeding fish are very light-shy. You select a few likely flies
and have them where you can get to them. You shorten your leader down to
six feet or so and ten- or twelve-pound test at the tippet. "The fish aren't
leader-shy at night. No need to mess around and lose a good fish on account
of using a light leader. Also helps to have a stiff tippet when you have to pull a
fly out of the trees."

He gave me—sold me, rather—some ugly, oversized flies that he had tied up
especially for night fishing and that he called, simply, Ivan's Specials. They were
big, hair-winged things designed to put a lot of silhouette on the water. He
threw in some bushy wet flies and a couple of Spuddlers to imitate baitfish. "If
you hear them feeding up on the surface, use the dries. Otherwise, fish the
wets the usual way on a short line. If you use the streamers, fish kind of fast
and try to move a lot of water. I think the fish come to the vibrations."

Later that night I smeared on some insect repellent, cut back on my normally too-long leader, and returned to the pool with the logjam and the big
trout. The sand and gravel bottoms of Michigan rivers are easy to wade, but in
the dark even the Pere Marquette felt strong and dangerous. I was aware, once
again in my life, of just how irresistible the surge of a river is. I made my way
carefully to a spot that seemed safe for standing and casting. As I stood there,
trying to accustom myself to all the new sensations, there was a heavy splash
out in the blackness of the pool. It was the sound you would expect from a
large rock thrown into water.

I waited several seconds, then there was another splash. It was, I realized
with my heart accelerating, a feeding fish. I began hastily stripping line. It took
me ten minutes or so to make a decent cast and to settle down to doing things
with the rhythms that I had developed in countless hours of daylight fishing.
By then the large trout was off his feed.

I fished on, and my senses became attuned to the night sensations around
me. The river smelled of some raw metal: copper or zinc. Bats passed overhead on invisible trajectories. Insects chirped on the unseen banks, a multitude

of fireflies blinked, and somewhere a frog groaned mournfully and an owl hooted one long, haunting note. I found I didn't need to see to fish. Near midnight I caught a trout of about two pounds.

Night fishing is more and more the way to go on many streams, not only because the big trout are out feeding then, but because it is almost the only time that the solitary fisherman can have a small piece of the river to himself. A good trout river like the Pere Marquette can get to be a very crowded place in mid-afternoon. The canoe hatch is reliable all season long, and more and more people want to ride even the gentlest rivers. But at night the stream is once again a lonely and wild place, even a little spooky. You can hear small animals moving around on the bank behind you, and you feel again the way you felt when you went fishing for the very first time.

Like tea dances and debutante balls, night fishing is more an eastern activity. The big fish out West can be caught during the daylight hours, and the rivers are generally too big and too fast to be fished safely at night. And the surrounding countryside is too spectacular to be missed.

Some men in the West are so spoiled that they fish exclusively for the very large trout that are common there. Charles Brooks is the author of three very good books on the subject of western rivers, large trout, and the special tactics he uses to catch them. He fishes with large nymphs, sinking lines, and heavy rods. Most of the time he fishes the surging channels with these rigs, and his methods—which would turn an English chalk stream man's hair white—work remarkably well. Brooks probably represents the furthest limit in trout fishing of the distinctly American school which preaches "Fish the water," whereas the classic English approach is "Fish the fish."

Brooks and most westerners—most Americans, for that matter—do things with a fly rod that in the early days of the sport simply were not done, certainly not by gentlemen. They do not do it merely to be heretical or crude. They are practical men, and they want to catch fish. Form follows function, and the Yellowstone is not the Test.

There was a time when anyone who could handle a fly rod and had read a book or two on the subject knew what a purist was. Many fly rodders back then were purists and proud of it. Those who were not were either ashamed of the fact or arrogantly proud of it, depending on whether they were cowed or incited by claims of aristocratic superiority. Real heresy, of course, got its start in America and became almost codified in the American West.

The definition of *purist* has always been elusive. The most extreme purist is the man who fishes only dry flies, tied to match the hatching naturals, and casts only upstream to a sighted fish. This strict orthodoxy came from England, where there is a tradition of that sort of thing and which has the streams for it. It took shallow roots in this country, hanging on most tenaciously in the Anglophile Northeast. The Northeast is also the seat of the publishing industry in America, so most of the early American literature of trout fishing was full of English orthodoxy.

But there are not enough streams in America that can be fished that way. Even in the East, most trout water is in fast freestone rivers where it is not possible to fish visible fish on a gentlemanly dead drift. So Americans learned to work the water and not the fish.

Nor were the opportunities for insufferable snobbery available here as they were in England, where a man could be thrown out of his fishing club for using a nymph. But that is not to say that Americans did not have the urge to become snobs. You can still find the occasional bore who thinks that dry-fly fishing is more virtuous than any other kind of fly-fishing. He claims that it is more natural, probably, and more difficult; but he is wrong on both counts. Fish feed on floating insects less than ten percent of the time, and it is far easier to fish a floating Adams than a dead-drifting pheasant tail. But who cares?

It is at another, more fundamental level that purism prospers in America. In this country you can find all sorts of water and many species of fish, and you

Pflueger tackle poster.

can fish for them with any of several methods. Hence the American form of fishing purism, which seeks to rank fishermen by the fish they seek and the methods they use. It is more sinister than the British form, because it is less comic.

I have known some trout fishermen who thought that bass fishermen were nothing but a bunch of trashy hill apes who probably didn't know any better and certainly couldn't be taught. They were patient with *smallmouth* bass fishermen, who could probably read, smoked pipes rather than chewed Red Man, and often used fly rods. Largemouth fishermen were beyond the pale.

And, coming from the South, I've known bass fishermen who were convinced that trout fishermen were all a bunch of sissies who lived on Fire Island when they weren't tiptoeing through some shallow mountain stream making limp-wristed casting motions. They collected pretty feathered little things that they kept in purses, don't you know, and most of them were too damned squeamish to kill a fish even if they did catch one. Smallmouth fishermen, on the other hand, might be OK.

Most of the literature of fishing is concerned with trout and salmon caught on fly tackle. Most fishermen are not trout fishermen and not even fly rodders. How do you explain that anomaly?

Well, for one thing, trout fishing is simply more cerebral and technical (not technological) than, say, trolling for walleyes. It is entirely possible that a dedicated trout man would know enough, or want to know enough, to build the rod he fishes with, to tie the flies he casts with that rod, to identify and code the insects those flies imitate, to know the history and the lore of the river those insects come from, and to try any of a dozen techniques that have worked on that river or other similar rivers. He may want to know as much about his sport as the protean Ernest Schwiebert, who, when he put it all down on paper, had two fat volumes and almost two thousand pages which he called, simply, *Trout*. There will never be a book called *Bass* that takes up two volumes and fills two thousand pages. There is no one who could write it, and if there were, there are not half a dozen fishermen who would even want to read it.

Furthermore, trout fishing breeds purists because the literature of fishing, which is firmly rooted and flourishing, begins with trout and trout fishing. Trout fishermen see themselves celebrated in prose that creates a lofty self-image even in the mind of the man who cannot cast forty feet without fouling his leader and has never caught a fish more than twelve inches long. Reading one's own notices is bad for authors, actors, presidents, and fishermen. We trout fishermen are not as noble as we imagine ourselves to be. But the Walton of bass fishing has not yet announced himself in print, so bass fishermen are still an unreflective bunch.

Finally, trout fishing and salmon fishing are largely affairs of rivers. There is no estimating the literary value of running water. Rivers are unknowable in any final sense, since it is their nature to change and remake themselves constantly and eternally—or until the Corps of Engineers intervenes. You cannot map or chart a river; you are reduced to suggesting it, evoking it. That is the whole business of fine writing, and that, I think, is the key to why so much fine writing—and less than fine writing—has been done about trout and salmon fishing. And why so little has been done on other kinds of fishing in this country.

But are walleyes inferior fish? Probably not. The art of trolling for them is less refined than the art of midge fishing for sipping trout. But after a few days of fine, fine leaders, and tiny, tiny hooks, and very particular if not fussy fish, fishing that is more basic can be just the thing. You find yourself, absurdly, needing to get away and relax. The best thing you can do then is take a butt-stiff glass fly rod and a handful of deer-hair and painted cork bugs and go fishing for bass. You can eyeball your leader down to about six- or eight-pound test, and you can stick a little muscle into your casts. Bass—largemouth and smallmouth—are not excessively delicate about the way they eat. Once they have taken a popping bug on the surface, they put up a Pittsburgh Steeler sort

A. Russell Ripley, *Fishing for Bass* (ca. 1935).

of resistance, and they are abundant, so should you decide that you want to eat a few, you don't have to worry about reducing the brood stock. They are excellent in the skillet.

Bass live in all kinds of interesting water, from the canals of the Everglades to the freestone streams of New England, to the farm ponds of the Midwest and the irrigation ditches of California. You can usually find good bass fishing when you don't want to fight the crowds or the prissy fish on a trout river.

Other species lack the bass's ubiquity but are still fine game fish—pike and muskies and panfish of all kinds. There is much more to the world of American fishing than fishing with a fly rod in running water.

The pride of the trout fisherman can be laughable. That is not true of the bass fisherman's sin, which is gluttony. Trout fishermen in most of the country have learned painfully that they must husband the resource and its habitat. So much has already been irretrievably lost. If he destroys a limitless number of fish, he will be left with the obscenity of hatchery fish on a put-and-take basis.

Trout fishermen tend to feel protective about their quarry. They release far more fish than they keep. It is rare to see a trout fisherman violating the game laws. No-kill regulations on a stream are virtually self-enforcing. Among trout fishermen, especially in the heavily burdened East, there is remarkable consent behind the laws.

Bass fishermen are coming along, but they have miles to go. They still like to call the big fish they are after "hawgs," and what you do with hogs is slaughter them. So you see a fisherman coming back to the dock with heavy stringers for bragging material and snapshots. They may eat a few of the fish and give a few away. Some of the fish go into the freezer. But a lot of them are planted in the garden for fertilizer, and some even go into the garbage.

The situation is gloomy but not yet dire. Bass are tough—much tougher than brook trout, for example. They spawn and multiply in all sorts of water, and they can endure heavy fishing pressure and even some pollution. And some bass fishermen are catching on. The big lakes are not as good as they once were, and there is only one explanation: fishing pressure. So the bass publications and organizations are now encouraging fishermen to release any fish they do not want to eat and to keep no more than five. Frozen fish, they say, you can buy at the supermarket.

Also, as bass fishing has boomed over the last few years, it has produced its own snobs. The big stringer is no longer the only measure of success. Bait casting was once the rule in bass fishing. It could put a plastic worm out there where you wanted it and horse that bass into the boat once he took. And you needed tough tackle in some of those lakes that were full of stumps and dead trees from drowned forests. Lately, many bass fishermen have been experimenting with the fly rod. What was once a fairly idiosyncratic activity on the bass lakes of the South is becoming more and more common. Most fishermen who use a fly rod admit that they can't catch as many fish as the bait casters and that they don't have a chance on the really big fish. But they believe that fly-fishing requires more skill and is, therefore, a greater challenge. That sounds familiar to any trout fisherman.

Does using a fly rod do some ineffable thing for the angler? Does his soul burn purer, is his hand steadier, does his mind grow sharper, his eye see more clearly, when he picks up a nine-foot Fenwick? Does he become a better husband and father, a better citizen, and a man of wisdom, wit, eloquence, and charm? Is there some virtue in doing things the hard way?

Well, you can get an awful lot of argument that fly-fishing is more difficult, hence more challenging, and therefore more noble than any other sort of fishing. But Lefty Kreh, who is generally regarded as one of the best fly casters around and whose book on the subject is a marvel of simplicity, says that fly casting isn't as hard as it is made out to be and is not even the most difficult way of fishing. It is much tougher, he says, to cast accurately with an open-faced spinning reel, feathering the spool with your index finger to control distance. Nor is he much impressed with the tricky manipulations he sees among the distance casters who double-haul eighty feet of line on a little trout

Illustration by Louis Rhead (1905).

stream—wasted effort and much ado about nothing, he says. Forty or fifty feet is all you will ever need under those circumstances, and if you have to double-haul to get that, you should quit.

Most fishermen who have tried fly-fishing and have stayed with it long enough to learn to use a fly rod comfortably begin to prefer it to other kinds of fishing. A man who can fly cast will find himself working the shores of a bass lake for smaller fish, while his old fishing buddies are out in the fiberglass boats looking for structure and ten-pounders to horse in on their speed sticks and Ambassador reels.

Casting a fly line (all the books and teachers insist that you cast the line and not the fly) is something like hitting a golf ball. The effort is made up of so many parts, and there are so many things that can go wrong, that when you are doing it right, it feels good. The line sings through the guides and rolls out in front of you so straight you could sight it with a plumb bob. The leader turns over perfectly. You fish out the cast, pick up the slack, and cast again. You false cast to dry the fly, shoot a little line, fish out the cast. The rhythm is seductive and gratifying in a way that flinging plastic worms on twenty-pound line can never be.

It is not the only way to fish, of course. A fisherman who refuses to fish any other way is putting some kind of purist obstacle between himself and a lot of pleasure. But a fisherman who does not want to try the fly rod, or thinks, once he has tried it, that it is too difficult to bother with, is not a man to whom fishing means very much. It is an alternative to other recreations, like bowling, not a way of life with its own traditions, rituals, and language.

When you fish with a fly rod, you make the sport more interesting and try for levels of excellence that are not available in other kinds of fishing. The rod is linked to craftsmen and techniques that predate the automobile. But it is good not to make too much of the fly rod. If you protest your virtue excessively, you are probably no better in the eyes of God than the prodigal son's insufferably self-righteous brother. If a fisherman seeks nobility, perhaps it is best that he borrow it from his quarry.

The greatest fish—for the mature fisherman—are those that were born in a river, swam to the sea when they grew, returned to the river to spawn and, in some cases, die. Certainly they are the most haunting and mysterious of all the game fish. They have the craftiness of river fish and the power of sea fish. It seems appropriate that they should be the supreme angling test and the fish most threatened by the modern world as well.

Atlantic salmon and steelhead are remembered individually by fishermen lucky enough to have caught them. You might remember a day when you caught thirty rainbows or a dozen browns, but you will remember this salmon or that steelhead. Done properly, this kind of fishing is the sport purified of all its immature excesses and frills. It comes down to the man and the fish and the river.

Steelhead are sea-run rainbow trout, caught mostly in west coast streams. They are tough fish, and you do not go after them with whippy rods made lovingly from split cane and animal glue. Nor do you make effortless casts with a flick of the wrist. What is tackle to the steelheader looks more like ordnance to the small-stream trout man. The fisherman frequently stands in icy water an inch or two from the lip of his waders and double-hauls a lead core shooting head in order to cover distances in the one-hundred-foot range. When a novice tries it, he is apt to get a tangle of line and monofilament or, worse, a bloody ear or neck. This fishing is not so much pretty as it is awesome, and not many people can do it well or have the stamina to learn. So most steelhead are not caught with a fly rod. But some are, enough to make it more than a freak occurrence and to give the fishermen who do it special status.

One of the very good steelhead fly fishermen is Russell Chatham, who is also a fine writer and artist. His book, *The Angler's Coast*, is a rich account of west coast fishing for steelhead and other species, including silver salmon, which he more or less proved would take.a fly. There is strong, sincere feeling

Black Bass Fishing by S. F. Denton (1889).

in Chatham's prose and no trace of frills, which is appropriate, given the kind of angling he does. We are talking here about big rivers with names like the Rogue ("Steelheading on the Rogue" simply *sounds* arduous). The fish are big and strong, and the tackle is built to match them and the conditions, which are often extreme. The word *fun* does not even begin to cover the satisfactions of fishing for steelhead with a fly.

Steelhead are, if not abundant, then certainly plentiful. (That doesn't make catching them on a fly easy.) They come up the rivers of the west coast to spawn, and if you want to fish for them you can find plenty of public water—some of it admittedly crowded—where you can do it. A man who works for a living can fish for steelhead on weekends without paying outrageously for the privilege and still have an honest chance at catching a fish.

Which is not true of the Atlantic salmon.

Somewhere in the considerable literature of fishing for salmon there is this suggestion to the angler: Spend a month if you want to be absolutely sure of a week's good fishing. Before dedication and determination, if you are going to fish for Atlantic salmon you had better have time and money.

That does not necessarily make fishing for Atlantic salmon the analog of country-club tennis or golf. There are plenty of devoted salmon fishermen who are not millionaires. I know one newspaperman who saves all year for his trip to New Brunswick. He is in every other aspect of his life a very frugal and unspectacular man, happy to drive a Chevrolet and wear Haspel suits. His one luxury is salmon fishing, and he would moonlight as a cabdriver, I'm sure, in order to afford it.

Though things are improving, there is little backyard salmon fishing for the American angler. A few small rivers in Maine have small spawning runs and a little fishing. But the numbers are not inspiring, and the Indian tribes along those riverbanks net the fish almost out of perversity—because it makes the biologists angry and keeps the sport fishermen off the river. And for the sheer hell of it, one supposes. The great salmon rivers outside Maine have been dammed and polluted until the salmon can no longer navigate them to their spawning grounds at the headwaters. This is slowly being corrected, and every year there is more optimism and good news about the once great salmon rivers. A few fish have even been seen in the mighty—and mightily polluted—Connecticut. But for now, if you want to fish for salmon, you need to leave the country.

The coastal provinces of Canada are the closest places that have good salmon fishing. New Brunswick and Quebec have several rivers where an American can fish with a guide on a beat that he has paid good money to reserve. Or he could travel to Iceland, Scotland, or Norway. The travel, needless to say, is expensive. Licenses, permits, guides, are all expensive too. Many salmon fisherman decide at some point that they might as well go first-class all the way and use very expensive equipment as well.

In a way, they feel they owe it to the fish. This salmon swims hundreds of miles to sea from the river where he was born, then returns unerringly to spawn. In the determined migrations of the salmon, the fisherman glimpses something of the life force itself. The drive, the imperative, is so great that one feels bound to honor it. Also, it is hard to think of a living creature that has been so foolishly abused by man. Majesty can exist only when we allow it. Of course, we know more now—that is, if you think of knowledge as an accumulation of laboratory-proven facts. There are some people, many of them fishermen, who would say we still don't know a thing.

Of all the books on fish and fishing, perhaps the finest is about the Atlantic salmon. William Humphrey's classic *The Spawning Run* is impossible to read without feeling a quiver of nearly religious awe for this great fish and the ordeal that is its life cycle. The man who has just tailed a twenty-pound salmon, its side as silver as a midwinter moon, and stands in the shallow water of a river wild enough and clean enough to support spawning fish, with the afterimage of the battle still running through his mind . . . he *knows* something. He is also the least and the last of the salmon's enemies and the only one who truly loves the fish. Moments like this are the apotheosis of a fisherman's life. They are beyond the power of a boy's understanding and too deeply pure to be appreciated by callow young men. To appreciate this kind of fishing, you almost have to begin by acknowledging that of the two of you, only the fish is noble. It is enough that for a few moments you are touched by his glory.

Pacific salmon etching by Sandy Scott (1981).

Norman Wilkinson, *The Bewitched Pool* (ca. 1920).

NATURAL LIMITS:
The Once and Future Atlantic Salmon
By Ted Williams

URSUING GAME FISH like Atlantic salmon (*Salmo salar*) with rod and reel is called a sport, only because modern languages lack a better word and because those who fish passionately and well have a certain reticence about using words that accurately describe fishing. Fishermen in general, and Atlantic salmon fishermen in particular, have a guilt complex about their passion. Ever since the great English moralist Samuel Johnson identified angling as a pastime for the dull-witted and indolent, it has carried with it a certain social stigma. Traditionally, it has been seen as contrary to the Protestant ethic—a pursuit of louts, dreamers, the idle rich . . . or of little boys like Dr. Seuss's Marco, wildly fantasizing on the banks of McElligot's Pool.

To admit that one fishes is one thing. To admit that one lives to fish—that one feels suddenly at peace with himself and at one with the earth when he takes up his "fish pole"—is quite another. When the angler feels the first surge of a wild fish in clean water, he is suddenly more alive than he has ever been. But even he calls the thing that makes him feel this way a sport. Bowling is a sport; fishing, when undertaken seriously, is much, much more.

Robert Traver, author of *Anatomy of a Murder*, says it best in his superior work, *Anatomy of a Fisherman*. He happens to be speaking in the context of trout fishing, but rare, if not nonexistent, is the Atlantic salmon angler who was not or is not also devoted to trout. And a trout, although not quite a salmon, is at least a salmonid—about as closely related as it can be without being a subspecies. But Traver's philosophy applies equally to any and all wild game fish and their followers.

"I fish," he writes, "because I love the environs where trout are found, which are invariably beautiful, and hate the environs where crowds of people are found, which are invariably ugly; because of all the television commercials, cocktail parties, and assorted social posturing I thus escape; because, in a world where most men seem to spend their lives doing things they hate, my fishing is at once an endless source of delight and an act of small rebellion; because trout do not lie or cheat and cannot be bought or bribed or impressed by power, but respond only to quietude and humility and endless patience; because I suspect that men are going along this way for the last time, and I for one don't want to waste the trip; because mercifully there are no telephones on trout waters; because only in the woods can I find solitude without loneliness; because bourbon out of an old tin cup always tastes better out there; because maybe one day I will catch a mermaid; and, finally, not because I regard fishing as being so terribly important but because I suspect that so many of the other concerns of men are equally unimportant—and not nearly so much fun."

It's a pity that more fishermen won't admit what Traver admits. Many can't admit it, even to themselves. If they could, perhaps the Michigan grayling that used to haunt Traver's beloved brook-trout water would still be with us. But because no one seemed to think the Michigan grayling or its pursuit was important, that brilliant spark of earth life is now gone forever, sacrificed to the rapacity of the timber industry. A century ago the suggestion that a mere fish—favored by a few idle, impractical romantics—should interfere with the important work of moonscaping Upper Peninsula watersheds would have elicited hoots of derision.

Things haven't really changed. Modern sport fishermen have no say whatever in the fate of giant bluefin tuna. Bluefins seem headed for oblivion, and those "rich elitists," as they are called, who like to hoist them in on rod and reel are not permitted to interfere with the important work of liquidating the last of the big breeders for Japanese gourmets.

We need fishermen because fishing is one of the few avenues by which large numbers of people gain love and understanding for the earth as man did not make it. Thoreau was a fisherman. So, too, was Aldo Leopold. Perhaps they would have learned to see without fishing; but fishing put them in the right place at the right time, and it helped them focus on the things that really matter.

The game fish themselves, important as they are, are only part of what's at stake. No one fishes for desert pupfish or snail darters, but fishermen, because they are among the few who understand, have come loudly to their defense. The challenge we face is not just saving things like the desert pupfish and the snail darter. It is learning enough about our planet and the way it works to *want* to save them. That's what fishing teaches us.

Much of what applies to other fish, however, does not apply to the Atlantic salmon. Here is a fish that has indeed roused the general public and whose plight has indeed interfered with business as usual. What is happening in America with Atlantic salmon began largely through the efforts of Atlantic salmon fishermen, a fact that renders the angler fully as valuable a resource as the fish. What is at hand is either the beginning of a bold political-biological experiment or, just possibly, the sudden awakening of a nation that slept for two centuries. The change in attitude has been possible, at least in part, because of a widespread fascination with Atlantic salmon as a species.

Throughout history the Atlantic salmon has been a creature that inspires, mystifies, and intrigues. Twenty thousand years ago—when three-hundred-pound dire wolves coursed the Pleistocene steppes, eviscerating ice-age megafauna, and mammoths uprooted oak trees with their trunks—southern European cave dwellers chose the Atlantic salmon as their symbol of strength and courage. Two thousand years ago Roman legionnaires marveled at this torch of life flashing from the rivers of their expanding empire, and they named him *Salmo*: "the leaper." Three hundred years ago Izaak Walton hailed him "king" of fish, a title he bears to this day.

Part of our fascination with *Salmo salar* lies in his ocean wanderings. "The ocean," writes Anthony Netboy, author of three definitive books on salmon, "remains as it was for the ancient Greeks: a mysterious part of the planet. In its depths dwell multifarious creatures with shapes and bodies and biological characteristics that puzzle and fascinate us. When the salmon plunges into the sea it becomes part of that mystery. . . ."

Then, in a river barren for a season or a year, the salmon appears who knows when from who knows where—a sudden, subtle shimmering seen only, if at all, by those who are looking hard. Where has he been and what has he seen? How does he navigate? Certainly it cannot be by smell alone, not from the coast of Greenland to, say, Duncan's Rock Pool on Newfoundland's upper Humber River. What *Iliad*s and *Odyssey*s we could read in his scales and glands and cells, if only we could understand.

But because we do not, we fill the wide gaps in our knowledge with mythology, like the ancients. It is widely believed for example, that *Salmo salar*'s long-secret winter lair—in the Davis Strait off west Greenland—was first discovered by U.S. atomic submarines that were cruising beneath the many icebergs in the area. The ships' crews noticed large silver fish suspended vertically from the bottom of the ice. As Montreal's *Weekend Magazine* reported on March 11, 1972: "These were salmon feeding on the myriad of small shrimps that abound in these frigid waters. Quite by accident the deep-sea feeding grounds of the Atlantic salmon had been discovered. The fishing boats were close behind." The fact that not a word of it is true spoils the story not in the least. Furthermore, grizzled anglers (who hunt sidehill badgers in the fall) have long known that when salmon find their migration routes blocked by especially high obstacles, they grip their tails in their teeth, tense, release, and hurtle skyward. Doubters need only consult Michael Drayton, who, three centuries ago, wrote in his *Polyolbion*:

> Here, when the labouring fish
> does at the foot arive,
>   And finds that by his strength
> he does but vainly strive,
>   His tail takes in his mouth,
> & bending like a bow
>   That's to full compass drawn,
> aloft himself doth throw. . . .

It was only about fifty years ago that it became clear that parr, smolts, and salmon were not separate species. When game and fish departments write to the lay public in their excruciatingly wordy communications about the selfishness and short-sightedness of our dam-building ancestors, they entirely miss the point. Most of the people who cut off our salmon runs simply never knew that the survival of Atlantic salmon depended on adults ascending rivers and smolts descending rivers.

They could have asked salmon fishermen. Like Traver pursuing his wild brook trout, they had entered the salmon's domain with quietude and humility. Because they had taken the time to watch and to learn, they had known all along about the salmon's life cycle. As far back as 1676, Walton, in *The Compleat Angler,* reported private tagging experiments that proved the connection between smolts and salmon: "Much of this [cycle] has been observed by tying a *Ribband* or some known *tape* or *thred,* in the tail of some young *Salmons,* which have been taken in Weirs as they have swimm'd toward the salt water, and then by taking a part of them again with the known mark at the same place at their return from the Sea. . . ." But Walton was neither widely read nor much believed. He was, after all, merely a fisherman. Fishermen were then, as they are now, a silent, secretive lot, and no one thought to consult them because it was assumed that they were dull-witted. They, like the fish, were a squandered resource.

Even today, despite the investment of millions of dollars in research, we know very little about *Salmo salar*. He remains one of earth's great unsolved mysteries, and it is this inscrutability, in

Norman Wilkinson, *Ghillie* (ca. 1925).

Ogden Pleissner, watercolor (1960s).

Ogden Pleissner, *Angler and Guide* (1950s).

part, that intrigues us.

We can't even answer the little, simple questions: What, for example, caused the crash of 1979 when great numbers of salmon throughout much of their range never returned to their rivers? Somehow, the Atlantic Ocean seemed to have swallowed them. Rod and commercial landings dipped to historic lows. Some wilderness rivers, subject to few abuses and little pressure, such as the storied Jupiter on remote Anticosti Island in the Gulf of St. Lawrence, were virtually without salmon. Had there been an unknown cataclysm at sea, as has been repeatedly suggested in salmon conservation circles? It seems too pat an answer. It is far more likely that some human excess or combination of excesses brought about the crash. Destruction of the food supply may be a partial explanation. While the world's salmon-producing nations were fighting high-seas salmon piracy by the Danes in the early 1970s, their self-regulating arm—the International Commission for North Atlantic Fisheries—was permitting the Soviets to extract annually more than 300,000 metric tons of capelin, the smeltlike fish that seafaring salmon depend on so heavily for forage. But why did salmon catches rebound the following year? Going back, why did 1978 produce some of the best runs in recent history? Who, for that matter, can even begin to explain why salmon all over the world were bigger than normal in 1980?

Biologists don't even know why Atlantic salmon take flies. It is not because they are hungry. Salmon running out of the sea do not feed in fresh water, so pursuing them is like pursuing no other fish. As Lee Wulff puts it, one must appeal to their minds instead of their stomachs. Do salmon strike out of anger? Perhaps; when one pricks a salmon, the fish sometimes seems to respond by striking again with greater ferocity. Does the vision of a natural or artificial fly evoke subliminal remembrances from parrhood, when the fish gorged on insects struggling in the surface film of tiny woodland rills? Maybe; in Iceland, where few surface insects are available to parr, it is extremely difficult to raise adult fish to dry flies. Every salmon follower has his theory about why salmon hit, and his delight in advancing it long into the firelight never ceases. Salmon commonly sip naturals and spit out the crushed body husks. The reason, say anglers who swear they know, is that the migrating fish derive strength from the brown juice inside the insects. It is true that one occasionally finds brown juice in the shrunken stomachs of bright river-caught salmon—proof positive, declare those who believe.

Why are fly pattern and size critical at some times and unimportant at others? Why do salmon sometimes play with dry flies, trying to sink them with their noses, seemingly taking perverse pleasure in the raging electrical storms they create in human nervous systems? These questions are not likely to be answered in the near future, but perhaps this is fortunate. If we knew the answers, our general fascination with Atlantic salmon would surely diminish. And wondering about the answers is part of the mystique of salmon fishing, an element in the maintenance of our salmon-angler resource.

One would be hard-pressed to find someone who knows more or cares more about Atlantic salmon than Dr. Wilfred M. Carter, who directs the International Atlantic Salmon Foundation, headquartered at St. Andrews, New Brunswick. He is, significantly, a salmon fisherman, and much of his dedication derives from what salmon fishing has taught him.

What intrigues Carter most about *Salmo salar* is the ability—unique among salmon—to recover after spawning. A few fish (about five percent) are able to return to the sea and make at least one more spawning run. Why?

"We don't know," says Carter, "but I wish we did, because I think part of the answer to the mystery of life itself may lie there. Perhaps it would provide a breakthrough in human medicine. If you follow the transformation of the principal glands of Atlantic salmon—the pituitary, adrenal, and kidney—through the spawning run from the time the fish enter the river until they actually spawn, what you see is increasingly intense activity in these glands. They're all furiously churning out hormones and various chemical products, many of which we don't even know. As the fish get close to spawning, these organs disintegrate. If you slice them very thin and look at them under a microscope, you can watch the cell walls breaking down. You can see the organs die right in front of your eyes. But some of the salmon—that five-percent fraction—are somehow able to reverse the process and come back from the brink. The glands then regenerate, like the glands of freshly born animals. To me it's the most fascinating thing there is about salmon."

What makes the occasional mending of spawned-out Atlantic salmon even more mysterious is that the ability apparently did not evolve as a unique adaptation in an isolated population. Instead, the six species of Pacific salmon—pink, chum, sockeye, chinook, coho, and Asian cherry—seem to have *lost* the ability. They are thought to be relatively recent offshoots of Atlantic salmon that strayed into the Pacific several million years ago when the Bering land bridge connecting North America and Asia was underwater. It is difficult even to guess at the environmental conditions that caused or permitted such change.

Some of our fascination with the Atlantic salmon derives from admiration—for his game and food qualities, which are unexcelled by any other fish. But our admiration runs a good deal deeper.

Norman Wilkinson, *Peter* (ca. 1925).

W. M. Bracken, oil painting (1864).

Frank E. Schoonover *Landing a Salmon* (1906).

Wilfred Carter touches on this when he observes that "in spite of our damnedest efforts, we haven't been able to kill the Atlantic salmon, to destroy them completely. That in itself is reason for a tremendous amount of admiration, because some of the things we've been doing would have meant extinction for weaker species long ago."

The things we've been doing include choking their rivers with pollution, drenching their watersheds with biocides, cutting off their spawning habitat with dams, exterminating them on the high seas. We have even attacked them with atomic bombs—this last insult by the Soviets, who recently rendered their magnificent Pechora River salmonless by blasting a canal with a nuclear device equal in force to 45,000 pounds of TNT, thereby reversing the river's flow so that it now discharges into the Caspian Sea instead of the Barents Sea. Still, bright sparks glow where old flames leaped, defying our efforts to extinguish.

No people tried harder to destroy their Atlantic salmon, or met with greater success in doing so, than the Americans. It is therefore fitting that we are now trying harder than anyone else to restore our Atlantic salmon. But vaunted technology, to which the salmon were sacrificed, is having great trouble rising to the occasion of restoration. It has not been enough to design and build modern fishways and elevators, to treat effluent, to build multimillion-dollar hatcheries and saturate rivers with their produce. This time the Americans are up against something they have never faced before: rebuilding a part of their biota that they destroyed. It is not a matter of merely laying hands off and letting nature heal herself, which is what happened with wood duck and beaver; it is a matter of laying hands *on*. The first requisite for success in this venture is not money, manpower, or machinery. It is the ability to learn about living things by moving quietly among them and patiently watching—an ability that can be acquired from fishing.

As we begin to recognize the difficulty of restoring Atlantic salmon, the value we place on them increases. But even those involved directly in the effort rarely grasp the enormity of the challenge or the significance of success or failure. Among those who do, however, is Dick Buck, the smart, tough political activist who directs Restoration of Atlantic Salmon in America (RASA), a group funded by salmon fishermen. Buck, and Wilfred Carter too, played an important role in forcing the Danes to curtail their salmon plundering in the Davis Strait—one of the rare instances when fishermen spoke and the world listened.

"With Atlantic salmon," says Buck, "we are progressing from the concept of conservation—keeping things from getting worse—to the concept of restoration. To me, that's exciting. There has never been a real *restoration* anywhere. You tell me one."

This is not the first time the Americans have tried to restore their salmon. More than one hundred years ago a federal hatchery was built in East Orland, Maine. What we now call the fish and game departments of New Hampshire and Massachusetts were established for the express purpose of restoring Atlantic salmon. In 1870 Maine, Massachusetts, and Connecticut formulated a pact that provided for the sharing of costs and labor in taking and hatching salmon eggs from Maine rivers. In 1874 the New England states released 1,359,000 parr in the Connecticut River system. A few adult fish returned, but commercial netters pounced upon them. The states got to bickering among themselves, and the whole restoration effort fizzled.

One reason for the failure was that biologists believed that a salmon is a salmon. Only in the 1970s were they to learn that this is not the case, that each of earth's Atlantic salmon rivers supports a genetically unique strain of *Salmo salar,* molded through millennia of natural selection to the environmental conditions in that river.

Immediately upon entering Dick Buck's home and office, nestled into a hillside in the Dublin, New Hampshire, grouse woods, one is confronted by a tracing of a very skinny salmon with very large fins that looks disturbingly like a spawned-out kelt. Of all the tactless utterances that ever issued from anglers' lips, none rivals the remark of a recent houseguest who did not know Dick Buck well: "Ah, you fish black salmon."

With the barest flicker of an eyebrow Buck explained that this was not a kelt, or slink, as he calls them, but a bright fish fresh from the Norwegian Sea. He had taken it from the River Laerdal, which crashes out of the glaciated mountains in Norway's high Fillefjell country and races fifty miles over wild cataracts and through breathtaking forested valleys to Sognefjord, one hundred miles northeast of Bergen. A salmon from, say, the Miramichi could never negotiate the fierce rush of water, but Laerdal fish have adapted to their unique environment by assuming streamlined bodies and extralarge fins.

Stocks that populate tributaries are distinct from stocks that populate main stems; thus, in a major river system like the Connecticut there may have been as many as twenty subspecies of Atlantic salmon. When a salmon run is extinguished, it does not just mean that a river is out of fish and needs to be restocked. It means that a unique life form has been rendered extinct. When just any salmon are thrown into a certain river, few, if any, will return to spawn. The only hope the Americans have is to work with strains that are as close as possible to the extinct stock. With luck, a few adult fish will return and may be used as brood stock to produce smolts that are better adapted to the river than the part of the parent generation that did not

Wood engraving by Dan Beard, from *Harper's Weekly* (1885).

return. With luck, this process will produce a second, better generaton of brood stock, the second a third, the third a fourth. To restore a salmon run one must essentially preside over the evolution of a new subspecies. It is an agonizingly slow process that tests the patience of sportsmen and politicians alike.

When the restoration of the Connecticut—probably the greatest Atlantic salmon river to grace the continent—was gathering momentum in the early 1970s, eyed eggs were extremely hard to come by. For want of more suitable stock, the restoration team, made up of fishery managers from Vermont, New Hampshire, Massachusetts, Connecticut, and the federal government, released smolts raised from the spawn of Gaspé Peninsula fish. The Connecticut River, lying at the southern extremity of *Salmo salar*'s historic range, warms quickly in the spring. For this reason its salmon traditionally ran very early in the year. But the Gaspé fish were genetically programmed to run a bit later. The few

that returned encountered warm water—and many promptly succumbed to fungus infections. Eggs from Maine's Penobscot fish, closer geographically and therefore genetically to the extinct Connecticut River salmon, became available; and as the beginning of a reborn Connecticut strain developed by natural selection, returns of healthy fish increased.

The International Atlantic Salmon Foundation, which has provided some of the eggs for the Connecticut program, is trying to shortcut this process. It has built "stock catalogs" for dead salmon rivers by collecting and assembling old data on migratory patterns, sizes, timing of runs, and growth rates. It is trying to re-create those stocks as accurately as possible with a series of crossbreeding programs. Wilfred Carter offers the example of a strain from southern New Brunswick's Big Salmon River. Because it is believed that the fish doesn't leave the Bay of Fundy, it is obviously a desirable species for restoration, since it doesn't expose itself to the

A. Russell Ripley, *Landlocked Salmon Waters* (ca. 1955).

perils of high-seas fishing operations. The International Atlantic Salmon Foundation is funded largely by fishermen.

Of all salmonids, none is more expensive or more difficult to propagate artificially than *Salmo salar*. This fact has tempted many eastern states to embark on what they see as an easy, politically expedient shortcut: Pacific salmon. Thus the fish has become, in the memorable words of Atlantic salmon crusader and fisherman the Reverend Robert A. Bryan, "a symbol of today's preoccupation with the spirit of instant gratification."

The seduction was effected by Michigan's stunning success with cohos in the late 1960s. Construction of the St. Lawrence Seaway had provided sea lampreys with access to Lake Ontario and thence, via the Welland Canal which bypasses the natural barrier of Niagara Falls, to the other Great Lakes. The sea lamprey—a primitive, eel-like fish with a rasping, tooth-studded disk instead of a mouth, the better to suck body fluids from its victims—virtually eliminated the native lake trout. This, in turn, enabled the population of alien alewives—introduced by fishery managers in the belief that they were alien shad—to explode in a predator-free environment. Massive alewife die-offs in Lake Michigan fouled beaches and clogged industrial and municipal water intakes. One aerial photographer reported a ribbon of dead alewives fifty feet wide and forty miles long.

Then, primarily as an alewife control measure, fishery managers introduced cohos. In one respect the experiment succeeded. With the lampreys largely under control by means of a selective poison administered in their nursery streams, the voracious cohos glutted themselves on alewives, balancing the population and increasing their own weight by a factor of ten in the first two months. Fishermen descended en masse on the lake. In March 1968 the Michigan Chamber of Commerce hosted a "Coho Victory Celebration" and predicted a billion dollars in assets by 1977. Suddenly, politicians from Eastport to Yonkers were clamoring for cohos.

Every New England state save Maine (the one that still had Atlantic salmon) and land-locked Vermont tried to duplicate Michigan's feat—and each failed spectacularly. Some coho success was realized in New York State, where Atlantic salmon were once so numerous that, as Anson Allen reported in 1848, it was "hazardous to ford with a young or spirited horse many of these streams on account of the many salmon which, either from natural courage or headlessness, would run against [the horse's] legs with great force and impetuosity."

The receptacle for New York's cohos (and later chinooks) was Lake Ontario, the only one of the Great Lakes that once sustained *Atlantic* salmon. Ontario's Atlantics had access to salt water via the St. Lawrence River, but they most likely wintered in the lake. In any case, they were big, deep-bodied fish, running to thirty-five pounds—nothing like "landlocks" as we know them today. New York has committed itself to an Atlantic salmon restoration program for the big lake, and the problems are even greater, if possible, than those faced on New England rivers. Lampreys, for instance, are a never-ending nightmare. If fishery managers slack off in their annual lampriciding of Lake Ontario's tributaries, the lamprey population rebounds. The cost of lampricide is soaring, and there is some thought that its use is causing selection for a strain of lamprey that breeds in river mouths—away from lethal concentrations of poison. Pollution used to be a particularly effective lamprey control, but as rivers are being cleaned up, lampreys are moving into and taking advantage of new spawning habitat.

About fifty exotic species of fish are now established in Lake Ontario, and it is not clear what effect they will have on Atlantics. With big runs of cohos and chinooks in former Atlantic salmon streams, the state lacks the manpower to pick up the carcasses of spawned-out fish. In order to prevent a health menace, it is forced to allow the public to snag the doomed salmon. Thus fishing has been replaced by something else, and the values fishing teaches have been lost. Deprogramming the snaggers, when and if Atlantics come along, will be a monumental public relations task.

The more we realize that we cannot have Atlantic salmon back quickly or cheaply, the more we wish we had saved them. Our fascination runs deep. Perhaps it is that the Atlantic salmon is not just an expression of the life force but a symbol of it as well. The plight of the salmon seems to mirror the plight of planet Earth.

Focus on a shoal of Atlantics shimmering through the icy currents of the Davis Strait. Here is a meeting and melding of life from thousands of watersheds segmented by oceans, mountains, and human politics. One boat from one nation, abiding by multinational agreement, sets eight hundred-foot gill nets within sight of the bright Greenland coast. That night the salmon of a dozen nations die in the nets, among them an entire run from a troubled Canadian river.

Netting in fresh water makes little sense, because a rod-caught salmon contributes roughly fifteen times more to the economy than a commercially caught one. But at least there is the chance for sound management, for adjusting the harvest to ensure the survival of a river's population. Netting in salt water, on the other hand, even in territorial seas, is madness. "Here," writes Dick Buck, "salmon stocks are inextricably intermingled. They come from different spawning streams, different river systems, different nations, different hemispheres. No man, and no type of fishing gear yet known to man, no method of control, can separate them out."

The diminished shoal continues, splits, and the two segments orient by some unknown natural beacon, one toward Europe, the other toward the coast of North America. On the European side Ireland takes fish from the United Kingdom, the United Kingdom takes fish from France, France takes fish from Spain. Off North America, Canada takes fish from the United States.

In the western North Atlantic the halved shoal shrinks quickly as "cod fishermen" catch salmon "by accident," and surviving fish drop out to filter into the cold, fast water veins of Labrador and Newfoundland or swing south to Quebec, New Brunswick, New England, and Nova Scotia.

In the brackish interface of the Atlantic and the Penobscot River several dozen salmon mill about, reprogramming their body chemistry for fresh water, scenting their natal tributaries, and overcoming their avoidance reaction to man's organic wastes, chemical effluent, and toxic metals.

The little pod holds in the Bangor Pool until anglers kill a third of the fish, then, with the first rain, moves upcurrent to Veazie and holds again. There, anglers again reduce it by a third. After more rain the fish press upriver, past weighted treble hooks that move over the log-strewn riverbed like panicked squid, under flashlights and gigs that strike like giant heron beaks.

After finning in shadowy lies through the long, tepid summer, a pair of fish move into a nameless tributary that cuts a steep course through shallow bedrock. The male has been a year at sea; the female, two. It is nature's way of guarding against the elimination of a year class.

Now the fish are lean and bronzed, their copper scales anchored tightly in their thickened hides. The lower jaw of the cockfish has lengthened and curved into a menacing hook. The thin flanks of the hen are stretched over bulging roe. Now, as night winds freshen from the north and the earth cools and slouches from the sun, the pair take a position in a pool below a gravel bar. In the wane of the rutting moon the cockfish prods the hen with his snout, and at length she glides up and over the gravel. There she turns on her side and, poising at a forty-five-degree angle to the flow, violently fans the gravel with her tail. She repeats this until she has excavated a circular depression in the gravel three feet in diameter and ten inches deep. With the cockfish at her side she crouches over the bed, flanked, as if in mimicry, by two thumb-sized male parr. Both adult fish open their mouths and, shuddering, release their eggs and milt simultaneously. The parr, sexually mature after only one year, dash into the redd, assisting in the fertilization. Now the cockfish moves away, and the hen edges upstream to cut another redd, thus burying the first.

Within a fortnight all the eggs are dead. The stream is one of hundreds in Scandinavia and North America that lack the capacity to buffer the acid fallout from air pollution. It is one of dozens that has been rendered too acidic to support *any* salmon. In Maine and Canada many of the hardwoods that once helped neutralize the poison rain have been herbicided in order to clear the way for conifers, which increase paper-company profits as well as acid runoff.

The acid disease, identified by some scientists as the most serious environmental threat of this century, originates not just in America's industrialized Midwest but also at nickel-smelting operations in Sudbury, Ontario. On the other side of the Atlantic it issues from more than half a dozen nations. The chilling global implications begin but hardly end with Atlantic salmon. Suddenly, the infection is in the bloodstream, coursing through the planet's system.

The Atlantic salmon has come to represent whatever it is that still holds the living earth together. It is a last ancient thread, a visible connection between unmolested land, clean air, healthy lakes and rivers, and the responsible, shared stewardship of the seas. He who angles for Atlantic salmon often learns to care about such things. Whether one calls it sport or religion, Atlantic salmon fishing teaches us that mirrored in the fate of the fish is the fate of water, earth, and atmosphere. Our fascination with Atlantic salmon has given us at least the beginnings of an understanding of something John Muir told us a century ago, when no one was listening: "When one tugs on a single thing in nature one finds it attached to the rest of the world."

Robert K. Abbett, *Glover's Rock, Matapedia* (1980).

Francis Golden, *Vancouver Island* (1980).

CATCHING ON:
Deeds Among the Steelhead
By Bill Barich

THE RIVER on which I live, the Russian in northern California, was named in honor of the fur traders who established settlements near it almost two centuries ago, beginning in 1812, when Ivan Kuskoff, a one-legged adventurer employed by the Russian-American Fur Company, leased several acres of coastal land from Pomo Indians, in exchange for blankets, breeches, horses, axes, and some beads. It flows southwest for 110 miles, from its headwaters in the mountains north of Redwood Valley to its terminus at Jenner on the Pacific Ocean. During the dry summer months, it is a slow green stream, thick with algae and pestered by canoers. But in November, when the winter rains start, the Russian is transformed and grows wide and deep and sometimes rises to the limits of its banks and then swamps them, flooding downriver towns like Guerneville. It looks majestic at flood stage, as broad across as the Mississippi; uprooted trees drift by, along with unmoored boats, fences, rusted agricultural implements, plastics, and hubcaps. If you stand on the cliffs above Jenner and watch the procession of objects sweeping past, you get the feeling that entire communities are being borne to oblivion on the tide. Sea lions congregate at the river mouth, dipping into the turbid, muddy water in search of migratory fish. Large numbers of salmon, shad, sturgeon, and striped bass used to ascend the Russian to spawn in its tributaries, but their runs have been depleted almost to the point of extinction. The only anadromous—"running upward," in Greek—fish that still persists in any quantity is the steelhead, a subspecies of rainbow trout.

Steelhead are members of the *Salmonidae* family, which includes all salmon, trout, and chars, and are classified as *Salmo gairdnerii gairdnerii*—*Salmo* from the Latin verb meaning "to leap," and *gairdnerii* for the nineteenth-century naturalist Meredith Gairdner, who helped Sir John Richardson collect specimens of Columbia River fish for the Hudson's Bay Company. They have a stronger migratory urge than most rainbows but are not dependent on an anadromous existence; if they're planted in a lake, they'll spawn in tributaries to that lake, skipping their saltwater wandering. Most Russian River steelhead opt for anadromy: they're born in fresh water, migrate into the Pacific between their first and third years—at sea, their upper bodies turn steel blue, which accounts for their common name—reach sexual maturity in another year or two, and return to their natal streams to spawn. They recognize the stream by its unique chemical composition and follow its trail like bloodhounds. Once they've paired off and chosen an in-stream spawning site, the female digs a nest, or redd, using her body and tail to clear away gravel, then deposits some of her two thousand eggs. Immediately, her mate fertilizes them with his milt, a chalky secretion of the reproductive glands. The process is repeated until the eggs are gone. Pacific salmon die after spawning, but some steelhead—about twenty percent—survive and may make the journey from ocean to river two, three, or even four times. Steelhead are notoriously elusive and seldom get snared in commercial salmon nets, although they frequent the same waters as salmon. Nobody knows how they avoid the nets, because marine researchers haven't been able to track them once they enter the Pacific. They disappear, off to the Bering Sea or Baja California or Japan. Anglers find them just as difficult to catch. In the winter of 1954–55, the California Department of Fish and Game sponsored a steelhead census on the Russian; it indicated that the average angler caught 0.55 fish per day. There are probably fewer steelhead in the river now—the annual run is estimated at 57,000—but the weather in which they thrive hasn't changed: cold, foggy mornings and evenings, relieved on occasion by brilliant afternoon sunshine that warms the bones and stipples the water with light.

Some years ago I picked up a copy of Zane Grey's *Tales of Fresh-Water Fishing* in a secondhand bookstore. I have come to treasure it for one story in particular, "Rocky Riffle," which is an account of fishing for steelhead on the Rogue River, "the most beautiful stream in Oregon." Grey was a zealous and talented angler—he was known to hire guides to guard favorite pools, so that nobody could fish them before he did—and his sagebrush prose seems to capture those qualities that are peculiar to steelheading: excess, enthusiasm, stamina, and a rhetorical approach to the universe. "The steelhead lay flat on the gravel. I stared, longing for the art of the painter, so as to perpetuate the exquisite hues and contours of that fish. All trout are beautiful. But this one of sea species seemed more than beautiful. He gaped, he quivered. . . ."

Once, I gave a copy of *Tales* to a man I'll call Paul Deeds, my friend and angling companion. I was acting as a missionary-for-literature, attempting to separate Deeds from the scandal sheets he so loves to read. He can tell you the medicinal properties of garlic, as well as the sexual preferences of major movie stars, but he has never opened even the most basic angling text. I thought I'd start him on Grey and escalate later to Hemingway. I had quite a plan in mind, but Deeds failed to cooperate. He flipped through the pages and looked at the pictures, grunting when he came to one that showed Grey, in fur chaps and flat-brimmed hat, standing on a snowy hillside cavorting with two bears. The photo was captioned "The Bears on the Way to Crater Lake—Tame, but Not Very!"

"What's this got to do with fishing?" Deeds inquired.

I explained that Grey, like Hemingway, was a larger-than-life character.

"I *hate* that expression," Deeds said disgustedly. "How can anybody be 'larger than life'? It's a contradiction in terms." He tossed the book onto the floor, where it joined some faded *Enquirers.* "The guy should have stuck to Westerns."

Deeds has little tolerance for pretense. He lives near me in the valley, on forty extremely unpretentious acres of prune orchard he bought with an inheritance from his father. There's a run-down farmhouse on his spread, with creaky screen doors and a grease-spattered kitchen ceiling from which insect-dappled flypaper strips are always dangling, and it suits him perfectly. He's the consummate bachelor, having sampled matrimony once, when he was in his twenties—he's forty-two now—and found it wanting. Only intrepid friends and relatives ever venture into his parlor. The room smells of camphor, of dogs, tobacco, and coffee, and in it Deeds sits happily by the hour, reading trash, tying streamers and bucktails, writing letters to his broker in San Francisco, and listening to vintage blues albums on a single-speaker blond mahogany hi-fi set he could easily afford to replace.

I met Deeds about five years ago, in December, shortly after I moved into my house. The river was up, and the first steelhead were running. I had never fished for them before, but I was eager to learn. I did some research on tackle and technique and then fell into an unvarying routine that occupied me for almost a month. Every day, I woke at dawn, built a small fire in the Ashley stove, ate a solitary breakfast, and dressed in what became my steelhead uniform: jeans, turtleneck, flannel shirt, Pendleton, jacket, two pairs of woolen socks, and a black knit watch cap. Outside, I slipped into my

Chet Renesor., *Steelhead* (1981).

waders and cinched them at the waist with a belt, buckling it tightly as a precautionary measure against seepage. I was very unstable in the water, often tripping over rocks or submerged branches, and had almost drowned on four or five occasions while pursuing trout in mountain streams. I had assembled a makeshift steelhead rig from my available gear—an eight-foot fiberglass rod (too short, really) and a medium-sized spinning reel wound with twelve-pound-test line—and I took it in hand, feeling my skin stick to the cold metal grip, and walked off into a seemingly static landscape that could have been painted by Hokusai: twisted live oaks, barren willows, green winter grass, vineyards laced with yellow mustard flowers, all cloaked in river mist.

It would be nice to report that I caught plenty of fish during those early excursions, but in fact I had no success. The lures I cast out were ineffectual; the diagrams in my books hadn't prepared me for the speed of the current or the snags I kept hooking. I was distracted, too, by the birds—herons, kingfishers, mallards, and mergansers—and by the does and fawns that browsed openly on a hillside across the river. Sometimes I saw a steel-blue back cruising past, in a manner that could only be interpreted as teasing. I became discouraged, even angry. One mid-morning, after hours of listless angling, I sat down to rest on a strip of sand. Moments later, I heard noises in the brush behind me, the scuffling of rubber boots over pebbles and then a hacking cough. Paul Deeds emerged from the trees. His beard was moist with drizzle; he was wiping his wet lips on his sleeve. When he noticed me, his eyes widened in murderous circles. He accused me of trespassing. I told him I'd just rented the old Fratelli place.

"You rented it?" he asked incredulously. "You rented it and you like to fish?"

He seemed crestfallen at the idea of competition. But after we talked for a while, and he realized that I was a rank amateur, he was much more accommodating and pleasant, and I invited him to come up to the house for lunch.

"Wait a minute," he said. He vanished into the willows and returned with a steelhead he'd caught that morning. The fish weighed nine pounds or so, about average for the Russian. It was steel blue along the spine; below, it had a bright silver color, which camouflaged it from ocean predators.

"Male or female?" I asked.

"Female," said Deeds. "Look at her mouth. See how nice and round it is? Bucks, they have hooked jaws."

"Has she been in the river long?"

"Nah, she's fresh-run. She'd be much darker and have a red streak on her side. She hasn't spawned yet. Feel," he said.

He jabbed my finger into the steelhead's belly. It was hard and protuberant, full of eggs. There were some gashes on her flank, between the ventral fins, and I asked about them.

"Sea lion almost got her," Deeds said.

At the house, I gave him a bourbon, while I made a couple of roast-beef sandwiches. The bourbon was a terrible mistake. Deeds seldom drinks anymore, because he tends to lose control. He's not a nasty drunk, not by any means; it's just that liquor unleashes torrential energies in him. He rambles on and on, discussing stride piano or prune horticulture, then suddenly loses his fear of travel and decides, around midnight, that absolutely the best thing to do is to jump into the pickup and drive to Reno, preferably at ninety miles an hour.

We ate the sandwiches, along with pickles, coleslaw, and a few underripe winter tomatoes, and had another drink, and then Deeds slapped his palm on the table and insisted that I visit *his* house, right away. So I got my introduction to that malodorous parlor. Deeds threw his coat over a chair and led me into the kitchen. He spread some pages from the *National Star* on the counter and proceeded to slit the steelhead's belly and remove her roe. It peeled away in two pearly salmon-pink slabs, which Deeds dusted with borax, then double-wrapped in cellophane and aluminum foil. "Best bait there is," he said, stuffing the package into the refrigerator and simultaneously extracting two beers. He told me how he shaped the roe into "berries": he cut a fingernail-sized chunk from one of the slabs, set it on a two-inch square of maline—a fine red mesh material that blends with the roe—twisted the maline tight at the top, and tied it securely with red thread. The finished product resembled a strawberry. "You got to fish 'em on a gold hook," he said. "Otherwise, you're wasting your time."

"Why do steelhead strike their own roe?"

"Cannibal instinct."

"Do you ever use flies instead of bait?"

"Listen," he said, "I'd rather fly-fish than anything. But the river's too high and discolored most of the time. If you want action, you go with bait."

We went back into the parlor, and Deeds brought down a quart of Jim Beam from an antique highboy. The bottle had spiderwebbing trailing from its cap; the tiny faces on the label were faded from the sun. I don't recall too much after this, although I know I stayed for dinner. Deeds fed me steelhead. I watched in awe as he concocted his special barbecue sauce—mayo, ketchup, A-1, Lea & Perrins, brown sugar, onions, garlic, and corn relish—slathered it on the skinned fish, and jammed the whole reeking mess under the broiler. But it tasted fine, at least to my jaded palate. After dinner, Deeds embarked on a lengthy monologue about the demise of the Russian. He showed me some photos in support of his case; they would have done Zane Grey proud. "That's 1964," he said, pointing to three big steelhead arranged on a bed of ferns. "I caught them in thirty minutes. You won't see that happen again. Too much *junk* in the river. Chemicals. Garbage. Sewage. Goddamn kids drive dune buggies down the creek beds, when there's still a little water left in 'em. Can you imagine that? They run over steelhead fry. Death by tires. It's incredible. I'm talking about *incredible.*" His mood became elevated, though, after he brought down the second bottle of Jim Beam. When I departed at last, he was slumped in his Barcalounger, using his rod tip to conduct the band that backed Bessie Smith on the record that was playing on the single-speaker blond mahogany hi-fi set.

I didn't expect to see Deeds for a few days, but he came over the next afternoon and apologized for not offering me a ride home.

"You offered, Paul," I said. "But I refused. You wanted to go by way of Reno."

Deeds laughed. "I meant to give you these," he said, digging into his pocket and handing over a jar containing five berries, "and these"—an assortment of lead weights—"and these"—three twenty-five-pound-test leaders. Each leader had a knot in it, so that it could be attached to regular monofilament by means of a swivel. Below the knot, the leaders were divided into two uneven strands. Deeds had snelled a gold hook to the longer strands. "You tie your weight on the short one," he said. "You want it to bounce along the river bottom, down where the fish are. Not too fast and not too slow: tick, tick, tick." He was demonstrating with an invisible rod, keeping his eyes fixed to the line. "The bait follows behind. If you feel the bait stop, *wham!*"— he jerked back the rod—"you set up. That drives the barb of the hook through the fish's lip."

"How should I play the fish?"

"With steelhead," said Deeds, "you don't play. You pray."

That evening, just as the sky was turning, I stationed myself near a deep pool below a rocky outcrop and started casting. Deeds's weights were much heavier than the lures I'd used previously; the one I tied to the shorter strand of leader bounced properly on the bottom—tick, tick, tick, like seconds passing. Suddenly, the berry stopped in transit, as if a fish had mouthed it. I lifted my rod, preparing to do battle, but I felt no resistance. Soon enough, I reeled in a fat sucker; it flopped onto the shore like a sack of mush. Suckers are trash fish, insults to divinity. They have chubby, humanoid lips and appear to be begging for cigars. It's possible to envision them wearing suspenders and sitting on park benches, acting like heirs to the continent's watershed. I released my sucker, stifling a desire to kick it, and moved toward the center of the pool. I placed my next cast under some willows on the opposite shore. Tick, tick, tick: again, the bait stopped, and again, I set the hook. This time, a steelhead shot out of the water.

I played, or prayed, the fish for ten minutes, certain that I'd lose it, but my luck held and I was able finally to draw it into the shallows and beach it. The steelhead was small, about four pounds, and male; so much milt leaked from him that a white puddle formed on the sand. I dispatched him quickly, suffused with guilt; but the guilt changed to atavistic pride once I threaded a willow branch through his mouth and out one of his gills and began the uphill trek to my house. I stopped on a rise and looked back at the valley, which was vanishing in purple haze. "The sunset was beautiful," wrote Zane Grey, "resembling ships of silver clouds with rosy sails that crossed the lilac sea of sky in the west. . . ."

Deeds became my nemesis as well as my friend. Never again would he grant me the license of undisturbed water. If I was fishing, he was fishing, often just ahead of me, combing the better pools and riffles before I had a chance at them. The situation would have been intolerable if I hadn't kept learning from him. He persuaded me to buy a longer, sturdier rod; taught me to use bobbers in bright red, pink, and chartreuse; instructed me in the basics of steelhead anatomy; and gave me a short course in how to cast a shooting head.

That first winter I caught ten fish; they were poached, baked, broiled, eaten as *sashimi,* and soaked in brine and smoked over hickory chips until their flesh was glazed and peeled away in savory chunks. Deeds caught forty-six; most were released, although a few prime specimens were subjected to the ignominy of his barbecue sauce. I thought my statistics would improve the following winter, but California entered a two-year drought, and steelhead fishing was dismal. When the drought ended, the rains were exceptionally heavy, and the Russian remained high, muddy, and inaccessible for most of the season. The year after *that,* rainfall tapered off, and the river was in excellent shape, but fish were scarce, because the drought had affected spawning adversely—in the low, clear water, steelhead eggs and fry had been more vulnerable than ever to predators and had suffered a high mortality rate because of soaring temperatures and a poor supply of oxygen. I tried to be hopeful, but in mid-September, right before the *next*—depressing? suicidal?—season was to begin, I cracked and said to Deeds, who was helping himself to my good French Roast coffee, "I can't take it anymore, Paul. I'm going to Oregon for some real fishing."

"I'll go with you," Deeds said.

I doubted his sincerity. "You dare to leave California?"

"I've done it before," he said defensively.

It happened that he had a sister in Portland, who'd been hounding him to visit. Her name was Joan, and she met us at the airport. She was a big woman, built like Deeds, with bony shoulders and elbows. She was ten years older than he, which showed in their relationship. She had a tendency to treat him in a mock-scolding manner, as if he were a bad boy in need of constant correction; he responded by acting petulant and making snide comments that elicited various rebukes. It was all very stylized, a residue from childhood. Joan took us to her house in a nice suburban neighborhood. Her husband, a machinist, told us he cared nothing about fishing. "If I want salmon," he said jovially, "I go to the supermarket." I suppose most families seem odd when viewed from the outside.

I made some phone calls while this family did its catching up and arranged for a guide to take Paul and me on a three-day drift trip down the Deschutes River. The Deschutes is a legendary steelhead stream known for its productivity; the lower portion we'd be fishing is wild and free-flowing. The guide assured me the river would be perfect for flies, unless we got some rain. I had a good night's sleep in the guest room and spent the next day purchasing tackle in Portland's sporting-goods stores. I wanted to rent a car, too, but Joan insisted I save the money; she volunteered to drive us to Maupin, where we were to launch the boat, and then pick us up at the mouth of the Deschutes—it empties into the Columbia River—at the end of the trip.

We got an early start in the morning. I'm never quite as happy as when I take off on a fishing trip, and I tried my best to ease the tension between Deeds and his sister. I made jokes and even did some whistling, but their bickering never slackened. About ten o'clock, we stopped for huckleberry pancakes at a restaurant near Mount Hood, then descended from the conifer-laden Cascades into a desert atmosphere of dry brown hills and clumps of sage.

"Zane Grey country, Paul," I said.

Deeds felt better when we reached Maupin. The guide was waiting for us outside a bar, holding a can of Blitz beer in his hand. His wooden drift boat—pale green, about thirteen feet long, with a slightly elevated prow—was attached to a trailer hitch and stacked high with supplies, to which we added our rods, tackle, sleeping bags, liquor, and sundries. We launched the boat at a ramp about a mile downstream from the bar. The Deschutes isn't really treacherous, except in its last five miles, when it drops briskly in elevation to join the Columbia and four sets of rapids are created, but I still experienced a few seconds' panic as we were tugged forward into the current. I was aware of the river's power, its swiftness, and of land falling irretrievably away behind us. The trip took on aspects of a childhood adventure. We drifted around a bend and into more primitive terrain: no cars, roads, or people, just craggy buttes and rattlesnakes and dust.

The guide worked his oars to keep us on the edges of the white water. He'd navigated the Deschutes a thousand times and claimed to know where the fish would be. "I don't guarantee they'll cooperate," he said, "only that they'll be in attendance." As we passed one likely riffle after another, we became fidgety and fumbled with our rods. Deeds lit a cigarette; I had a nip of whiskey. Finally, the guide stopped near a moderately fast stretch that seemed the perfect habitat for steelhead. We were out of the boat before its prow touched the ground. I had trouble keeping my balance at first. I listed to the left in concord with the river's flow, drawn unavoidably in its governing direction.

Deeds beat me to the water, of course, and, after a false cast or two, laid out thirty feet of weight-forward line. He was using a nine-foot rod and a wet fly I'd bought in Portland, a Skykomish Sunrise. The fly was a beauty. It was supposed to represent the colors of a sunrise along the Skykomish River in Washington—red, yellow, and silver, dressed with white bucktail wings on a no. 4 hook. I'm sure I chose the fly for its metaphoric content rather than its resemblance to a baitfish or a bit of free-floating roe. I was particularly susceptible to aesthetic considerations when purchasing flies. Once, I'd filled a paper sack with tiny jassids, because they reminded me of Egyptian scarabs. I'd never caught a fish with any of them. Probably I'd never catch a fish with my Skykomish Sunrise, but it pleased me to watch it cut through the clear water, just beneath the surface. I asked the guide if the fly should run deeper; no, he said, the steelhead would come up to take it, if they were curious enough.

Deeds was working the slicks about twenty yards above me. I imitated his style: cast, quarter the line, retrieve, take two steps to the left; cast, quarter the line, retrieve, take two steps to the left. We looked like a comedy dance team practicing for the Elks' annual picnic. Deeds was concentrating so hard he didn't hear the guide announce that we were moving on to another spot. I had to wade over and tap him on the shoulder. "What is it?" he asked irritably, his eyes black behind the tinted lenses of his glasses.

Late that afternoon, in some frothy riffles, I nailed our first steelhead on a Deschutes Skunk, a dry fly the guide had lent me. The Skunk was sparsely tied and didn't ride as high on the water as dries ordinarily do. The fish inhaled it on the retrieve, with such abandon that I almost lost control of my rod. I managed to tighten my grip before the rod escaped, and I passed the next quarter-hour dashing back and forth along the bank, following the steelhead when it made its runs. The runs were long and dramatic, often punctuated by aerial high jinks. I should have cupped my hand around my reel to provide some drag, the necessary resistance, but I hadn't played many steelhead on a fly rod, so I compensated by jogging. Deeds

Richard Schlecht, *Steelhead Fishing, Klamath River* (ca. 1955).

thought this was very funny. He laughed even harder when the guide started jogging behind me, brandishing a landing net. No doubt the guide would have been laughing, too, but I hadn't paid him yet; he was forced to maintain his professional composure. Gradually, the fish began to tire, and I drew him toward the shallows, where the guide scooped him up—a six-pound buck whose dorsal fin was stubby and malformed.

"Hatchery fish," the guide said, touching the fin. "They rub up against each other in the holding tanks and nip off each other's fins."

I wiped the sweat from my brow and glanced at Deeds; his laughter had turned to envy.

We set up camp in a grove of river oaks. The buttes across the water were red; the water itself was dissolving in blackness. I shucked off my waders and did some stretching exercises, glad to be free of constriction. Deeds brewed coffee in a dented tin pot; the guide and I shared the bourbon. "You gentlemen are lucky," the guide said, after his third drink, "for I am an excellent cook." Indeed he was, in the grand campground tradition of abundance. He filleted the steelhead, then broiled it over a wood fire and served it with skillet-fried potatoes and a tossed green salad. We applauded his culinary skills and awarded him another bourbon. Magpies flitted about over the camp, diving now and again into the sage. "Dessert, gentlemen," the guide said, serving us wedges of Sara Lee cheesecake on pink paper plates. The moon appeared over the buttes. It was almost full and shed a soft, pale light that rippled on the ripples of the water. The guide washed his pots in a plastic basin, singing a many-versed song about love and death in the wilderness. I awarded him a final bourbon, on the condition that he drink it in silence, and rolled out my sleeping bag near Deeds. I woke just once during the night, when a Union Pacific freight train wailed in the distance, beyond the buttes. The sound was so melancholy it gave me the chills. It reminded me of somebody weeping in a darkened theater, long after the movie has ended. I sat up and looked at the moon and the smoke rising from the fire.

The guide nudged me at dawn. "Fishing time," he said wryly. I had no melancholy left, only aching bones and sore joints. Deeds was polishing the lenses of his glasses with a dish towel. He put on his waders and vest and walked into the river. I followed him. I could see the sun shining on the ridges of the buttes, but down below, in the canyon, it was still cold and gray. Two steps and cast, two steps and cast—we took thirty fishless steps before the guide called us to breakfast. After eating, we broke camp, drifted downstream for a mile or so, and waded into the water again. By three that afternoon, we'd hooked five steelhead and released all but one, the dinner fish. "I feel pretty damn decent," said Deeds, resting on shore. He

had the country person's compactness of expression, saving his superlatives for truly earth-shattering events like wars, hurricanes, famines, and the failure of his pickup to start on demand.

That evening, we had our fish poached in wine and chicken broth. At Deeds's request, I read aloud from *Tales of Fresh-Water Fishing.* I chose a passage describing a nine-pound Rogue River buck. "He looked exactly what he was, a fish-spirit incarnate, fresh run from the sea, with opal and pearl hues of such delicate loveliness that no pen or brush could portray them. He brought the sea with him and had taken on the beauty of the river. He had a wild savage head, game as that of an eagle, jaws of a wolf, eyes of black jewel, full of mystic fire."

"Very ripe," said Deeds, chewing contentedly on a cheroot.

"Jaws of a wolf?" the guide asked. "Full of mystic fire?"

We took three more fish on our last day, not counting the monster Deeds lost, a huge steelhead that sounded three times, made a crazed run upstream, and snapped Deeds's leader at the tippet. Usually, this would have thrown Deeds into a funk, but for once he accepted his fate with equanimity. He even smiled a little. The smile was rueful, haunted. "You'll get the bastard next trip," the guide said. "Jay-sus, what a monster!"

He advised us to fasten the clasps on our life jackets, because the Deschutes was dropping quickly and we were about to shoot the rapids. White water loomed ahead, great furls of it; boulders were visible in the spume. "I'm going to have to pay attention here for a minute," the guide said, working his oars to position us. The roar of the water grew louder and louder. I looked at Deeds; he had his fingers in his ears. My muscles tensed involuntarily. I held tightly to the seat. "Wooden boat's more trouble than those rubber rafts," the guide said. "If we hit a rock, we splinter." The current accelerated, pulling us ahead with a vengeance, until we were sucked forward into the gush and tumble and then expelled a few seconds later on the other side. The guide brushed some water off his nose. "Gentlemen," he said, "we have cheated death." He negotiated the next three rapids with the same sort of understated flair, keeping us in quiet pockets in the surging foam. The sensation was akin to the one surfers get when they're riding inside the curl of a wave. I felt protected, enclosed in a husk of space. After the final rapid, the noise level diminished, and the river widened by degrees, and we saw people fishing along the shore. The guide drew in his oars, and we glided effortlessly toward home.

We reached the landing about noon. I paid the guide, awarded him a congratulatory snort, and helped Deeds unload the gear. Joan was waiting for us in the parking lot. I think we frightened her, stomping to the car all sunburned and exuding primitive energies. But this may be a masculine conceit; it's equally possible that she was offended by our dirty clothes and—in my case—unshaved cheeks. She and Deeds began arguing right away. She wanted him to wrap the steelhead steaks in newspaper before putting them into the cooler; he said newspaper was unnecessary, the plastic bags would keep them just fine. Then a funny look crossed his face. "No, Joan," he said, "you're right. I'll wrap them."

We unwrapped them later that night and cooked them in Joan's kitchen. Her husband was impressed. "These are as good as the market kind," he said. I coughed, and a bit of garlicky butter dribbled down my chin. Later, I sat in a lawn chair on the porch and watched the traffic drift by: round headlights and fluttering moths. Deeds joined me after a while. He'd taken a bath, and his skin smelled incongruously of the perfumed soap he'd borrowed from his sister. Naturally, he was smoking. He cupped his hand and used it as an ashtray. This was a civilized gesture to make, but a sudden breeze came up and ruined everything by scattering ashes all over the furniture. Again, Deeds flashed his haunted smile. "I wish the hell we'd never left that river," he said, flipping his cigarette butt into the yard.

Deeds's words were prophetic. We descended from the sublimity of the Deschutes into another miserable winter's fishing. When it was over, I consulted a biologist about the future of steelhead in the Russian. We met in his office at the Department of Fish and Game, in Yountville, California. Behind him on a shelf were several jars containing specimens of fish commonly found in California streams—bass, squawfish, even suckers. The specimens were bleached and rubbery-looking, as though they'd been made in Hong Kong for the express purpose of filling large jars in offices. When I stared at the jars, I perceived a sort of whiteness. I don't know how else to put it: *a whiteness.*

The biologist told me first about salmon and their evolutionary efficiency, how in their run upstream to spawn, they literally consume themselves, digesting even the protein in their scales in an effort to continue. Salmon fingerlings are nourished by the corpses of spawned-out elders, in a macabre yet elegant loop. Because salmon have attained such perfection, they cannot easily adapt to changes in their environment, whereas steelhead, being less evolved, are more malleable. But

this didn't ensure the steelhead's survival in coastal rivers, the biologist said. Myriad factors combined to threaten the fish with extinction: poor timbering practices, which cause erosion and siltation; pollution, both industrial and agricultural; gravel extraction from creeks and streams; development, and the demand it places on the water table; dams; greater fishing pressure; and so on, through a catalog of familiar woes. The steelhead trout was not an endangered species, but its existence at present was decidedly precarious.

I conveyed none of this information to Deeds. He was already morose and taciturn. One sweltering August evening he informed me that he was thinking about selling his land to some pinhead—his word—from the city, thereby earning an enormous profit, which in turn would let him relocate in the Pacific Northwest, probably in Washington, not Oregon, because Joan was in Oregon, and though he loved her dearly, he could not abide sharing a state with her.

"Why not Canada?" I asked. "Why not a cabin on the Babine River? You could eat berry pies and chat with the loons."

He grumbled something about pissant fishermen and played his Bessie Smith album, rather loudly. A few days later I saw a realtor's car parked in front of his house. I phoned him that night and asked if he was serious about selling. "I don't wish to discuss it," he said, and hung up. I lost touch with him then. I spent September back East, visiting my family. In October, the first frost hit the valley, and the grapevines performed their annual elegiac wilt, as brilliantly as maples. It rained on November 4, two inches; the creeks started flowing. It rained again on the sixth, and then, on the eleventh, it poured. The sky was dark and ominous until noon, when the storm broke. About one o'clock, Deeds knocked on my door. He was wearing a yellow slicker and an old-fashioned rain hat of the type favored by New England sea captains. He invited me to accompany him to Jenner. We drove there in his truck, with the wind blowing intermittent showers across the glass, filling the cab with the scent of fecund earth. We parked above the river; junk and scuds of foam drifted toward the Pacific. There were sea lions at the river mouth. "I had an offer on my place," Deeds said, "but all this early rain, you know, we could have a terrific season." I agreed. It was the best thing to do. Dire prophecies were swept to sea; the steelhead were returning.

WINTER

Except for a choice few, fishermen grow restless now.
Where's the acton, where's the bite? To the older
fisherman, however, it's different. Why, there's
plenty to do! He tells stories to the boys.
He prays for the water. He tries to give back
to the sport all he has taken from it.

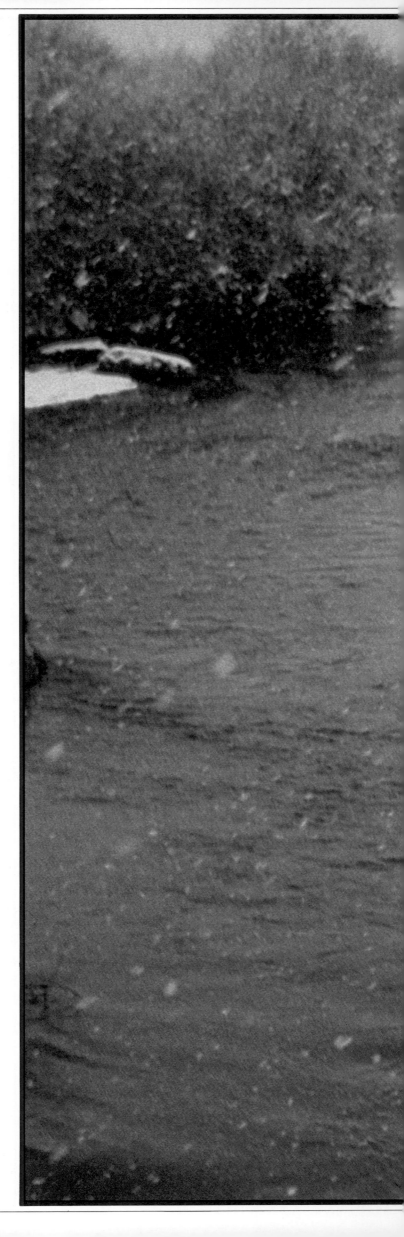

There is never a season of absolutely no fishing. But when winter comes there is not very much fishing, and what fishing there is becomes very specialized. In the deep part of winter a fisherman usually looks for substitutes, or travels to a better climate, or simply goes through the motions when there is no ice. It is a slow time. He reads and remembers, fiddles with his tackle, and studies the catalogs.

When a fisherman begins to know that he is near the end, he seems paradoxically to care less about actually fishing and more about the spirit and traditions of his sport. They seem important then, and he wants to make sure that they survive, even if he does not.

Fishermen past a certain age—which is very hard to pinpoint with numbers—go on fishing trips and seldom wet a line. Or if the fisherman does actually fish, it is merely for the sake of having done it, in order to be able to say that he did. After a few casts he can put up the rod and go back to the fire and the kitchen and the satisfactions of storytelling.

This is not necessarily the behavior of a feeble man, though the water does seem a little colder to the bones every year. Fishing is not so painful or taxing that you must simply give it up after a certain age. There are many vigorous ninety-year-old fishermen. But many old fishermen are like Fred Bear, the great archer (and a fine trout fisherman as well), who never really stopped hunting late in his life but who did stop killing a lot of game and began spending more and more time around camp telling stories and listening to them. Everyone in camp knew that if he chose to pick up a bow and go off into the woods, it would be the same old Fred Bear and he would probably come back in a few hours with meat. But he just didn't seem to want to do that. "I got to where I liked sitting around better," he told me once, as if that were all he needed to say.

When you have a lifetime of fishing behind you, your ambition is probably not so much to catch more fish or bigger fish. It is to honor the tradition that has given you so much satisfaction, and perhaps to give something back to it. So old men teach young boys how to fish, passing along some of the things they have spent a lifetime learning.

There are excellent reasons for young boys and old men to fish together. For one, both are very casual about time. Neither is in a hurry, though for wildly different reasons. For another, the old man usually wants the young boy to catch all the fish. He is genuinely content to row the boat if one is involved, or to coach from the bank if the boy is wading and casting. He does not pressure the boy or compete with him. Old men don't often ruin fishing for boys the way young men frequently do.

One of the most touching volumes in all sports literature is Robert Ruark's *The Old Man and the Boy,* which tells of the relationship and experiences of an eager young buck and a savvy old man. Everything that the boy has to learn the old man already knows. He also knows that he cannot teach the boy very much of it; he will have to learn most of it on his own. But the old man can be there to point the boy gently in the right direction and to make sure that he does not make any disastrous mistakes. This he does with great wisdom and wit, and with the dignity of those who have aged well.

It is also possible to give something back to the sport by writing about it. With some spectacular exceptions, the best writing about fishing seems to have been done by authors who were looking back. Fishing memoirs are much more affecting and wear much better than the expert treatises of fishermen who are in the prime of life and looking for the conceptual key that will unlock all of angling's secrets. One thinks of the prose of Roderick Haig-Brown, which is as cold and clear and bracing as the flow of a glacier-fed stream; or the fussy good humor of Robert Traver; or the almost epic purity of Norman MacLean. Their writing seems so much worthier of the sport than all the new research into insects and rise forms and tackle combinations that is published and forgotten every year.

Not every fisherman writes, of course, but if he lives long enough, a fisher-

Franklin Jones, *Waiting for the Rise* (1980).

Thomas Aquinas Daly, *Jigging for Perch* (1978).

Kent Day Coes, *Winter Village* (ca. 1965).

man almost always comes back to reading about the sport. I managed a few years ago to acquire a considerable library of fishing books from the estate of a man who lived a long life in Scotland and America. He had been successful in business and used his money to travel and to fish. He also used it to acquire many fine things, of which I was able to afford his fishing books. I went through them—more than one hundred in all—and it was apparent that they were well loved and read. Many of them had notations in the margins and on the title pages, reflections written in ink in a precise, disciplined hand.

He would have been more than fifty years older than I. Many of his favorite books will be part of my library, and when I die they will, I trust, pass into the hands of another young man who is interested in fishing, not merely as an activity, but as a way of life. I have the Scotsman's copies of Walton and Skues and Sawyer and Halford, his complete set of Haig-Brown. I have added my own favorites by American writers of my generation: Russell Chatham's anthology *Silent Seasons,* Nick Lyons's *Fishing Widows* and *Bright Rivers,* and some titles by Arnold Gingrich, whom I met once, the day I went to work for *Esquire* magazine, which he had founded some forty years earlier.

There is no indispensable man in any field as rich as angling, but it is fair to say that the sport and its literature would not be what they are today without Nick Lyons and the late Arnold Gingrich. Lyons's sweetly melancholy prose captures precisely the frustrations of a man with the heart of an angler trapped in the body of an urban office worker. Most people who write about fishing either fish all the time or could if they really wanted to. The condition of most people who love to fish is precisely the opposite. (Remember the first great law of fishing: *No fisherman ever fishes as much as he wants to.*) Lyons captures this frustration perfectly and with considerable wit, which in some measure eases the pain. But his own books are only a part of his enormous contribution to the spirit and literature of the sport. As an editor, he has kept the good old books in print and brought good new books to the attention of their proper public. In the world of conglomerate publishing that is a heroic achievement.

Arnold Gingrich wrote, among other things, a wonderful volume called simply *The Fishing in Print.* Gingrich, who published Fitzgerald and Hemingway in their time, also made the pages of his magazine available to Lee Wulff and Ernest Schwiebert. He was a great enthusiast and was generous with his enthusiasm. His contributions to the sport went beyond his labors as an editor.

Which brings us to the realization that sooner or later strikes any fisherman: there is no certain future for the sport. It is not enough to initiate young boys or even to celebrate the mysteries in print. This is, sadly, the modern world, and it is not necessarily the fittest who survive but the best organized. If you love the sport, it is important that you work to protect it. This means politics, which is the grim antithesis of fishing.

Front page from *Gleason's Pictorial* (1854). In its account of pike fishing, *Gleason's* noted the many methods used by sportsmen: "snaring, trimmering, huxing, or fastening live bait to a distended ox-bladder, trolling, and even shooting them."

GLEASON'S PICTORIAL

F. GLEASON, {CORNER OF TREMONT AND BROMFIELD STS.} BOSTON, SATURDAY, FEBRUARY 11, 1854. $3 00 PER ANNUM. 6 CENTS SINGLE. {VOL. VI. No. 6.—WHOLE No. 136.

PIKE FISHING.

Below we present another of our American sporting scenes. The pike, jack, or pickerel, with the trout, may be considered the universal fish of the world. It appears to inhabit the inland waters of all northern countries. They are found in nearly all our streams, ponds and lakes, from one extremity of the Union to the other, and do not materially differ from the same species in other countries. The largest fish are taken in our Western lakes, frequently of thirty pounds weight, and occasionally of forty. They generally spawn in the months of March and April. During the height of the season their colors are extremely brilliant, being green, diversified with bright yellow spots. They are fond of still, shady spots, under and near the weed called pickerel-weed, and appear to grow better and larger in ponds and lakes than in swift-running streams. In winter, they retreat to the deep holes, and under rocky projections, stumps of trees, roots, etc., from which places, by making a hole in the ice, they are readily taken with a drop-line with a small live fish for bait. At this season of the year their colors are less brilliant, and their spots of a darker hue. During the summer they are listless, and affect the surface of the water, where, in warm, sunny weather, they seem to bask in a sleepy state for hours together. At these periods, no bait, however tempting, can allure him. Generally speaking, the months of September and October are found to be the best months for angling. There is, perhaps, more angling for the pike than for any other of the finny tribe; insomuch that it is almost impossible to mention a section of the country—except within some of our more southern States—which do not furnish fine grounds for pike of moderate size. The most common mode of taking them in the ponds and lakes is with a stiff rod of ash or bamboo about twelve feet long, accompanied with a reel containing from fifty to one hundred yards of strong flax or grass line, with a small fish, or the leg of a frog, for bait. There are many other methods adopted by sportsmen in fishing for the pike—such as snaring, trimmering, huxing, or fastening live bait to a distended ox-bladder, trolling with a rod ten or twelve feet long, and even shooting them. In this last method, a light charge is put into the gun, and all the art displayed in the performance consists in making due allowance for the refraction of the water, according to the depth and distance of the fish. A love of this sport is fast increasing in this country, and is also a very profitable employment for the sportsman, who finds a ready market for his game.

PIKE FISHING.

Take the case of Charlie Fox, who is in his seventies now. Fox lives on the banks of the Letort River, which he no longer fishes so much as manages. If you have ever fished that remarkable limestone stream, you almost certainly know about Fox and have probably spent some time talking with him. In his life he has seen the countryside around the Letort change radically. It was once simply a gentle spring run in the middle of farm country that flowed over beds of watercress and *Elodea* and held a fine population of trout. Then civilization grew up around it like a fungus. The crowning blow was the four-lane interstate highway bridge about a mile upstream from Fox's home.

In addition to the runoff from badly planned developments, sewage, trash, and the other normal by-products of civilization that are such a threat to trout, Fox had to fight the state wildlife managers who wanted to stock the stream and turn it into a put-and-take operation. The idea is a sacrilege. Fox fought the biologists politically and worked physically to keep the stream a fit habitat for wild trout. After years of struggling with the bureaucrats, he won and the stream was placed under special trophy regulations. It is now full of wild trout that live less than a mile from a K-Mart. Fox has built casting platforms in the stream for the fishermen and spawning beds for the fish. He keeps the banks clean and watches for the rare violator. The Letort flows through Carlisle, Pennsylvania, like a secret, thanks in large part to the efforts of Charles Fox.

Not all fishermen can do as much. But there are organizations to be joined, meetings to be attended, letters to be written to congressmen and other politicians, who might not be able to tell a rainbow from a brown but know exactly what a pressure group looks like. All this takes time, and it is a bleak way to spend it. Older fishermen with time and a cultivated sense of their duty do much of the work. Most younger men are too busy or not yet convinced of the need.

But the work must be done. There is an ill-advised development a day, and it sometimes seems that the contractors outnumber the fish three or four to one. Sometimes the enemy is not a fast-buck hustler at all but somebody who should be on the right side. It was the fishery experts, after all, who introduced the carp to this country. Charles Fox found the biologists to be much more stubborn than the developers, who only wanted to make money, not commit science. Today, fish biologists in the New England states are working on programs to transplant Pacific salmon into the rivers of the Atlantic, and Atlantic salmon fishermen are fighting the proposal. They believe, with good reason, that the coho is not as fine a fish as the Atlantic and that it will likely take over the spawning streams and finish what man has started. The fight promises to be strenuous and long.

Finally, there is a nascent movement to outlaw sport fishing. If it is not the obvious enemy or the unlikely enemy, it is simple wrongheaded sentimentality. Jacques Cousteau has lent his prestige to the campaign as if to say that the sea

A snapshot of Arnold Gingrich with a grilse,
taken on a fishing trip in Iceland (1950s).

should be the playground solely of subsidized researchers. The campaign is not aimed so much at saving and restoring fish habitat—fishermen have already staked out that turf. The effort is moralistic in the worst sense of that word, the plaything of people who find fishing obscene.

It is not enough to outvote them now, which is easy enough. The important business is to make a case for fishing, not as something that is morally indifferent but as something positive and, in some cases, ennobling. Fish hogs and other boors give fishing a bad name even among fishermen, but gentlemen like Charles Fox and Arnold Gingrich are nearly irresistible moral models.

There is a man in his eighties who lives in the little Vermont town I call home. He is Welsh by birth. The First World War was the end of his youth, as it was for most of the men of his generation. He spent months behind Turkish lines, spying and operating as a guerrilla in the theater of the war that produced men like T. E. Lawrence while in France their contemporaries died anonymously by the hundreds of thousands. My neighbor escaped the Turks dozens of times but barely survived cholera.

While he convalesced after the war, he learned about fishing and became a skillful and resourceful fisherman. When he was well, he left Wales for good. The war had made a traveler out of him. But the peace had made him a fisherman, and he fished all over the world before he retired near the Battenkill, one of the most famous American trout rivers. On the day he moved into his retirement home, he wandered down to the river and quickly caught a five-pound brown trout. "That's more than ten years, now," he says when he tells the story, "and I'm still trying to catch another like it."

He fished every year in New Brunswick, and out of his love for salmon he became active in several different organizations that lobbied for restoration. He gave money and time generously and flooded the mails with correspondence. There finally came a year when he could not make his annual salmon trip. He had been ill most of the winter and simply did not feel up to it. So he went out to the local rivers with a weepy old Hardy rod and some snelled wet flies that must have been fifty years old. He was without a doubt the only man in those parts and perhaps in all of America who wore a necktie while he fished.

Evenings, he would drop by the house of one local fisherman or another with a fourteen- or fifteen-inch rainbow in his creel. The fish was a gift, he would say. He did not want it for himself, but it seemed a shame to let it go to waste. He would be invited in for a drink and perhaps for dinner, and after he had refused once or twice, he would accept the invitation and put down his tackle. As he sipped his drink, he would recall when he had hooked the fish and where, and he would recount each step of the battle that followed. "A very near thing," he would say. "A very near thing. Purest sort of luck I landed him at all."

During dinner he would tell stories about his time in Turkey and about rivers he had fished all over the globe. "Today's fish was just as fine as any of them," he would always say. "If I live long enough I'll be telling people about this river and that fish, too. Lovely. Just lovely. What a wonderful thing fishing is. A gift and one of God's finest."

We of the poplin shirt and fast rod set would talk about his visit the next day and smile over the necktie and wicker creel and old wet flies. Then we would sneak down to the river where he said he had caught the fish to see if there was another one there. We would also tell each other that old age was nothing to fear if you could be sure of winding up like that.

There are many reasons for a fisherman to look forward eagerly to the last years. There are regrets, of course, and loneliness. Angling may be his solace. The first rule of fishing is less emphatic and cruel. Old men may even defy the rule entirely and fish just as much as they want to. They have more time and less of the burning desire that makes the lives of young anglers such torment. Anglers can defy the instructions of Dylan Thomas—what did he know about old age?—and go gently into the good night. And why not? You will be going anyway, and kicking and screaming cannot change that.

I sometimes try to imagine myself as an old man, still fishing in spite of the years. Lately I have been able to see the picture of myself with such clarity that I can even make out trade names on the equipment I use. I know what brand of pipe tobacco I will smoke if I should decide to start smoking a pipe, which is the kind of affectation old men can indulge in without drawing too much attention to themselves or looking foolish.

The first characteristic of my old age as an angler will be wisdom. It is preeminent in my vision of the future, virtually nonexistent in the present. When I am old, I will know things about which I am now confused, ignorant, or just plain wrong. I will have learned much and learned it painfully. And I won't be selfish with what I know, either. If you ask me a question, I, by God, will give you an answer. I will be arch and probably a little patronizing about it, too.

By that time I will have caught enough fish to know when it is not worth the trouble to go fishing. I'll stay home. When I do go out, I will know exactly what to carry with me to the stream, and I'll leave everything else at home. I'll know when a fish can be fooled and when it is a waste of time to cast to him. In short, I will be an angling minimalist. No wasted motion or false starts. I will not allow myself to be frustrated. There won't be enough time left for that. Desperation is an indulgence for young bucks.

I will have a library of fishing books that I will go back to when I am not rereading Shelby Foote's trilogy on the American Civil War or Proust's seven volumes. I will pick from among the titles as the mood suits me and sit in a leather-upholstered chair in front of a fire—old men chill easily—and read my favorites again and again: the Hemingway stories, of course; Ruark's *The Old Man and the Boy*; *A River Runs Through It* by Norman MacLean and William Humphrey's *The Spawning Run*; Nick Lyons's *Fishing Widows* and Robert Traver's stories in *Trout Magic* and *Trout Madness*; all of Haig-Brown.

Perhaps I'll teach a noncredit course at some local college, the Literature of Angling or some such. We will read all of those books and make the obvious comparisons with Thoreau and Twain. There will be no tests. We might discuss some of the angling passages that appear as mood sweeteners in books by contemporary authors such as Thomas McGuane and Philip Caputo. I will wear a tweed jacket with elbow patches to class and smoke the pipe that I shall have mastered by then. My course will be among the most popular in the curriculum as much for the anecdotal abilities of the professor as for the quality of the texts.

Not far from my home there will be a stream that is neither too big nor too famous. It will hold some nice trout if you know where to look for them, and, of course, I will know—as will my three or four local companions, all of whom will be approximately my age and will have devoted as much of their lives to fishing as I have.

We will probably not fish the local stream together. It will be more of a private business, done on a whim. But we will go off together for one or two annual trips and fish for a week or two, probably for salmon. One of my companions will be the group's self-appointed cook. Another will provide essential supplies, such as good liquor and smoked sausage. My role will be rather vague—sweeping and fussing around with the cabin chores, helping to fix broken tackle, keeping the card game going, providing wisdom and advice upon request. I will bring along the books and music.

My companions and I will begin planning the trip three or four months in advance. I will be on the phone with at least one of them every day during the planning stage. There are thousands of contingencies, and I don't intend to overlook any of them. My companions will be exasperated with me before we are ever ready to depart.

Once we have arrived at the camp, I will fish less than anybody, except perhaps the cook. I'll complain about what wading in cold water does to my knees, and I'll stay behind to help around the kitchen or read. I'll take my first drink of Irish whiskey sometimes as early as four in the afternoon.

But I will catch my share of fish, one or two of which I will kill without guilt. At home, on the local stream, I will kill a dozen or so a year for breakfast. An old man should be allowed a few wild fish to eat.

I will own thousands of flies by then and will not be able to remember the names of most of the patterns. They will be classified simply as "little black bushy ones" or "wispy yellow ones." For local fishing I'll own one truly fine rod by one of the contemporary makers such as Hoagy Carmichael, Jr. There will be a closet full of other rods which I'll seldom use and will often find a reason to give away.

I will have made several trips to the places that trout fishermen like to talk about when they get together, and I will have caught at least one permit on a fly rod. I will have no politics and will not know who won the Academy Awards. I will follow football only during the play-offs and baseball only during the World Series. I will give money to organizations that are attempting to save very small parts of the world, particularly rivers. I hope to have made some sort of peace with God and to have grandchildren, one or two of whom will come to me to learn how to fish.

With the coming of a new spring, I will realize that I was not going blind, after all—that it was merely winter that made everything look gray and dim as ash; also that I am not near paralysis—merely stiff with cold. I will rouse myself from the leather chair and the books and the Irish whiskey and rummage through the epic collection of tackle. I will go down to the courthouse or tackle store and buy a license. Then I will pick up my vest and waders and rod case and head for the local river, ambling and taking my time in order to admire the wild flowers, mushrooms, and newly returned birds. My fingers will be knobby, but they will still quiver with the old excitement as I tie on a fly. The water will feel alive when I step into it. All the old sensations will wash over me in a wave of association and memory, and I will be thankful for the day.

The life of a fisherman ends, but fishing does not. No fisherman can escape the comforting, haunting feeling that the world is eternal and that as it continues, some part of him will continue with it, wandering across the planet perhaps, like a migrating salmon that always knows the way home. If an epitaph is needed, let it come from an Irish poet who loved the world extravagantly and at the same time understood that it is always mysterious.

THE FISHERMAN

Although I can see him still,
The freckled man who goes
To a grey place on a hill
In grey Connemara clothes
At dawn to cast his flies,
It's long since I began
To call up to the eyes
This wise and simple man.
All day I'd looked in the face
What I had hoped 'twould be
To write for my own race
And the reality;
The living men that I hate
The dead man that I loved,
The craven man in his seat,
The insolent unreproved,
And no knave brought to book
Who has won a drunken cheer,
The witty man and his joke
Aimed at the commonest ear,
The clever man who cries
The catch-cries of the clown,
The beating down of the wise
And great Art beaten down.

Maybe a twelvemonth since
Suddenly I began,
In scorn of his audience,
Imagining a man,
And his sun-freckled face,
And grey Connemara cloth,
Climbing up to a place
Where stone is dark under froth,
And the down-turn of his wrist
When the flies drop in the stream;
A man who does not exist,
A man who is but a dream;
And cried, "Before I am old
I shall have written him one
Poem maybe as cold
And passionate as the dawn."

—William Butler Yeats

Illustration by Russell Buzzell (1981).

REMEMBERED LESSONS:
Down-Home Bass
By Geoffrey Norman

Y FATHER went where the navy told him to go, and when there was time for recreation, he enjoyed what was available locally. He was a carrier pilot and, in spite of long months at sea, a good father. When he was on shore, while the air group and the carrier refitted for another cruise, he liked to spend time with his family and to go fishing with his friends.

He would probably have been a fine trout fisherman. He was English, and he had a passion for order and precision. Except for some salty language, which was routine with aviators, he was always correct and almost formal. And he had an eye for beauty. Whenever he came home from a European cruise, he would bring a painting or two that he had picked up somewhere. They were not always realistic depictions, but there was certainly never any surrealism, either. He liked landscapes best, done in a vaguely impressionistic fashion, with light diffused across the canvas. He was English, as I said, and I suspect his favorite painter would have been Turner.

So, he might have been a good trout fisherman. But the navy does not have any ports that are near good trout waters. The forty-thousand-ton aircraft carriers that he flew from were based in places like Norfolk, Virginia, and Jacksonville, Florida. There was fishing nearby, but none of it for cold-water trout.

So my father fished for bass, which was fine with him. It would never have occurred to him to complain about *that.* Recreation and sport were held in their proper regard, and if you were not resourceful enough to make the best of what you were given in that part of your life, you were probably not the kind of man who could land a Banshee on the *Bonhomme Richard.* If bass fishing was the only fishing available, then bass fishing would just, by God, have to do.

He started fly-fishing for bass after the war in the Pacific, when we lived in Virginia. Like many of the men who survived that war and had grown up in the depression that preceded it, he was ready to have some fun. A squadron mate had to teach him how to fly cast, since he had never done any fishing at all when he was growing up. But he

practiced and learned and soon became an able fly caster.

The man who taught him was also his favorite fishing partner, and they would go off in the very early morning, before the sun was up, and come home late, usually with a few fish and sometimes many. I don't remember the fishing partner's name—Tom, I think—but he was an enthusiast and a great pal to all boys. He was lean and athletic and looked just right for the job of flying jet fighters. He had a sort of roguish grin and a big horse laugh. He called me "sport" and I loved it. A couple of years after he and my father started going fishing together, he was transferred back to the Pacific to fly Panthers over Korea. His plane was badly shot up on one mission, and before he could make it back to the carrier, he was forced to ditch. It was winter, and helicopters were new to the navy and not very reliable. While two of them sat on the flight deck with engine trouble, Tom froze to death in the Sea of Japan.

I was old enough to understand, I think. I realized what a risky thing my father did for a job, and it made me want more than ever to be his partner . . . his wingman in my young boy's scheme of things. I wanted, at the very least, to go with him on those early morning fishing trips.

He had taken me fishing many times and outfitted me so that I could go alone or with some of the boys I played with. But those trips were always to tame little ponds where we caught panfish until it got to be old stuff. Then we skipped rocks, went for a swim, or looked for a snake to kill. It was fun, and I went every chance I got. But it wasn't the same as getting up before dawn and going off somewhere down on the coast to fly cast for bass. *That* is what I wanted to do.

But in my father's world you did not simply go off and do something. First, you trained and practiced and rehearsed. Mistakes were inevitable in his world and you lived with that; but avoidable mistakes were something else. He could not tolerate or forgive them. It was a long time before I understood why, but in the meantime I had no choice. Either I went along with the way he did things, or I did not go fishing.

So I learned to fly cast on the lawn, the same way he had. Practice, practice, practice. "You get so you can do it without thinking," he would say. "Then, when the time comes and you are casting to a spot where you've just seen a fish strike, you'll be able to do it without panicking." I practiced and he coached, and after three or four weeks of it I was doing an acceptable job.

Then we checked all my equipment to make sure that no hooks were rusty and no leaders were frayed. "Right now," he said, "when you are at home and have all the tools you need to repair what is broken, is the best time to make sure of your tackle. Later, when you are in a boat, out on the water, it will be too late." So I got all my gear in shape, and the night before we finally went bass fishing together, I laid out my clothes so that I could dress quickly in the morning. I set my own alarm clock even though I knew that he would come upstairs to wake me. I wanted to be dressed and ready when he opened the door to my room.

I was, and perhaps as a reward, he let me drink half a cup of coffee, which I filled the rest of the way with milk and sugar. It tasted surprisingly good, and the warmth and the caffeine kept me awake on the drive to the landing.

My father had an old car, some sort of Ford, I think, from the thirties. For some reason, navy pilots in those days—the ones with families, anyway—always owned two cars. One was a fairly recent model, which the wife used to do the shopping and transport the kids from school to Little League and so forth. The other car was an old clunker, which the husband used to get to the base and back and to take on fishing trips. The parking lot at the Officers' Club was always filled with this strange mix of old black Fords and bright new sports cars that belonged to the young, unmarried pilots.

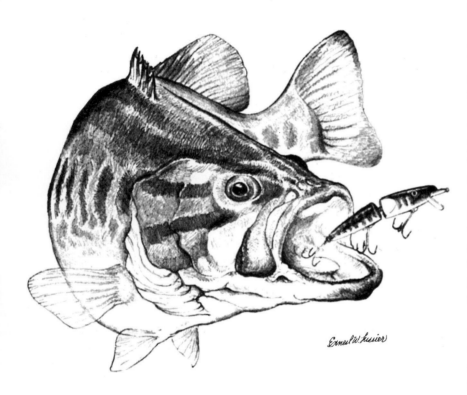

The heater on the Ford was broken—or maybe the car didn't have one—and one of the windows would close only about halfway. It was an hour's drive to the landing, and I was cold to the bone the entire way. Cold and disoriented. I wished mightily that I had stayed in my bed, even though I would have had to do all my chores before I could play baseball. As it was, I had the day off because I was going fishing with my father. In the cold, dark, rattling old Ford at four in the morning, it did not seem worth it.

It was still dark when we got to the landing. My father bolted his outboard motor to the transom of a rented juniper skiff, then I handed our rods and tackle boxes and lunch down from the dock. He stowed them carefully in the boat. "There isn't room in a boat," he said, "to just throw things around. Leave a tackle box in the middle of the deck, and sure as hell you'll trip over it." I huddled in the bow as he cranked the little Mercury, and we headed off into the darkness of Back Bay.

The sun rose spectacularly. First there was a band of silver light above the horizon, and then the blackness around us softened a little to ash gray.

The flat orange disk of the sun appeared above the land. It was the color of coals in a dying hardwood fire, and we could look directly into it. There was still a heavy chill in the air, and it was possible to imagine briefly that the sun had gone cold. But as it rose, almost perceptibly, it brightened and the air warmed, and all around us a maze of coastal islands and inlets materialized like a world being born.

I was overwhelmed, at ten years old, by Back Bay. It spread out from horizon to horizon, flat and unchanging as a prairie. It was almost all water, and what earth there was could barely hold its own against the water. The islands were grass and a few stark cypress trees. Eelgrass, saw grass, and cattails, as far as we could see. Most of the grass was brown and dry, waving a little in the morning breeze like a great field of grain ready for harvest.

Where there was no grass, there was water— glinting, steel-colored water that stretched off in wide, flat bays or narrow channels in every direction. It was a maze of water, and I thought that it would be impossible for anyone to navigate or know it except a pirate. Being ten, I thought a lot about pirates, and for once it was appropriate. I was in the right place. Back Bay had been a notorious pirate hideout a couple of centuries earlier.

The shallow, brackish water was laced with underwater grass and dotted with duck blinds. In the fall Back Bay had some of the best waterfowling in the East. There were huge rafts of diving ducks, flocks of geese, and large flights of puddle ducks, especially blacks and mallards. Now, in the late spring, there were only some coots, rafted in the middle of the bays and scattered everywhere in singles and pairs. They would race along in front of the boat, leaving little white wakes behind them as they struggled to get airborne. We put up dozens of them on the way to the place where my father wanted to start fishing.

"Looks like those coots could use a catapult," he said after he'd cut the engine. I agreed and sat in the bow with my ears still ringing and my senses trying to adjust and find equilibrium in the midst of so much that was strange. I was fairly tingling with excitement. So this was it. Finally.

We fished the bank of an island for the first hour of full light, after the pink pigment had left the sky. At first he paddled and I fished. That was the drill, he said. We would change after one hour or after the man who was fishing had boated two fish. It seemed like a good system, especially since I had the first watch.

My father kept the boat in close to the bank, not quite paralleling it. The bow was in a little closer than the stern to give me a better casting angle. I did all right, considering my nervousness and the fact that I was awestruck by the wildness of Back Bay. "Just concentrate on what you're doing, son," my father said. "We'll be out here all day. There will be plenty of time for sightseeing."

I missed a good strike because I had slack in my line and because I was so surprised I didn't even try to set the hook until the fish had spit out the cork bug and run for shelter. I probably didn't really believe that it ever happened, but it had happened now to me, less than an hour after I had started fishing.

"Pay attention, son," my father said gently. "The worst mistakes come from not paying attention. That was a nice fish."

My heart was beating wildly and my throat was tight with excitement and frustration. I was unhappy, nearly tearful, about losing that fish. But if I had managed to get one to strike, then surely another would try it, too. And this time I would set the hook and land him. That was the proper progression.

"OK, son, that's your hour."

I thought it was unfair, naturally. I wanted to fish. I cared as much about paddling my father around while he fished as I cared about washing and waxing his car, which was one of my many chores. I sullenly took the stern.

"A little closer," my father would say quietly over his shoulder as he worked the bank with a popping bug. Or, "Not so fast, son." I did what he told me. Barely. I knew that I was doing a bad job, but I didn't care. I was going to show him. Then he missed a strike. He was coiled all the way around toward the stern of the boat, watching his motionless bug. He'd made a perfect cast, putting it snugly up against an old cypress tree. The spot looked like ordained bass water. My father was waiting for the ripples to settle where his bug had hit the surface, counting carefully to fifteen, before he gave it that first twitch.

If I had been doing my job instead of doping off, as they say in the navy, I would have held the boat almost motionless while he waited to put some action to the bug. I would have kept the paddle blade in the water, backing and prying to keep him in position to work the bug and, with a little luck, to hook and play the fish when it struck. But in the vernacular of my generation, I blew it. While I did nothing, the boat kept sliding across the water, and my father took a deeper and deeper coil to face the bug. Finally, when he could turn no further, he twitched it. The water around the stump erupted in oily foam. Coiled and off balance as he was, my father could make only an awkward, backhand attempt to set the hook. He missed the strike. The water settled and everything was quiet again. Very quiet. He began false casting, looking for another target. He didn't say a word. Sitting in the stern, I felt like a very small boy who had no business being where he was. I bit my lip and swallowed hard and decided to "bear down"—one more navy expression that I'd heard often enough but was just now beginning to understand. For the last fifteen minutes of my watch, I concentrated on the paddle the way my baseball coach had taught me to concentrate on the bat. But there were no more splashy strikes on my father's popping bug.

"All right, son," he said, bringing in line, "that's my hour. Pull over to the bank and we'll change positions."

"That's OK, Dad. I don't mind paddling."

"No. It's your turn to fish. That's the way we work it."

"But I made you miss that strike."

"Those things happen, son. Just forget about it. Best thing for you to do now is catch your two fish. Then I'll get another chance early."

I felt even smaller. I stood in the bow with my gleaming waxed rod and forgot everything. It was as though I had never held that rod before in my life. I could not control the loop, shoot line, or straighten the leader. I was tangled in fly line, trying harder and harder, which only made it worse. Much worse.

"Just settle down, son. Reel in. Change flies and untie that wind knot in your leader. Put on another fly. Take your time. One of the best things about fishing is that you don't have to hurry."

He let the boat drift and poured some coffee from a thermos. He sipped it and remarked that it was a beautiful day, a perfect day to be on the water. This sort of wild, coastal, pirate's water was so much more satisfying than the monotonous open oceans that he was used to, he said. And a warm, windless day like this one made it just perfect. Fishing, he said, really was just an excuse to get out on water when you had a beautiful day to enjoy.

While he talked, I did what he told me, and when I was standing again, ready to fish, I felt better. He nosed the boat around into a wide inlet that was deep on one bank and had an old channel running through the middle. There was a broken-down duck blind in the shallow water off the other bank. It looked as if it had not been used for a season or two.

"Work the deep parts," he said. "And keep it slow."

I began casting, and my new skills came back slowly. Each cast was a little longer and a little straighter, and I began to feel confident about the mechanics of the thing.

This time when I got a strike, I was ready. It was a splashy hit and the bass jumped almost immediately. A largemouth bass is not an exceedingly refined fish. It has the finesse of a linebacker, which is why you use stout tackle that would be out of place on almost any trout stream. Bass like a mouthful, so you use a rod that is big enough to power a large bug and strong enough to horse the fish out of the grass. You really need to snub them.

Which is exactly what I did, even though my fish was not especially big—just game. He jumped a

couple of times, made a short run, and then tried to go into some weeds. I stopped him and he went under the boat. Then he came to the surface, on his side. To me, he was a marvel. All two pounds of him, with a profile like that of Rocky Marciano, who was the heavyweight boxing champion then. The fish was green and white with big scales and bulging eyes. He smelled like wet earth. I could hardly believe that I had done it when my father netted him and handed him to me. He patted me on the back and congratulated me. He was prouder, probably, than I was. I realized that he had kept the boat perfectly positioned the entire time. I never had to make a difficult cast or one that was too long. When I hooked the fish, I had been in just the right position. I had never once thought about the boat.

So when my turn came again, I worked on my paddling. I was bearing down all the way. I didn't make any mistakes that cost my father a fish . . . but, then, he didn't get any strikes.

We ate lunch in the late morning with the boat tied to a duck blind. We spread ham sandwiches, hard-boiled eggs, oranges, and a thermos of tea on the middle seat of the boat and ate hungrily.

"You're doing a fine job," my father said.

"But you still haven't caught anything."

"That's something you get used to after you've fished for a few years."

"How big do you think that one at the stump was?"

"Hard to tell. Sometimes a small fish will make a real spectacular strike and a big one will just sort of suck the bait in."

"I don't think that one was small."

"Maybe not."

We ate and sipped tea and watched big, billowing cumulus clouds roll across that vast, lonely tidal stretch of the Atlantic coast. It is wild and remote, the starting place for all sorts of living things, a hatchery and incubator for thousands of creatures. It felt oddly peaceful and alive at the same time.

"How do you feel?" my father asked when we had finished the tea. "Tired?"

"No."

"You sure? We could go on back. It's been a pretty long day."

"I'd like to fish some more."

"OK, son. But if you get tired, let me know. You've done just fine and you've been a good sport."

The missed fish still bothered me. Ironically, the ten-year-old boy wanted desperately for his old man to catch a fish. I wanted it to be a good day for him too, and I would have paddled all afternoon if he had let me.

But we kept to his schedule, with no success. The hot, flat stretch of the afternoon wore on, and I felt bone-tired. My soft palms were beginning to blister from gripping the paddle. I dunked them

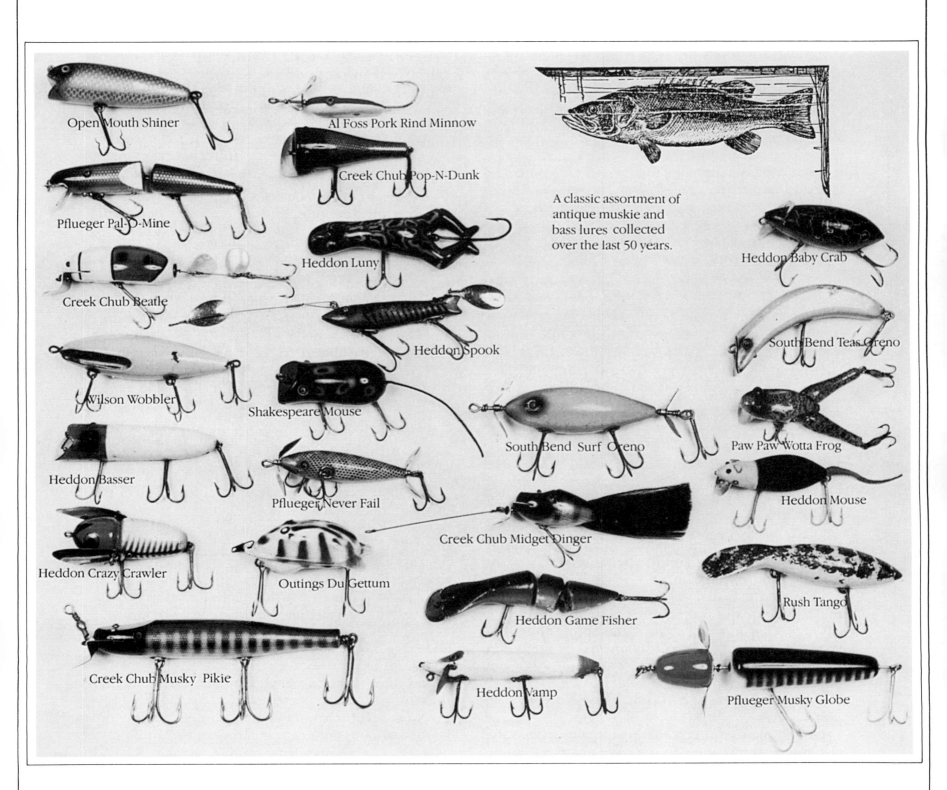

Open Mouth Shiner

Al Foss Pork Rind Minnow

Pflueger Pal-O-Mine

Creek Chub Pop-N-Dunk

Creek Chub Beatle

Heddon Luny

A classic assortment of
antique muskie and
bass lures collected
over the last 50 years.

Heddon Baby Crab

Heddon Spook

South Bend Teas Oreno

Wilson Wobbler

Shakespeare Mouse

South Bend Surf Oreno

Paw Paw Wotta Frog

Heddon Basser

Pflueger Never Fail

Heddon Mouse

Heddon Crazy Crawler

Creek Chub Midget Dinger

Outings Du Gettum

Rush Tango

Heddon Game Fisher

Creek Chub Musky Pikie

Heddon Vamp

Pflueger Musky Globe

into the water for relief, then splashed a little water on my face to stay alert. There was a persistent ache in the small of my back.

Late in the day, when the sun had leached the last of my enthusiasm, my father took the bow for his final turn. I paddled . . . more and more like a ten-year-old boy.

We were moving too fast and too close to a shallow bank when my father said over his shoulder, "There it is."

"What?"

"The place where I am going to break this slump and catch a fish."

I looked ahead. A long spar stuck out from the bank at a shallow angle. One end had gouged a small pocket in the bank; the other was anchored and invisible in five feet of water. This was bass cover that could have been lifted straight from the pages of *Field and Stream* as an example of a typical hot spot.

"Looks great," I said.

"Right. So ease me in close and then hold what you've got." My father was talking to me as I imagined he talked to his wingman. I was alert now, and nervous. My hands went a little white around the paddle, and I bit down on my lower lip. I used a cross draw to ease the bow out from the bank and a pry to hold the boat stationary. They worked just the way the scout manual said they were supposed to. The boat was in position, and my father began false casting and shooting line. Then he spotted his bug right in the apex of the angle between the bank and the spar, one foot out. Perfect.

I could see his lips move as he silently counted to fifteen. His shoulders took a slight forward roll. A little twitch from his line hand was transmitted down thirty feet of line to the bug and . . . *splash!* He was hooked tight and the bass jumped, shaking his head and rattling his gills.

I backed the boat away from the bank and moved the bow with the direction in which the fish ran. My father let him tire against the strain of a nine-foot rod, and when it was time, he asked me to net the fish. I used all the caution of catching a last-out pop fly.

"Damn fine job, son. Damn fine. Now let's go home."

He ran the motor and the boat planed across the water into the orange sunset. We scattered some rafting coots, and I watched a distant osprey making its way heavily home with a fish in its talons. In the car my father talked about other fishing trips we could take when he got a turn of shore duty and, ultimately, when he retired from the service altogether.

With a kind of lingering, melancholy satisfaction, I cleaned the fish when we got home. My father said that was a boy's job, and it was one that I didn't mind. When I was finished, I bathed with my last ration of energy. Before I went to bed, my father rubbed my tired shoulders and put some antiseptic on my blistered hands. After I had gone to bed, he said to my mother, but loud enough for me to hear, "Well, I found myself a new fishing partner today." I went to sleep in glory.

We flew high and wide for the next ten years, a couple of hot rods from out of Norfolk, Virginia (Virginia Beach, actually). We fished whenever the carrier was in port and the season was right. I got better at fishing and paddling and just being a companion. There is a time—paraphrasing the Preacher—to talk and a time to keep your mouth shut; and it takes a little boy some time to learn the difference. There is one way to act when you are catching most of the fish and another when your partner is. A boat is a small place when you are in it all day long, and a good part of making the day enjoyable is simply being a good companion and knowing how to act.

I learned how to be a better fisherman, too. In fact, I worked harder at it than my partner did, largely because he had other things on his mind. He was doing dangerous work to support a family and, not least in my eyes, pay for the boats and tackle and gasoline that kept us fishing. Since he was performing all those logistical functions, I took it upon myself to do the research. I became a one-man intelligence section and did the reading for both of us.

It wasn't quite the job then that it would be now. There was *Field and Stream*, which I read devotedly, especially the articles about bass fishing. I also read a little magazine on Virginia wildlife that was put out by some state agency. Every other issue, it seemed, had something on Back Bay. There were the fishing annuals, which always had some features on bass fishing and sometimes narrowed it down to fly-fishing for bass. I read them all with real dedication. Today, just the magazines devoted exclusively to bass fishing would wear a boy down.

I condensed the information from all the articles and gave my father verbal reports. If I had read about some devastating new bass bug, my father would shop around for a few and we would try them out on the next trip. I don't remember that we were ever astounded by the results. When I learned about some new technique, we would give it a try on the next trip, usually when it was my turn to fish. We actually learned some things that way. I remember somebody advising that you should add a foot or two of leader to the normal six feet when you are fishing in clear water, then let the bug lie on the water without working it at all. Bass will often hit a motionless bug in clear water when they would flee one that looks too busy.

Most lessons, though, we learned ourselves out on those flat, shallow grass beds between the islands of waving grass. We learned how to swim a bug instead of merely popping it, stripping line with a hand retrieve that seemed to work when there was a lot of bait in the water. We also learned how to work a bug very gently from pad to pad when we were casting to a clump of water lilies. We saw more than one bass come all the way out of the water to take the bug off a lily pad. We also learned that you can fish for bass with a very short line so that casting, especially in a wind, is not such a workout. And we learned that the best thing to do some days is to put up the bass bugs, tie on something small, and catch bluegills.

There were many days when we didn't see any other fly fishermen, at the dock or out on the water. Those days, in those parts, most bass were caught on large minnows, some of them almost a foot long, and heavy bait-casting gear. We always stayed with the fly rods, even when it was windy and the water was high and dirty. We could always find a lee someplace in that maze of islands, and if the water was too dark for popping bugs, we would use big, gaudy bucktails and swim them like crippled minnows.

Some days we would come back to the dock with more fish than the bait fishermen, or with fish that were at least as good as theirs. I would lift the stringer and the men would gather around on the dock to appraise our work.

"Caught 'em on those fly rods, eh?" some fellow would say.

"That's right," my father would answer.

"Youngster catch them with a fly rod too?"

"Ask him."

The man would look at me, all five feet nothing of me, and ask, "How about it, son? You catch those fish with a fly rod?"

"Yes, sir."

"How many?"

"About half of them, I guess."

"Well, isn't that something," the man would say, meaning it.

"The biggest one is his," my father would say, whether it was or not.

"I'll be damned," the man would say.

Everything comes to an end, of course. For a military family, everything comes to an end every two years or so when your father gets transferred. But we were going to Florida. The biggest bass in the world were in Florida; I knew because I had read it—many times—in *Field and Stream*. Also, every little roadside pothole was fair game for the fly rodder. You could catch big bass out of the little ditches down around Miami and the Everglades. I figured my wingman and I would mop up.

And we did, although there wasn't as much fishing as I'd hoped there would be. But we caught fish in rivers, lakes, and even in the roadside potholes of my dreams. We learned some new tactics—fishing from an inner tube and fishing at night, among them. And on one brackish-water river, we switched from artificials to bait when we were finally convinced that was the only way.

The bait to use, an old-timer told us, was shrimp. Live shrimp. He sold us some, and we hooked them with a single hook, just under the hard, sharp spine at the top of their heads. I was always sticking myself in the thumb with the hook or that spine. We slung the shrimp up against the cut banks with an underhand motion and let them run freely. Sometimes we could see the swirl where a bass would take a shrimp and head for deep water with it. It was as thrilling in its way as the oily splash of a bass taking a bug on the surface.

Several things happened, not simultaneously but close together so that they have become fused in my memory. I grew up enough to get interested in things other than fishing. My father finished out his navy career and retired. Then I went away to school. We were living in the middle of all that great bass water, but we weren't fishing much anymore. It seemed a waste.

I remember one trip, sometime before I went off to college. We went with some other men and their sons to a big lake on the Florida-Georgia line. It was late winter and still cold, or what passes for cold in Florida. We camped on the shore of the lake and got up early every morning. After eating smoky ham and eggs and drinking a couple of cups of sawmill coffee, we paired off, father and son, and climbed into our boats for a day of fishing. There were three boats of cane-pole fishermen who were after shellcrackers—a big-eared panfish— which were on the beds and taking live crickets at that time of year. There was a team of bait casters. My father and I were the only fly rodders, and I wasn't letting anyone forget it.

So, we fished, and on the first day the cane polers came back loaded. The bait casters didn't catch anything, and neither did the fly casters. That night we ate fried shellcrackers, hush puppies, tomato-and-onion salad, and more sawmill coffee. The boys were allowed to put an ounce of bourbon in with their coffee, and for most of us it was the first sanctioned drink of whiskey.

The next morning when we were leaving the dock, we saw a pair of fishermen loading their boat. They were bait casters, and their rods were rigged with plastic worms about a foot long and the color of a Concord grape. They looked like party novelties, the sort of thing you would drop down the back of a squeamish girl's dress.

"You going to fish with those?" I asked.

"That's right," one of the men said. "That worm is the hottest thing I have ever seen on bass. You ought to try 'em. Here," he said, reaching into his tackle box and coming up with a handful of the absurd plastic worms, "take you a couple and try 'em out."

"No thanks," I said, "I'm fly-fishing."

"Well, good luck to you then, son. This time of year those fish are all in deep water. I don't think you've got a chance with a fly rod."

I shrugged. I'd heard that one before. And I was sure that he had even less chance with his worms.

We all left the dock and ran off in various directions across the lake, which was still covered with a milk-white morning fog. Once we were in it, we couldn't see anything, not even the water six feet from our bow. The other boats disappeared, and the only evidence we had that they were there at all was the hollow whine of their outboards. "The worst storm I ever saw at sea didn't scare me as much as fog," my father said. "Once a storm gets started, you pretty much know what to expect—more of the same. But fog . . . you never know what might suddenly appear out of a fog. Another ship. The beach. Very frightening."

Even though the lake we were fishing was no wider than two or three miles at the waist, I felt I knew what he was talking about. And I wondered if he missed ships and the sea and, especially, airplanes now that he was retired. Probably he did. But he never mentioned it.

The morning sun eventually burned off the fog, and we worked the likely-looking shorelines using everything we had learned in six or seven years of doing this together. We barely broke for lunch, taking our ham sandwiches and hot tea on the run. We tried the mouths of the creeks and the steep drops near points of land. We fished in the stumps and on the packed shallow bottoms. Except for a couple of big bluegills, we came up empty.

The man who had wanted to give me the plastic worms and his partner were already at the dock when we got there. They had a long stringer of big fish, one of which must have weighed seven pounds. "I told you, son," the man said cheerfully. "Did you do any good with that buggy whip of yours?"

I told him that I hadn't.

"Don't feel bad. This ain't the time of year, and it ain't really the water neither. You got to fish where they are, and in a place like this they're deep—over the old roadbeds and brush piles."

He explained the rudiments of how he fished and offered to lead us to a couple of good spots in the morning. Of course, we would have to fish the plastic worms, and of course we did, using borrowed equipment. And, of course, we caught fish.

That was the last day of the trip, and in the car on the way home that night my father said, "Well, hell, I'd always rather catch fish than not. But that is the least interesting way to catch fish I have ever seen."

I agreed. It was all deep water, slow retrieve, and half the time when I struck at what I though was a fish, I had buried my hook in an old submerged hickory tree. It had its refinements and its own skills. But everything does. It was to fly-fishing what flying for the airlines would be to landing hot jets on aircraft carriers. It was ponderous fishing, and we were deft fishermen, a pair of hot rods who had caught fish all over the state and in Virginia besides. We cared about the form more than the numbers.

I lost my partner in a cruel way. A telegram came saying that he had cancer. I was at Marine Corps officers' training at Quantico, Virginia. (If the son of a navy man truly wants to rebel, he becomes a Marine.) We were graduating in three days, and I waited to fly home. My father and I talked once before he went into surgery. He was never the same afterward and died less than four months later.

The last time we went fishing together was just before I left for Quantico. I was full of talk about Vietnam, which was drawing young men like me with a kind of gravitational inevitability. He was telling me to watch myself and not be so eager to get into something I didn't know anything about. He had flown close support at Tarawa, and he knew a lot I didn't know about what happens to Marines at war. I listened about as much as any cocky young stud in history ever has, which is damned little.

We did OK that day, caught four or five nice fish on popping bugs. My father took the last one from an old crooked cypress stump. He made a false cast or two while I held the boat steady with a cross draw on the paddle. The little frog-colored bug dropped four inches from the old bleached stump, the ripples working themselves out across the water and dying like a breeze. My father tensed a little and put a twitch down the line that traveled to the bug and made it kick just so. The water erupted, and we yelled "All right!" simultaneously. The fish came out of the water in an angry, head-shaking jump, and . . . I shall never in my life forget that moment or that day.

Richard La Barre Goodwin, *Small-Mouth Bass* (ca. 1900).

William J. Schaldach, *Leaping Tarpon* (ca. 1930).

SALTIER TALES:
Along the Shoreline, Lightly Armed
By Charles F. Waterman

T HE OLD HOUSEBOAT is certainly gone now, either broken up for kindling or nearly rotted away at some backwoods dock. It had always leaked anyway, its plywood hulk an affront to marine architecture.

We lived on it long ago where the mangrove swamp joins the freshwater Everglades to the Gulf of Mexico, thirty miles from the closest marina, where a passing boat was a rarity. It was near what was a nameless channel then, a marked and busy route now.

At night in the tiny protected bay we could feel a gentle rise and fall with a passing tarpon's wake or, contentedly half-conscious in our bunks, listen to the wheezing sigh of a curious porpoise. Nearly always there would be the endless assertions of a chuck-will's-widow atop a nearby buttonwood tree; the pistol shot of a snook taking a mullet against the far shore; the skiff bobbing at its tether and nudging the bigger boat's side with a gentle thump.

"This is a good place," my wife said.

Estuaries and their marshes, the most fertile of the world's waters, are the nurseries of the sea, sometimes wild but ever fragile in their balance, and none is more dramatic or has had a more profound influence than the Everglades. South Florida is an estuary, the broad and shallow river of grass flowing through the great cypresses, then the mangroves, and on to the gently shelving Gulf bottom and the bright flats of the Florida Keys. The salt and fresh water mix, the mixture changing constantly with rainfall, wind, and tide. So does the aquatic population change.

All such estuaries and their marshes have risen from the status of wastelands and useless swamps to that of recognized monitors of the sea's welfare, and the angler of a distant shore benefits from a marsh he has never heard of. A tiny bonefish found off Canada has little effect on the year's salmon run, but it marks a link in the food chain, which, after all, is endless. Environmentalists become poetic about estuaries, although many once regarded the term *brackish* as an indication of some sort of impurity.

It is here that no angler is more obsessed than the inlander who discovers the narrow frontier of mangrove country, a brackish mystery that belts the world at these latitudes—part land and part water, with its own wild residents and constant visitors from both land and sea. The black-tipped shark meets largemouth bass from some prairie pothole; a giant sawfish weaves his awkward way along a narrow creek, seeming puzzled that he has wandered so far from the swells of the open Gulf.

To a fisherman, the mangrove country is a paradox of tiny streams and placid bays producing fish that seem out of scale with their surroundings. By squinting his eyes a little he can turn a narrow tidal creek into a trout stream, but when his fly is taken by a hundred-pound tarpon instead of a nine-inch trout, he loses his perspective on the whole thing in a sort of crashing illogic. It doesn't cool his ardor for the nine-inch trout, but he finds it hard to describe.

After I experienced the backcountry fish, I had a passion for showing them to others. It is the tarpon that makes the most dramatic show, and I recall the old freshwater friend I took by outboard into a creek near Broad River. Captain Ted Smallwood, Bunyanesque dean of Everglades guides, had told me of the place, and the time and tide that would find the fish, fifty miles from a dock through mangrove rivers, passes, and bays.

Some of the bays are a mile wide and some of the creeks less than twenty feet wide on the way to Broad River. In the bays there are likely to be little rafts of bluebills that rise ahead of the skiff and peel swiftly to one side or the other, generally coming back to rest behind the wake. As the boat drops to an idle in a crooked, narrow creek, there may be big unseen fish or a porpoise pushing silent swells ahead of it. At the creek mouths you watch for manatees. A collision could be dangerous.

My friend and I welcomed cobwebs in one narrows, a sure sign that no one was ahead of us. We came to the mouth of the nameless creek at the right tide. We had felt lonely during the last crooked twenty miles; there were no channel markers then. It was so quiet under the loose canopy of mangroves and buttonwoods (really a kind of mangrove too, but named separately in the swamps) that it was a "trout stream scene." An anhinga plunged from a limb overhead, croaking

Stanley Meltzoff, *Snook Belize* (1968).

John P. Cowan, *Thin Gin* (1978).

in outrage at our invasion, into the black water.

The tarpon were here, a school of them, and they were big fish, large for so small a creek. We approached with careful oars; they were rolling with gurgles and sighing breaths.

They competed wildly for anything we offered. They leaped thunderously, smashing into the mangrove branches, crashing back into the creek, drenching us with brackish water. Within minutes the shallow creek bottom had been stirred, and we seemed afloat on swirling creamed coffee. We broke leaders and landed no fish. Finally a hooked giant leaped above us over the stern of the skiff, gill covers clanking, trailing a gout of muddy water. Its huge scales gleamed in a streak of sunlight. I stared at the ten-foot-wide foamy splash where the fish had disappeared and started the motor without comment. We did not belong here.

Tarpon fishing in the mangroves has its special problems, different from those of deepwater fishing or those of fishing in the offshore flats. The fish are no bigger than they are at sea, but when one weighing more than a hundred pounds has learned a few acres of creek, oyster bar, bay, and root tangle, the record-seeking fisherman becomes a worried soul. Whoever handles the boat must make decisions.

The Miami Metropolitan Fishing Tournament offers no cash prizes. Still, devotees come year after year to spend time and money in pursuit of winning catches. The fly-rod tarpon class is especially ardent. The winner, which must be well over a hundred pounds, almost invariably comes from the Keys flats or duplicate waters nearby. Only once, as far as I know, has the winner come from the mangrove country.

I tried it once, after weeks of predawn runs to fishing grounds, more than fifty miles from a dock, marked on a chart by the aforementioned Captain Smallwood. I came nowhere near a competitive entry, but I can still see the potential winners leaping above my head and feel the slack line as leaders snapped, the fish swimming up creeks, around points, or under mangrove branches—or simply taking advantage of my flustered ineptitude. After I gave up, I was almost haggard. The largest fish I had landed weighed less than one hundred pounds. My favorite fishing region had begun to seem uncooperative.

The southern Florida mix of sea and fresh water is among America's most dynamic. Society's use of fresh water upstream has changed the Everglades and allowed more and more intrusion of salinity as the drained land has been turned into truck farms, cattle ranches, housing developments, and pastel cities. Thus the mangrove belt grows wider, the groping roots coming farther inland during dry seasons, while rainwater is shunted off through canals in the name of flood control. During drought the mucklands of the inland glades burn like peat, and the smell of smoke and flecks of ash reach far offshore.

The mangrove community is made of trees that build their own unstable, shivery land. Mangrove bulbs float with the tides until their tentacle roots can find a little purchase, and when they become anchored "bushes," they reach out for sustenance from either water or mud to make an interlaced, spidery network, eerily depressing to those who do not love it, especially in half-light.

Mangrove swamps, with their labyrinth of waterways and their predaceous insects, have been unattractive to both the landsman and the deepwater sailor and have hosted a strange assortment of societies. On the Florida coast were mysterious Indian tribes before the Seminoles, pirates, and then the blockade runners of the Civil War. There were fugitive murderers, the rumrunners, and the draft dodgers from World War II, and one can commune with their ghosts at dusk on a leaky houseboat in a nameless bay.

Today there are the dope runners and the agents looking for them, and things have changed because of the millions of small boats Americans have bought for pleasure. The National Park Service and other agencies have marked the inland boat trails across the places we once navigated with pride because not everyone knew the way. But leave the staked channel, and in seconds the creek can narrow and darken, the cobwebs glisten in streaks of sun, and somewhere ahead may be a widened place where no one has cast a fly for months. There was the time we rounded the river bend and saw a panther, his clan almost gone from the glades now, sitting tall like a proud house cat atop the remains of an old cistern. That little plot of high ground had once been occupied by settlers, but the bushes have reclaimed it.

The mangrove country is no longer as remote as it once was, but it is still an outlaw land. I held the boat just off a little mangrove point five miles from the Gulf, and my wife Debie cast the white-and-red streamer to where there was a pocket in the facade of roots groping into dark water, roots that showed a reddish tint from the sun, almost down now. The distant gunfire began then, dull booms deadened by miles of mangroves, measured shooting that has echoed through the swamps for all these years, ever since the plume hunters of a dying century slaughtered birds for New York ladies' hats. We paused in our fishing to listen to the familiar, depressing sound. The plumes are no longer sold, but outlaw gunners still "shoot the roosts" in their own defiant tradition and serve the curved-bill curlews for Sunday dinner.

But protection has caused an increase in the number of curlews (white ibises), and when they travel toward the rookeries in the evening, they go in little flocks, often following the creeks to keep below treetops and avoid the wind. They come with a soft rush of wings and flare at the sight of intent fishermen in a drifting boat.

The fisherman's main attraction here is the snook, one of the world's great fly fish that is found in much of the mangrove belt. Its name does not fit its image. In this it is kin to the mutton snapper, reel wrecker of the Keys flats. *Mutton snapper* sounds like something to be hoisted aboard a party boat with a handline. *Snook* sounds like some kind of joke; its Spanish name, *robalo,* has not caught on.

In early summer the big migrating snook come in from deep water or up from the south, or both, and leave their eggs in the offshore passes; at other times the occasional fisherman simply says, "The snook aren't running." But there are resident snook all year in the backcountry, powerful, olive-hued fish that know their home and, unlike the tarpon, make deliberate runs for the mangrove roots or the sunken logs. It is true that the "inside" snook don't average as large as the silvery "outside" snook of the passes, outer islands, fishing piers, and highway bridges, but fishing for them is somewhat of a magnification of fishing a shoreline for black bass.

The fly, popping bug, or bait-casting lure is cast as close as possible to the edges, a matter of inches, and the fly caster may overline his rod to gain efficiency in the short throws. The heavier line makes the rod work and slaps the lure in the chosen size—a four-inch streamer in bucktail or feathers, or a three-inch popping bug.

Hooked in the open or in strange territory, the snook is just another game fish that makes short runs and occasional violent jumps. But when he comes for a fly from beneath the shade of mangrove roots, he comes with the intent of returning with his prize. He takes it in a surly swirl or an explosive pop or both, and it is in those seconds that he somehow calls upon more power than anything else near his size.

You set the hook hard, but it isn't really necessary, for the snook's mouth is not armored. Once hooked, he may even run along the shore for a short distance, but when he turns in his slant for the undercut beneath the roots, he is incredibly hard to stop, breaking lines and leaders with a strength that seems overpowering for a seven-pound fish.

And seven pounds is the terrorizing size for simple but seldom considered reasons. A seven-pound fish has the thrust to bring your rod tip down (giving line if the take is close to the roots is usually fatal), and he is small enough to have quarters far back under the bank. The bigger fish, although he squalls the reel in the open, must find a bigger hole, and it seems he is more likely to be a traveler with skimpy knowledge of local fortresses.

If you are at the oars, you head for open water when your fisherman strikes, and if you have an electric motor you test it. If you have time, you can get the main power plant started, but time is what you seldom have. At such moments there is a customary quotation, so routine that it is classified along with "Set!" by a quarterback or "Pull!" by a trapshooter. The words are:

"Keep him out of the bushes!"

This is much like a man struggling with a stuck umbrella and announcing, "It's beginning to rain!"

But I use the order as everyone else does, and when I said it one day as I labored at the oars, my friend Jim Henely turned to me, his snapped line draped about his shoulders and the mangrove roots still waving along the route of the departing snook.

"Don't just say that!" Jim grumbled. "Point at the damned mangroves! Point!"

The snook has no noticeable teeth, but he has some honed gill covers that can shear lines or leaders. The shock tippet isn't for shock at all but is a heavy section to resist cutting, generally of monofilament.

After several break-offs even the veteran angler becomes a bit gun-shy. Henely once met several aggressive fish along a short piece of mangrove shoreline and then found the boat drifting past a narrow indentation that obviously contained sunken snags. He cast gingerly two feet outside the little gap. Then he flipped a little closer. Nothing. The obvious next move was a cast right into the hole. Jim appraised it and said nervously, "You don't suppose he thinks I don't know he's in there, do you?"

Until recent years, many believed that both snook and tarpon spawned in the shallows of the backcountry, simply because when very small specimens were found they were invariably far back from open water. But in these cases at least, it appears the mangrove belt is a nursery rather than a hatchery. Both tarpon and snook are now believed to do most of their spawning at sea or in the open passes. It is the juveniles that come ashore—or almost ashore—to make their early growth.

Fluctuations in the populations of saltwater fish are observed over such long periods (several human generations have sometimes passed between peaks of coastal populations of bluefish and striped bass) that the trend in the Everglades is hard to follow, but generally it has seemed to be downward, despite periods of recovery.

At the inland beginnings of the tidal rivers along the Gulf coast there are times when the overlap of salt and fresh water can be observed in capsule form. It happens only when a chain of circumstances is linked just so.

Give the saw-grass prairies good rainfall for two or three years, coming gradually so that there is not too much human meddling. The marshes have their water and the alligator holes are full. The black bass thrive, and there are bluegills and other sunfish as their prey.

Chet Reneson, *On the Flats* (1976).

Stanley Meltzoff, *Tarpon Daisy Chain* (1968).

Then the rains stop and drought begins. The shallow grass prairies begin to dry up, and the bass move down to the gator holes and on to the heads of the rivers, where the water has a taste of salt but is still mostly fresh. Down there the mangrove trees are little more than bushes, following the narrow rivers up toward the grass and the cypress stands where the sky is huge, decorated by high, dry-weather clouds and the jet contrails that converge toward Miami.

The bass are displaced and they go farther down where there is a distinct tidal effect, and there they are met by saltwater residents that have somehow followed the seawater up from the Gulf. I have seen it four times, this fishing carnival, formed from a series of meshing weather events.

Row silently up the ever narrowing watercourse where the freshwater grasses have been growing. There are more birds than there were farther down—herons, egrets, and fidgety coots arguing in the shallow sections where the grass is clogged.

A black bass strikes in the shade of a tree, and your streamer is taken on the next cast, but you suspect it is not the fish you saw strike at first, for there are several subtle water movements in the blot of shade. The fish is fat and a glistening green, completely different from the dark fish found in the tannic stained water of the region. A saw-grass bass.

You find yourself fishing for bass and are completely surprised when a fifty-pound tarpon smashes at the same lure that drew the attention of a six-inch bluegill a moment earlier. In a deep, clear spot you see a black-tipped shark under the boat, and there will be spotted weakfish, channel bass, and snook, all gathered at the river's head to feed on what has come down from the freshwater marshes.

But as an angler's paradise it is temporary, filled with foreboding. If the drought continues, the saltwater fish will destroy most of the bass and the water will finally become so salty the others will die, unless new rain takes them back to the alligator holes and marshy ponds with their cattails, rushes, and lily pads. Because so much water has been diverted by dams and canals, that has not happened much lately.

The story is much the same all along the western mangrove coast on the Gulf side, and the conditions are most pronounced in Everglades National Park, which is a wild oasis free of development, even though the boat channels have been marked.

To the south of the park the mixing effect is similar, although the scene is different. There is Florida Bay between the mainland and the Florida Keys proper. The bay has had varied fishing fortunes, but in spring, if you can find them, there are big tarpon in a true flats area where the master fisherman can show them streamers with all the perfection of rod, knots, approach, and casting developed in twenty years of tournaments.

The fast backcountry skiff crossing the bay between the mainland and the Keys begins to seem a little out of place. This is not an ocean, but it is so broad and featureless that, as one guide says, "I seem to be going over a big, continuous curve"—which he is—"and I'm surprised when I see my landmarks."

The occasional tiny islands and the annoying shoals seem to add to the expanse rather than reduce it. When you look back and see your progress traced by a lingering streak of mud across the flats, you become uncomfortable in the thought that you may have misjudged tide or route or both.

The newcomer to the flats sees first the horizontal shimmer and the varied colors of different depths and bottoms, from white sand to dark turtle grass. It is minutes later that he begins to see the bottom itself and a hint of its varied life. It is hours later that he begins to see the true detail as he looks through the water instead of at it. It is days later that he begins to pick out the broad but gentle disturbance on the surface caused by what moves near the bottom. It is probably weeks later that he begins to see that a school of tiny fish makes a delicate riffle and that even less noticeable "nervous water" can mean a hundred pounds of tarpon. He analyzes movements and wonders whether he really sees them or feels them with some new instinct.

And finally, the flats veteran knows a panorama of life in bits and pieces of lights and shadows, automatically converting visual hints into fish that now appear plainly in his view. Now he cannot understand why the newcomer sees only shimmers of blues and greens and blotches of sand and grass bottoms.

The Keys themselves are not remote, although there are broad expanses of flats seldom visited. There the mangroves are generally smaller and the water saltier than in the Everglades backcountry. The tarpon sought on the flats are easier to play than those of the mangrove pockets, but they tend to be moving fish, and a successful guide must know a great many holding spots and a great many routes, for the fish come in and out for a list of seasonal, tidal, and weather reasons.

Fishermen come from around the world to try the tarpon, not because there are none elsewhere, but because the flats fish are special, seemingly made for the streamer caster. The task force changes, and the fast flats boat with its big outboard, its fiberglass push pole, and its casting deck now has the poling platform above its stern, a working crow's nest for the man with the pole. But the treasured skill of those who can head off moving fish is being sullied by a new advance, the powerful electric motor, and one guide stands atop his perch not only with his push pole but with two-foot switches that control twin electric motors.

The tarpon (the beast) is sometimes compared with the Atlantic salmon (the beauty)—I believe Mark Sosin first used those terms—for some of the skills of fishing for them are the same. Of course the games are so different that neither fish suffers from the comparison, and a big tarpon taking a fly in clear, shallow water is never really what the newcomer expects.

The sudden caldron of a big tarpon's turning strike is a wider swirl than anyone can anticipate, but it is other things that surprise. There is the school of slow-moving or motionless big fish, amost invisible in four feet of wind-riffled water only a few yards away, seen as bits and pieces, shades of gray moving in an underwater mirage of shifting light that shows uncertainly a fin or a section of scales to staring eyes—vagrant and unsure shadows.

Then, when the fish turns to follow the nervously stripped streamer, there is its bulging series of swirls on the surface with perhaps a fin breaking now and then. And there is the sudden great dark spot that appears in back of the fly when the fish is hard to make out otherwise. The dark spot is the inside of the fish's mouth, and when it appears, there is a nervous urge to strike too soon—before the fish has taken and turned so that the streamer will be pulled into a corner of its jaw.

Tarpon fishing should not be compared with salmon fishing. There are no sighing pine trees, no roaring rapids, and the flies are not the delicate structures with colorful names that mysteriously attract a fish that is not supposed to feed at all. But there are the palm islands floating in haze, and there are the unfolding miracles of the shallow bottom with its coral and other living inhabitants.

But the flats also belong to the bonefish, a quarry more subtle than the tarpon, and fishing for it is a little less of the circus, but just as much of the hunt, if on a somewhat smaller scale. Bonefish affect fly fishermen in a sequence of attitudes. At first there is the novelty of a fish that takes a small fly in inches of water and runs for more than a hundred yards. Usually the first bonefish is the result of experienced guiding. Then the fisherman may fish for tarpon or permit or a hundred other saltwater varieties, and he probably takes a trip to some Caribbean resort where bonefish catches are counted by dozens. Then there comes a time when he wants to find the big fish of the Keys, learned fish that have watched thousands of boats and as many fishermen, and he wants to stalk them on his own and memorize their movements with the tide.

There is a shallow point in the flats that faces southward toward the open sea, guarding bays that are almost out of water at low tide. The breakers there are miniatures, because the point is protected by a row of reefs that reduce the swells to impotency. The heavy upper Keys bonefish, subtly tinted gray cigars of power, go around very close to the point as they move up the coast during lower tides. At low tide the bay flats come alive with bonefish food that is hidden when the water is deeper. There is a constant crackle of newly exposed shoreline barnacles, and crabs and tiny fish are busy on the shallow bottom. The fisherman, his boat anchored at the point, wades out so that the light is right.

A cruising bonefish can be there suddenly, the way a motionless deer suddenly appears in a forest, as if flashed onto a screen, and the fisherman often wonders where he came from. He looks for moving fish, and experience has taught him which way they will be going, but in the scant inches of shallows near the low mangrove shoreline he is likely to see a tailer, a preoccupied fish that is working the bottom industriously, possibly tipping up in more than a foot of water, but also possibly wallowing at a depth that does not quite cover him.

For the tailing fish there is a stalk and a careful cast, or several casts, to get the fly just close enough but not too close; the bonefish can be remarkably watchful, but sometimes remarkably naive if the stalk has been careful enough. Close to shore the scene suddenly becomes memorable—the gleaming shaft of the fish's tail above water, quivering like some newfangled antenna attuned to food or danger. In the background are the lumpy coral shoreline and its border of scattered flotsam—the lost crab-trap float and the battered vegetable crate from some offshore freighter. And perhaps there is the haunting hoot of a white-crowned fruit pigeon.

If the fish takes and goes toward deep water, the slack line is drawn up in a heart-stopping swish, and if it does not catch upon the thousand things a swinging loop looks for, the fish is on the crying reel and leaves a boiling streak of mud and sand pointing toward the open sea.

If the fish breaks off or roots loose in sea fans or seaweed in water almost too deep to wade, a fisherman begins to crank in his backing, still shaking, and as he watches his line come in from out past the miniature breakers, he sees a hazy freighter and its smudge of smoke at the edge of the world where two shades of blue meet.

The freighter moves in deep water with marlin and dolphin on a sea that is a mix of the world's rains and snows, but it is dependent upon a gently moving river that flows across the grasslands and the marshes and the shining flats—a dependency we still do not fully understand.

Some of the water the freighter uses comes down through the mangroves, through the interlaced creeks and the shallow bays. It runs past where the old houseboat was anchored. By day there is the sound of boats as they pass close by on their way to Alligator Bay. At night it is much as it was before, when the gentle tidal current gurgled a little against the old houseboat's hull.

Francis Golden, *Tarpon* (1975).

Lyne Bogue Hunt, *Tarpon* (ca. 1930).

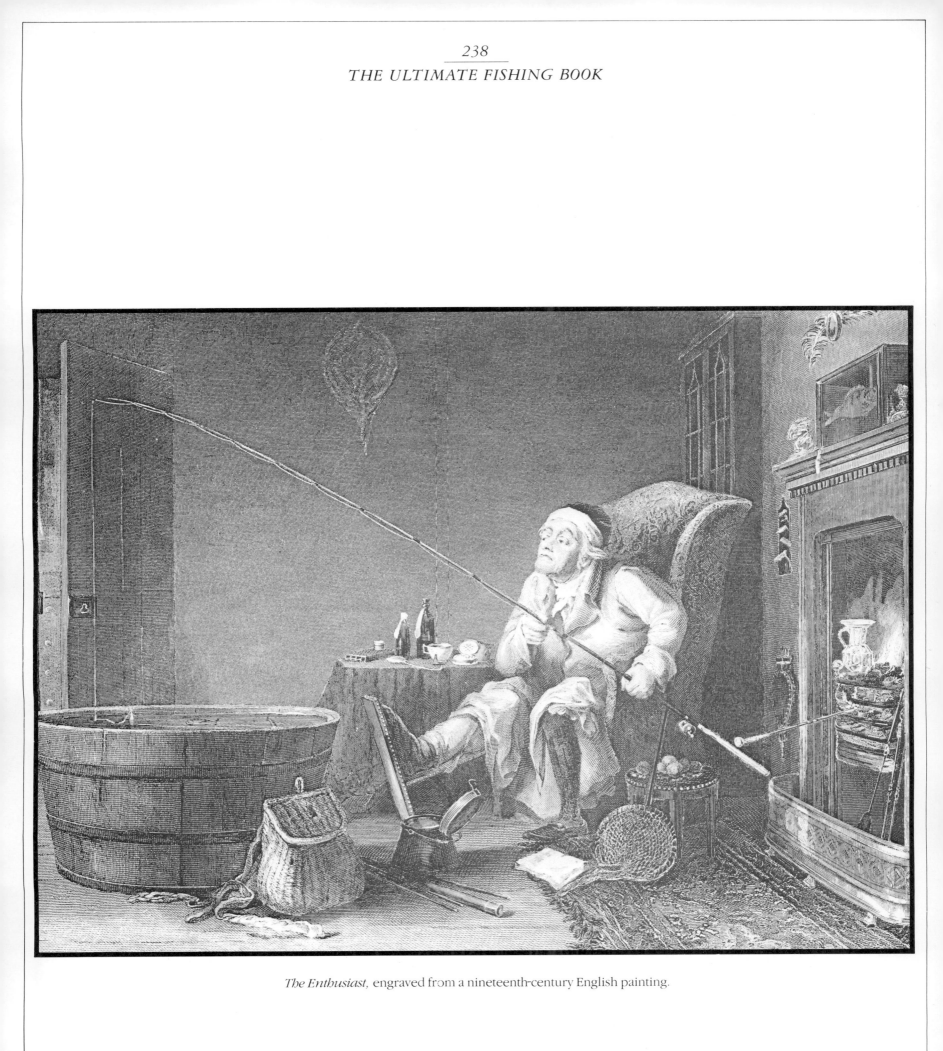

The Enthusiast, engraved from a nineteenth-century English painting.

NIGHT SCHEMES:
Getting Through Winter
By Christopher Lehmann-Haupt

NE OF THE most enticing stretches of water I know is the stream that runs behind my house. It meanders out of a copse to the east; pauses to punctuate itself with a series of shallow, circular pools; then cascades between two angular boulders into a broad oval pond whose sandy floor is so gently inclined that a fisherman might stand at its center and strike the hours of the clock with his casts. At the foot of this pool, the water ripples over the pebbly bottom, gathers speed, and rushes down a bouldered chute into a long, placid run along whose banks the foliage sprawls languidly, trailing its green tresses over dark, trouty caverns below. Next a grassy island rises up to divide the stream into two bubbling parentheses, whose feet contend in crazy crosscurrents that defy the floating of a drag-free fly. Then a footbridge casts its shadow where the currents compromise and agree to race ahead, tumbling and rolling in unison down mossy steps, then easing around a gradual bend that ends where a slab of rock thrusts out and drops the water sighing into the tumult of froth below.

Just below this lies my favorite pool, its surface smooth as poured glass, its mysterious depths alive with the promise of big fish. Whenever I look at this run, I see myself wading beside the brush that entangles its banks and dragging forth a dinghy that holds my rod, my fishing vest, and a small picnic basket. When the boat is free of the bank, I leap aboard it, catch my balance, set the oars to their locks, and row softly upstream until I get as close to the waterfall as I dare. Then I drift slowly down the middle of the run, working the pockets along the shore with silent sixty-foot casts, until giant boulders obstruct my way and my stream goes boiling toward the river below.

I often dream of doing this, especially in winter when the snow along the banks absorbs the light and seems to turn the water inky black. And I would, but for an insurmountable problem. Though it has all the contours of a classic river, the stream that runs behind my house in the Bronx is only sixty feet long from copse to waterfall, with an average width of maybe fourteen inches. I was once encouraged to think of it in grander terms when a Chicago firm expressed reluctance to insure the title of ownership on my house on the ground that the house stood hard by a right-of-way. But in truth it's a mere rivulet. Moreover, the apartment houses upstream from us have so polluted it with oil and detergents that not even a tough city trout, if there were such a thing, could survive in it for more than a few minutes.

Still, my stream looks enough like the real thing to provide me food for fantasy. So I pace its shores like Lemuel Gulliver in Lilliput. Just above the island, the water reminds me of the famous Ledge Pool of the Brodheads River in Henryville, Pennsylvania. So, hoping that none of the neighbors will catch me staring in a trance at my little stream, I visualize a fisherman six inches high, set him down in the murmuring current, and re-create the summer years ago at Henryville when I hooked my biggest trout.

I imagine it is just after sundown again. Gone is the golden light that minutes earlier turned the water bronze and made a hatch of caddis flies seem an inverted snowstorm. Having been skunked all evening—because the fish in their perverse way have been ignoring the hatching caddises and feeding on something beneath the water's surface—the little fisherman has given up hope of catching anything and is practicing roll casts. Just practicing. But he finds pleasure in it, because the night air is soft and caressing, the sudden hush of the forest is peaceful, and the powers that control such matters have decreed that the fisherman shall achieve competence. In short, it is one of those rare moments when everything he does is graceful and right. His line has stopped wrapping itself around his rod tip on every second cast. As far as he can tell in the swiftly gathering darkness, his leader is uncoiling its full length instead of collapsing on itself in a snarl. His arm is moving effortlessly, and he isn't tripping over every submerged boulder he encounters. He's at one with himself, his equipment, and nature. The taking of fish has become irrelevant.

And then, as if he were being rewarded for his indifference, he hears a heavy splash out there where he has just thrown his fly. Can it possibly be? Before the words have formed in his mind, he twitches his rod back and . . . no, he has snared his

A fly tier's bench.

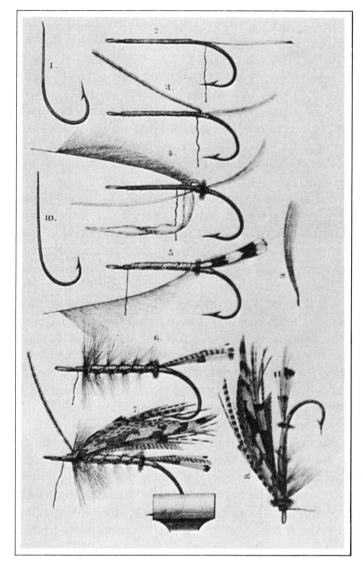

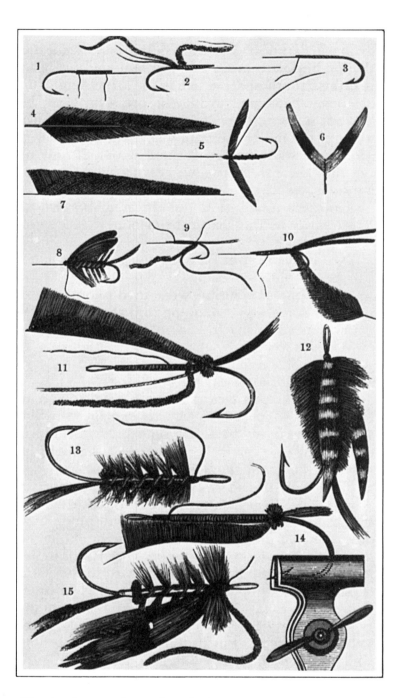

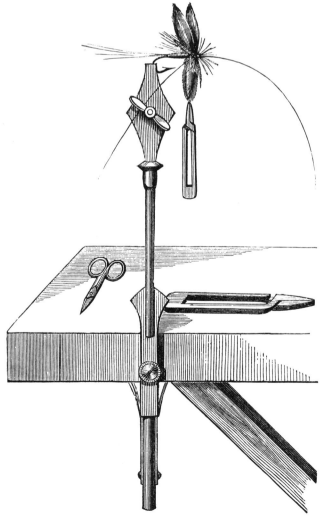

Fly tying has not changed much since
these step-by-step illustrations appeared
in *A Book on Angling* (1867) by Francis Francis,
Fishing in American Waters by Genio C. Scott (1869),
and *Ogden On Fly Tying* (1887).

line on an underwater log or boulder, for there is nothing of the telltale electric spasm that lets you know when you are onto a fish. Damn it; he will have to wade out to midstream and grope blindly in the water. Or break off his leader and call it a night, since he'll never be able to tie on another fly in the darkness. But then slowly and inexorably the log begins to move downstream, and his heart is in his mouth and his hands are trembling. This has never happened to him before. Oh, God, let him not screw up. The thing is heading for the fast water at the tail of the pool where the current will add to the strain on the delicate tippet. If only he can turn the fish before he gets to the fast water by the island.

"Good evening," calls out the neighbor whose house is across the stream from mine. "Have you seen our dog?"

"No, I haven't. But I'll keep an eye out for her."

"Little cool this evening."

"I was just wondering what to do about these soapsuds somebody's draining into the brook."

"You mean it isn't frozen yet?"

"It never freezes."

"Well, don't catch cold now."

"Thanks. I'll look out for your dog."

The look on his face must be a suspicious one, for there's no plausible way to explain why I'm sitting alone in my backyard on a snowy evening.

But how else is a fisherman to get through the winter if not with the sustenance of dreams such as mine? The dream is everything in the sport of fishing. You dream with every cast of your fly that the shadowy form will finally rise to your lure. You dream as you drop off to sleep at night about the lunker that got loose just as you were about to net it. As Jim Deren, the presiding wizard of the Manhattan tackle shop Angler's Roost, has written: "There don't have to be a thousand fish in the river. Let me locate a single good one and I'll get a thousand dreams out of him before I catch him. And if I catch him I'll let him go." You dream most of all when you are far away from fishing; so winter is the best time for dreaming.

Of course there are fishermen who refuse to put up with the inactivity required for dreaming. Those who can afford it simply go to where it's summer in the winter: to New Zealand, where unspeakably huge fish are apparently waiting in every puddle; or to Tierra del Fuego, at the lower tip of South America. Others, who can't afford or haven't the time to fly halfway around the world, resort to mooning over their favorite pools, even when the snow is piled a foot deep along their banks. One member of a private fishing club—let us call him the Demon Angler—took to pacing the banks of his most beloved stream whenever his legal practice allowed him to get away. One warm December day the Demon Angler encountered the club's caretaker making his rounds through the woods.

They fell into conversation—about fishing, naturally enough—and the caretaker said he had observed a curious thing. On warm winter days, the fish appeared to be feeding on the surface just as actively as they did in the summer. In fact, just this past Christmas Day, which happened to be unseasonably warm, as the weatherman says, he had tried casting a fly—purely by way of experiment, mind you—and damned if the fish hadn't hit it! Good ones, too.

That so! said the Demon Angler. Purely in the interest of science, what sort of fly was it they happened to hit? Well, said the caretaker, a stone fly, a small stone fly. Smaller, that is, than the ones you see in March and April. I'll be damned, said the Demon Angler, and went straight home, tied up a batch of small stone flies—Off-season Stone Flies, he immediately named them—and returned to the stream to see if what the caretaker had told him was true. It was, and the Demon Angler continued to experiment until he was caught by the local warden and reported to the other members of the club, who gently hinted that the Demon Angler had better cease and desist. The depth of his passion for fishing can be measured by the fact that he told this story without a trace of shame.

Others seek fellowship—or good works—in the wintertime. They join the Fly Fisherman's Club, the American League of Anglers, the Federation of Fly Fishermen, the Theodore Gordon Flyfishers, Trout Unlimited, the Fly Tiers Society of Upper Saddle River, New Jersey. I picture the jolly members of the Anglers' Club of New York collected around the fireplace in their quarters above the Fraunces Tavern in lower Manhattan—prosperous-looking men in soft Scottish tweeds and ties monogrammed with leaping trout, regaling each other in the arch language of fishing; proposing toasts to the carbuncled judge who slipped and submerged himself in the West Branch of the Neversink last summer; dipping their heads for a moment of silence in memory of the gaunt stockbroker who passed away this fall and whose ashes were scattered over the Home Pool of the Beaverkill he loved so well. This Dickensian scene must be reflected in ten thousand sportsmen's clubs across America—in Laconia, New Hampshire, where grizzled dairymen and gas-pump attendants in forest-green coveralls gather in the back room of the VFW hall to get peacefully sozzled over memories of the time Walter Nutley's Myrtle hooked a seven-pound rainbow in the Winnipesaukee River and was dragged downstream all the way to Tilton before she triumphantly beached the monster, which now hangs above the counter in the Nutleys' kitchen, a permanent, glass-eyed reproach to Walter's sense of male superiority; or in Red Oak, Michigan, where at every monthly meeting of the Oscoda County sportsmen's club, Fred Enderby eventually falls to muttering over the evening

Louis Rhead, *A Christmas Garland* (ca. 1900).

twenty years ago when he spent a full half hour fighting something in the deep water below Foote Dam on the Au Sable River, only to land a water-logged Styrofoam mattress.

I salute them—those men in groups—especially the ones who band together to preserve the noble trout by legislating no-kill waters, where you have to put back everything you catch; by fighting the tract developers and power authorities who view all bodies of water as parts of a vast sewage system; or by studying ways to breed a trout so tough and canny that it might conceivably even survive in the stream that flows behind my house. I salute their fraternity. But the pleasure of fly-fishing for me lies in its solitude—the chance it provides to lose oneself in nature. I grant that I've spent happy interludes fishing within fifty feet of a companion and sharing observations of what flies seem to be hatching and where the fish are feeding. And I particularly relish memories of passing a flask back and forth at streamside after sundown. But fishing means solitude to me. So anything I do about fishing in the winter also should be done alone. Besides, if I had ever joined a fishing club or gotten otherwise communally involved with the sport, I would never have had a chance to try the Master Plan.

Not everyone who fishes needs the Master Plan. The members of the sportsmen's clubs certainly don't need it. They tend to be practical. If you were to ask one of them how to prepare for Opening Day, he would think for only a moment before telling you how to get your equipment squared away. Check your waders for leaks by putting them on and lowering yourself into a filled bathtub. (You might want to wait until your family is out of the house before you do this.) Patch any holes that show up, no matter how tiny they may seem. Replace the felt on the soles if it's worked itself loose or worn away. Be sure your flies are in shape. Boil up a kettle of water and hold your used ones in the jet of steam with a pair of tweezers. You'll be surprised how even the most bedraggled ones spring back to life. Tie up some new ones in whatever patterns and sizes you're running low on. Good way to pass a winter evening. You need only about fifteen basic patterns—what they are depends on where you fish—but you ought to have plenty of what you do use, and in a wide range of sizes. Check the guide windings of your rods to be sure they haven't started to fray. Rewind them and lacquer them if they have. Push your hand into your net to test it for rot. Oil your reels. Tie up a big supply of leaders with a good variety of tippets. Make sure there's fly floatant and insect repellent in the pockets of your vest. Put fresh batteries in your night-light. That ought to do it. An evening's work. A couple if you tie your own flies. Plenty of time left over for reading or shooting the breeze.

Oh, you run into the occasional fanatic among these citizens—the fellow who ransacks old attics for discarded women's hats decorated with dyed swan flanks or the brilliant waxy feathers of the blue chatterer (especially good for salmon flies). Or the man who insists on raising his own blue-dun hens. And there are people who faithfully keep streamside diaries and pore over them on winter evenings, not so much to recapture past joys as to see if nature is sending any messages they haven't yet deciphered. But even the most zealous among these folk would never waste his time with the Master Plan.

It came to me as a consequence of meeting the Master Fisherman. We sat together by a stream during an hour of the afternoon when the fish didn't seem to be doing very much . . . according to him. (According to me, they are *never* doing very much.) He announced that it was a transitional time of day between terrestrials and the first evening hatches. I said if he said so, it was good enough for me. We stared at the stream for a while. I saw water and trees and bushes and shrubbery. He saw a geological formation whose principal components were sandstone and slate, cut through by a flat streambed, along whose banks grew hemlocks, alders, willows, oaks, sycamores, rhododendrons, laurels, early violets, white adder's-tongues, wild onions, and pink bellworts. He said there would shortly be a hatch of *Ephemerella dorothea*—in fact, a few were beginning to come off the water even now—to be followed by a spinnerfall of *Stenonema fuscum* and *Stenonema vicarium*. He said there were already three trout beginning to feed at the base of the sycamore on the far side of the river, two more over there, and possibly four or five up yonder. They were not splashing the surface, he explained, because they were sipping from the surface whatever they were feeding on, which was probably three-quarter-inch green inchworms, judging by the one that had just dropped from a tree and been consumed by a smallish trout on our side of the stream. Let's see, he said, and heaved himself up, tied on an inchworm imitation, and worked his way to the middle of the stream. Inside of ten minutes he had taken and released three good-sized fish. I still saw water and trees and bushes and shrubbery. But I felt inspired.

Later on, when I had gone off on my own to work the water above where the inchworms were raining, I felt less inspired. It was one of those wrong times. First, the inchworm failed to work—because, it finally dawned on me, there were no branches overhead for them to drop from. Then, after I had run my way troutlessly through a no. 14 and a no. 16 Sulphur, a no. 10 and a no. 12 March Brown, a no. 12 Ginger Quill, a no. 16 black beetle, two Light Cahills, a caddis pupa, and a no. 14 Breadcrust, I stepped my leader down to a 7X tippet, tied on a no. 28 nymph midge, and, failing to allow for the extra leader I had just tied

H. L. Driscole, *Trout* (ca. 1890).

on, promptly snared my fly in some unidentifiable shrubbery along the bank behind me. Having finally located the minuscule fly and untangled its cobweb-fine tippet from around the twig on which it had impaled itself, I brought my next cast back too low and wrapped the fly a half-dozen times around my rod tip, which created such a bird's nest of a snarl that by the time I had unwoven it my eyes would no longer focus at a distance, and, disoriented by the current, I fell dizzily to my knees and barely avoided filling my waders with cold water. On my next cast, the outermost section of my rod, apparently loosened by the untangling maneuver, flew off and landed seven feet in front of me with an ignoble plop. Finally, in a cold fury, I tied on a Mickey Finn streamer, began to lash it viciously through the water, and to my astonishment hooked onto something substantial, which immediately broke off because, forgetting that I still had on a delicate 7X tippet, I tugged at it too hard.

It was then, while sitting on a rock and trying to hold back tears, that I conceived, designed, and decided to implement the Master Plan, a winter program of study that would carry me in a single great leap forward from the depth of my incompetence to the height of mastery. It would have two phases: a theoretical one and a practical one. The first would involve merely reading—a solid introduction to geology, a couple of field guides to the flora and fauna of the eastern seaboard, an advanced text on entomology, and as many practical books on trout fishing as I knew were already waiting for me in my haphazardly collected library: Izaak Walton's *The Compleat Angler;* Charles Ritz's *A Fly Fisher's Life;* A. J. McClane's *New Standard Fishing Encyclopedia;* Ray Bergman's *Trout;* Ernest Schwiebert, Jr.'s, *Matching the Hatch, Nymphs,* and two-volume *Trout;* Leonard M .Wright, Jr.'s, *Fishing the Dry Fly As a Living Insect;* Vincent C. Marinaro's *A Modern Dry-Fly Code;* Ray Ovington's *Tactics on Trout;* Art Flick's *Master Fly-Tying Guide;* Doug Swisher and Carl Richard's *Selective Trout;* and Brian Clarke and John Goddard's *The Trout and the Fly: A New Approach.* In addition, I would subscribe to *Fly Fisherman, Rod and Reel, Gray's Sporting Journal,* and any publications I hadn't yet heard of and read them from cover to cover whenever they showed up on my doorstep. A command of these materials, I reasoned, would enable me to cast my eyes on any streamside scene and, like the God of Genesis gazing upon the void, inhabit it with my very thoughts.

To supplement my reading, I would put into action the practical phase of the Master Plan. First, I would learn to cast properly, even if it meant tying a bright red plastic bead to the tip of my leader and practicing in snow up to my knees. And not just the simple single haul, but also the tight loop and open loop, the sidearm and backhand, the right hook and left hook, the check, the serpentine, the corkscrew curve, the wiggle, the parachute, the change of direction, the reverse, the steeple, the bow and arrow, the simple roll, the Argentine roll, the Belgian wind stroke, the Ritz storm cast, the double haul, and whatever else they'd come up with while I wasn't looking. I'd wear one of those Wristloks to keep "the wrist from falling back at the critical 'loading point,'" as they put it in the advertisement, and I'd even keep an actual drinking glass locked between my elbow and my side.

Then I'd learn to tie a decent fly—not just the standard patterns, like the Quill Gordon and the March Brown, but any design that nature could conceive. I'd gather up all the materials I could lay my hands on—if necessary I'd ransack the attic for old hats decorated with silver pheasant feathers or dyed swan flanks; why, I'd even start raising blue-dun hens—I'd stow them all in the trunk of my car, and I'd challenge nature to produce any insect I couldn't imitate in a matter of minutes. Finally, I'd put on my waders and vest, balance myself on an upright cinder block, and practice tying blood knots and double turles in a howling gale. Never again would I get out there on a stream and be surprised by the difference between fishing in reality and fishing in the mind.

Such were the rudiments of my Master Plan, but of course it didn't pan out. Once back in civilization, I found that there were other things to think about than becoming the trout-fishing god of the creation. And once my competitiveness had subsided, I realized that the course of study I had set myself was not just a program for a single winter, but a plan for a lifetime of fishing. Besides, a little reflection made me see why not even two lifetimes would suffice to give me the Master Fisherman's command of the sport: what stood in the way of the knowledge I sought were precisely those things I loved most about fishing. The Master went fishing to establish his dominion over nature, to reduce her sensuous commotion to categories of his mind. I went fishing for reasons directly opposed—to submit myself to nature's dominion, to lose myself in her colors, textures, and sounds. In short, the Master was a classicist, whereas I was a romantic.

And so in the years since that awful seizure of resolution, my winters have relaxed into seasons of moods and indulgences. In the fall, after the last October outing, I comb through my gear as I store it away, and I am invariably stricken with an attack of equipment fetishism, as if the lack of fish that summer could be explained by the shortness of my rod or the lightness of my line or the lack of some elegant little gadget or other. So I browse through the pile of catalogs and magazines that have accumulated over the year, to see what solutions they've come up with to needs I never knew I had. "MINI-FORCEPS—HOOK DISPENSER . . . with serrated jaws and 3-stop locking device"? Granted,

An H. T. Webster cartoon (late 1940s).

the precision-tooled stainless-steel instrument would look impressive dangling from the retractable chain that holds my Angler's Clip, but I've never had a problem removing flies from fishes' mouths, and by some miracle not of my own making I've never yet succeeded in impaling myself. No, I'll do without the mini-forceps for the time being, though I'll order one of those Richardson Chest Fly Boxes just as soon as I'm convinced that my skill as a fly caster is sufficient to compensate for my looking like an organ grinder gone wading without his monkey.

As winter approaches, I'm drawn like a salmon on a spawning run to Jim Deren's Angler's Roost, where I invariably find in the riot of his one-room shop another piece of equipment that I really don't need. Once I even bought myself a micrometer— a lovely little instrument that looks something like a pocket watch—to be absolutely certain that my leaders tapered down uniformly. To have it in my vest made me feel . . . precise. But after numerous dunkings its delicate mechanism rusted, and to tell the truth its breakdown hasn't made any difference.

The first snowfall seems to bring on an itch to read—not the books of instruction I once promised myself I'd devour, but other fishermen's adventures: Nick Lyons's poignant recollections of battles won and lost; William Humphreys's *The Spawning Run* and *My Moby Dick;* Norman McLean's haunting autobiographical novella, *A River Runs Through It.* Once in a great while I'll even read an account in *Rod and Reel* or *Fly Fisherman* of fishing for browns on the Madison River in Yellowstone Park or on Iceland's Laxa I Laxádalur, as if I'll ever get to those faraway places. Oh, yes, I'll get to Wyoming and Iceland someday. And to New Zealand and Tierra del Fuego, too. Anything seems possible as a new year comes around and the memories of last year's frustrations fade into oblivion. But February and March are cruel months, breeding dead thoughts out of the dead land. The stream behind my house is swollen now with melting slush, a miniature replica of a thousand turbid and unfishable torrents in the Catskills, the Poconos, the Adirondacks, and the Green Mountains. The mind has been feeding so long now on fantasies that it is down to sucking dry bones. Sometimes I even forget why I bother to go fishing.

Why do I bother to fish? After all, there are plenty of simpler ways to immerse oneself in nature than to spend many hundreds of dollars on objects made of plastic and cane and bits of colored feathers, and to fight the law of thermodynamics which says that all systems must sooner or later deteriorate. It isn't that I aim to stock my freezer full of trout for the winter. I don't care for the taste of fish all that much, and anyway the future of good fishing lies in those streams where you have to release your catch. Nor is it that I wish to prove

my superiority to the need for food, which is how Thorstein Veblen would no doubt have explained the evolution of the fly caster who cares more about fishing than about fish. And I don't believe it's heredity that has programmed me to hunt, else why would I so loathe the prospect of shooting guns at animals?

No theory will adequately serve to explain why a person goes fishing. Whenever I try to think about it rationally, I am flooded with emotions—in particular the memory of a trout I failed to catch. During World War II, when meat for the table was scarce and gasoline to fetch it even scarcer, I used to get up at sunrise several mornings a week, dig a batch of worms from the compost heap in the garden, dunk them in several pools of a brook that flowed through our summer place in Connecticut, and come home with enough small trout for my mother to serve as a meal. It was a routine though by no means unpleasant chore, and after a while it became a habit.

One summer after the war, when my father was off teaching at some midwestern college, I began to have trouble with one pool in particular. It was broader and deeper than the rest because my father and some friends had dammed it up in the hope of creating a lair for larger trout to grow in. I would always fish it the way he had taught me—from the side where a steep, overhanging bank made it possible to drop a worm into its deepest water without being seen by any fish that might be hiding there. Invariably, morning after morning, I would get a powerful strike just as my worm disappeared beneath the overhang, and just as invariably the fish would break loose, leaving my hook stripped clean. This ritual continued all summer long, no matter how I tried to vary the angle and strength of my strike or the length of time I allowed that fish to chew on the bait. He would always get the worm, and I would always end up with my bare hook tangled in a branch above me.

Then, late in August, when my father came home, he asked me one day in a mock-serious way if I would serve as his official guide to our little brook, since I, with a summer's experience under my belt, must now know its secrets better than he did. I took my charge with pride and seriousness and, when we had arrived at the deep pool, explained as exactly as I could the trouble I had been having. My father gazed at the water thoughtfully for a minute, then told me to stay where I was and walked away into the woods upstream from where I was standing. A good five minutes later he emerged from the trees on the other side of the stream. I understood at once that he had circled around with the idea of going after my fish from the opposite side of the pool. But I didn't see how he was going to get near it without being seen, since the bank on that side was absolutely level and provided no cover whatsoever.

Drawing by Ernest Lussier (1980).

But as I stood wondering, my father got down on all fours and slowly crawled to within about thirty feet of the water's edge. Then he lay down flat on his stomach and literally snaked his way another twenty-five feet until he had come up behind a rock that was large enough at least to obscure the whiteness of his face. Finally, he thrust his rod out awkwardly with his right hand, grasped the hook in his left hand, pulled the line toward him until the tip of the rod bent over to form a bow, and let the hook go like an archer releasing an arrow. It was a weak sling, and the worm fell short of the channel that ran beneath the embankment. But the fish, overconfident by now, went after it anyway and fell into my father's trap. For with the changed direction of the cast, maneuvers that would normally have caused the line to go slack now served to set the hook in the fish's mouth. After a brief and furious struggle, the fight was over and my father stood triumphantly holding up a sixteen-inch brookie, the biggest by at least four inches that had ever been caught in our stream.

At first it filled me with pride that I had been responsible for my father's taking such an enormous fish. After all, by feeding that trout all summer I had practically created it. But if I had created it, why hadn't I caught it? Why hadn't I been the one to cross over to the other side of the brook? The more I thought about it, the angrier I grew at myself for getting stuck in the groove of habit. By the following spring I no longer looked upon fishing as a functional routine. I was passionate to kill a still bigger fish. I think I've been looking for it ever since.

Trout painting from S. A. Kilburne's *Game Fishes of the United States* (1878).

But such memories seem sterile in the winter of my forty-fifth year. For in the intervening time I've caught many bigger fish, yet the longing for that moment of electric connection remains as powerful as ever. And there will always be still bigger fish waiting in some yet undiscovered pool. Can it be that the only reason I want to hook and torture them is to satisfy a young boy's yearning to grow up? If that is true, then fishing is a childish thing.

But with the first warm days of April, the world returns to normal again. The water in the stream in back of my house is down, and the ground along its bank is drying and beginning to turn green. At dusk I pace its length, dreaming the old dreams. At the head of the little island, the water once again reminds me of the Ledge Pool at Henryville. And I can see myself still fighting to turn my big fish before he reaches the fast water at the tail of the pool, as I actually did so many years ago. Perhaps this time my neighbor won't come along to interrupt the memory.

Gently, I increase the pressure on the line—ever so cautiously. Will the tippet break, or will the fish turn around? At last I can feel my rod tip quiver as he begins to exhaust his run. For the first time I feel I have a chance to catch him. Then he comes to a stop, and the line actually seems to stretch as we pull at each other with equal force for what feels like a full minute. Here is the critical moment. Either the leader will part, or the fish will come back to me. Abruptly, the pressure is gone.

Have I lost him? Or has he changed the direction of his run? Frantically, I reel in line . . . so much line that it seems impossible that he can still be attached to it. Then behold—the pressure is there again, and I can feel the line moving through the water toward me. My fish has turned.

Twenty minutes later, I am still fighting him as he cruises the perimeter of the pool in slowly diminishing circles. I can hardly see in the dark, so I don't dare stab at him with my net for fear that I will break the tippet with a clumsy thrust. But another fisherman, who has been casting upstream from me and has heard my whoops of excitement, is now waiting on the bank behind me. So when I have reduced the diameter of the fish's circles to a mere six feet, he is able to hold his net in the water and wait for the fish to swim into it.

God, he is big! I can't see him in the dark, but it takes both my hands to lift him out of the net and set him down on the bank. As I feel for the tiny hook in his mouth, he gives a mighty flop, and, kneeling over him now, I can feel his tail slap me way down at my knees. The hook slips out easily, and I lift him into the shallow water by the bank and cradle him in my hands. For one panicky instant, I feel him tilt as if he is going to go belly up. But when I right him again and nose him into the faster current farther out, he shudders and begins to slide from my hands like a submarine moving out of its pen. For a stupid moment I wonder if he feels gratitude for being allowed to go free. Then I push the thought aside and I see that the feeling of gratitude is mine.

Picture Credits

Frontispiece: The Museum of American Fly Fishing, Manchester, VT; *The South Side Sportsmen's Club,* illustrations by S. F. Denton (1896)

P. 3: The Museum of American Fly Fishing, Manchester, VT; *The Speckled Brook Trout,* illustrations by Louis Rhead (1902)

P. 4: Kennedy Galleries, New York, NY; oil painting by Arthur Parton (1887)

P. 5: Grand Central Art Galleries, New York, NY; oil painting by George Inness (1865); collection, Judge Paul H. Buchanan

P. 8: Douglas Allen, Neshanic Station, NJ; oil painting by N. C. Wyeth (1913)

P. 10: Russell Buzzell, West Brookfield, MA; pen and ink drawing (1978)

Pp. 12–13: Photo by Bill Browning, Sedona, AZ

P. 15: Ernest Lussier, East Meredith, NY; wash drawing (1979)

P. 16: L.L. Bean, Freeport, ME; catalog cover, illustrator unknown (1933)

P. 17: New York Herald Tribune; H. T. Webster (1940)

P. 18: The Museum of American Fly Fishing, Manchester, VT

P. 19: Collectors Choice, Santa Ana, CA; etching by William J. Schaldach (1930)

P. 21: Old Print Shop, New York, NY; Martin L. Bradford Company catalog (1910)

P. 23: Gifford B. Pinchot, M.D., Guilford, CT.; *Just Fishing Talk,* by Gifford Pinchot

P. 25: U.P.I., New York, NY; photo of Zane Grey (1936)

P. 27: Madelaine Hemingway Miller, Petoskey, MI

P. 28: The Museum of American Fly Fishing, Manchester, VT; *The Speckled Brook Trout,* illustrations by Louis Rhead (1902)

P. 29: The Museum of American Fly Fishing, Manchester, VT; *The Speckled Brook Trout,* illustrations by Louis Rhead (1902)

P. 31: Collectors Choice, Santa Ana, CA; etching by William J. Schaldach (1937)

P. 32: The Museum of American Fly Fishing, Manchester, VT; *The Speckled Brook Trout,* illustrations by Louis Rhead (1902)

P. 33: Russell Buzzell, West Brookfield, MA; pen and ink drawing (1978)

P. 34: Francis Golden, Weston, CT; watercolor painting (1980)

P. 36: The Museum of American Fly Fishing; Manchester, VT; *Fishing in American Waters,* by Genio C. Scott, published by Harper & Brothers, New York, NY (1869)

P. 37: Ernest Lussier, East Meredith, NY; from a stone lithographic print (1980)

Pp. 38–39 (top): Hirschl and Adler Galleries, New York, NY; miniature oil painting on an ivory fan blade, signed on the back by Winslow Homer (ca. 1900)

Pp. 38–39 (bottom): The Adirondack Museum, Blue Mountain Lake, NY; watercolor painting by Winslow Homer (1889)

P. 40 (top): Russell Buzzell, West Brookfield, MA; pencil drawing (1977)

P. 40 (bottom): The Museum of American Fly Fishing, Manchester, VT; unknown photographer (ca. 1890)

P. 41: Kienbusch Collection, Princeton University Library, Princeton, NJ; *Game Fishes of the United States* by G. Brown Goode, illustrations by S. A. Kilburne (1878)

P. 42: Kienbusch Collection, Princeton University Library, Princeton, NH; salmon flies, English (late nineteenth century)

P. 43: The Museum of American Fly Fishing, Manchester, VT; S. Allcock and Company, Redditch, England, a catalog page (1887)

P. 45 (top): The Adirondack Museum, Blue Mountain Lake, NY; illustration by Frederick Remington (ca. 1900)

P. 45 (bottom): The Museum of American Fly Fishing, Manchester, VT; *The Speckled Brook Trout* illustrated by Louis Rhead (1902)

P. 46 (top): The Adirondack Museum, Blue Mountain Lake, NY; daguerreotype (ca. 1855)

P. 46 (bottom): Kienbusch Collection, Princeton University Library, Princeton, NJ; oil painting by A. F. Tait (1863)

P. 47: Sportsman's Edge, Ltd., New York, NY; oil painting by C. E. Monroe (1979)

P. 48: The Museum of American Fly Fishing, Manchester, VT

P. 48 (bottom left): Stanley Read, Vancouver, B.C.

Pp. 50–51: The Museum of American Fly Fishing, Manchester, VT; *American Game Fishes* by G. O. Shields (1892)

P. 53: John Dodge Antique Prints and Photos, Bedford, MA

P. 54: The Museum of American Fly Fishing: *The Scientific Angler* by David Foster (1883)

P. 55: The Museum of American Fly Fishing, Manchester, VT; an old fishing log (1865)

P. 57: Collectors Choice, Santa Ana, CA; etching by William J. Schaldach (1929)

P. 59: The Museum of Fly Fishing, Manchester, VT; *A Book of Angling* by Francis Francis (1867)

Pp. 60–61: U.P.I., New York, NY

P. 63: The Museum of American Fly Fishing, Manchester, VT; *Sport with Gun and Rod* by Alfred M. Mayer (1883)

P. 65: The Museum of American Fly Fishing, Manchester, VT

P. 67: National Park Service, Yellowstone Park Files (ca. 1901)

P. 68: Russell Buzzell, West Brookfield, MA; pen and ink drawing (1978)

P. 69: The Museum of American Fly Fishing, Manchester, VT; *Complete Manual for Young Sportsmen* by Frank Forester (1863)

P. 70: The Museum of American Fly Fishing, Manchester, VT; *Adventures in the Wilderness* by William H. H. Murray (1869)

P. 71: The Museum of American Fly Fishing, Manchester, VT; *The Speckled Brook Trout,* illustrations by Louis Rhead (1902)

Pp. 72–73: The Museum of American Fly Fishing, Manchester, VT; *The American Angler,* newspaper (1882)

P. 74: Russell Buzzell, West Brookfield, MA; scratchboard drawing (1981)

P. 77: Sandy Scott, El Paso, TX; etching (1978)

P. 79: The Museum of American Fly Fishing, Manchester, VT; *The South Side Sportsmen's Club,* illustrations by S. F. Denton (1896)

P. 81: The Museum of American Fly Fishing, Manchester, VT; *The Basses, Freshwater and Marine* by Louis Rhead (1905)

Pp. 82–83: Photo by Michel Fong, San Francisco, CA

P. 85: The Museum of American Fly Fishing, Manchester, VT; *The Speckled Brook Trout,* illustrations by Louis Rhead (1902)

Pp. 86–87: Museum of Fine Arts, Boston, MA, William Wilkens Warren Fund; watercolor painting by Winslow Homer (1897)

P. 89: Copyright 1981 The Curtis Publishing Company, reprinted with permission from *The Saturday Evening Post*

Pp. 90–91: Delaware Art Museum, Wilmington, DE; oil painting by George Luks (1919)

Pp. 92–93: William Greenbaum Fine Prints, Gloucester, MA; Etching by George Marples (1924)

P. 94: The Fogg Art Museum, Harvard University Bequest—Grenville L. Winthrop; watercolor painting by Winslow Homer (1891)

Pp. 94–95 (bottom): The Museum of American Fly Fishing, Manchester, VT; Winslow Homer's Rod (ca. 1890). Photo by Bill Cheney, Pawlet, VT

P. 95 (top): Museum of Fine Arts, Boston, MA, Williams Wilkens Warren Fund; watercolor by Winslow Homer (1889)

P. 96: William Greenbaum Fine Prints, Gloucester, MA; etching by Robert Nisbet (1955)

P. 97: William Greenbaum Fine Prints, Gloucester, MA; etching by Phillip Little (1929)

P. 100: William Greenbaum Fine Prints, Gloucester, MA; *American Turf Register,* engraving (1839)

P. 101: The Museum of American Fly Fishing, Manchester, VT; *Fishing Tackle* by J. H. Keanne (1885)

Pp. 102–103: The Museum of American Fly Fishing, Manchester, VT; photo by Bill Cheney, Pawlet, VT

P. 107: The Museum of American Fly Fishing, Manchester, VT; Stoddard and Kendall catalog cover

P. 109: The Museum of American Fly Fishing, Manchester, VT; S. Allcock and Company, Redditch, England, a catalog page (1887)

Pp. 104, 105, 106, 110, 111: The Museum of American Fly Fishing, Manchester, VT; *The Speckled Brook Trout,* illustrations by Louis Rhead (1902)

P. 113: The Museum of American Fly Fishing, Manchester, VT; *National Sportsman* magazine, illustrator unknown (1933)

Pp. 114–115: Peter Keyser, The Keyser Gallery, Cirencester, England; watercolor by Ernest Briggs (ca. 1900)

Pp. 116–117: The Tryon Gallery, London, England, and Rodney Wilkinson; drypoints by Norman Wilkinson (1878–1971)

P. 118: The Tryon Gallery, London, England; oil painting by William Garfait (1980)

P. 119: The Tryon Gallery, London, England, and Rodney Wilkinson; watercolor by Norman Wilkinson (ca. 1955)

P. 120 (top): Punch's Almanac (1850s)

P. 120 (bottom): Kienbusch Collection, Princeton University Library, Princeton, NJ; *Mr. Briggs and His Doings* by John Leech (mid–nineteenth century)

P. 121: Block prints by Charles Keene (1823–1891)

P. 122: Jim and Judy Kaiser, Newark, DE; oil painting by Frank Schoonover for *Popular Magazine* cover (1913)

P. 125: The Museum of American Fly Fishing, Manchester, VT; *Rural Sports, Part I* by Rev. Wm. B. Daniel (1803)

P. 126: Kennedy Galleries, New York, NY; oil painting by Oliver Kemp (1930)

P. 127: The Fogg Art Museum, Harvard University Bequest—Grenville L. Winthrop; watercolor painting by Winslow Homer (1897)

P. 130: U.P.I., New York, NY; photo of Ted Williams (ca. 1948)

P. 133: The Museum of American Fly Fishing, Manchester, VT; *Fish and Fishing of the United States and British Provinces of North America* by Frank Forester (1866)

P. 134: Sandy Scott, El Paso, TX; detail of an etching done for *Gray's Sporting Journal* (1979)

Pp. 136–137: Ernest Lussier, East Meredith, NY; pencil drawing (1980)

P. 139: Copyright 1981 The Curtis Publishing Company, reprinted with permission from *The Saturday Evening Post*

P. 141: George Luther Schelling, Laceyville, PA; oil painting reproduced here in black–and–white (1980)

P. 143: The Museum of American Fly Fishing, Manchester, VT; *The Basses, Fresh–Water and Marine* illustrations by Louis Rhead (1905)

P. 144 (top): The Museum of American Fly Fishing, Manchester, VT; Thomas Chubb catalog (1888)

P. 144 (bottom): The Museum of American Fly Fishing, Manchester, VT; *Familiar Fish* by Eugene McCarthy (1900)

P. 145: Ernest Lussier, East Meredith, NY; pencil drawing (1980)

P. 146: Photograph by Bill Browning, Sedona, AZ

P. 149: The Museum of American Fly Fishing, Manchester, VT; *Favorite Flies* by Mary Orvis Marbury (1896)

P. 150: Eldridge Hardie, Denver, CO; watercolor painting (1981)

P. 151: Robert K. Abbett, Bridgewater, CT; oil painting (1981)

P. 153: The Museum of American Fly Fishing, Manchester, VT; *The Speckled Brook Trout* illustrations by Louis Rhead (1902)

P. 154: Grand Central Art Galleries, New York, NY; watercolor by Tom Daly (1978), Jack S. Parker Collection

P. 155: Grand Central Art Galleries, New York, NY; watercolor by Tom Daly (1978), Joyce and Elliot Liskin Collection

P. 157: The Museum of American Fly Fishing, Manchester, VT; catalog cover (1919)

P. 158: Carolyn Wyeth, Chadds Ford, PA; oil painting by N. C. Wyeth (1916)

P. 159: Schweitzer Gallery, Inc., New York, NY; oil painting by George Inness (1866)

P. 161: Ernest Lussier, East Meredith, NY; pencil drawing (1980)

Pp. 162–163: Russell Buzzell, West Brookfield, MA; scratchboard drawing for *Gray's Sporting Journal* (1981)

P. 164: The Museum of American Fly Fishing, Manchester, VT; catalog cover for Pflueger (ca. 1900)

P. 167: Coe Kerr Gallery, New York, NY; watercolor by A. Lassell Ripley, reproduced here in black–and–white (1935)

P. 167 (bottom): The Museum of American Fly Fishing, Manchester, VT; *Familiar Fish* by Eugene McCarthy (1900)

P. 169: The Museum of American Fly Fishing, Manchester, VT; *The Speckled Brook Trout,* illustration by Louis Rhead (1902)

P. 171: Old Print Shop, New York, NY; lithographic print from a painting by S. F. Denton (1889)

P. 173: Sandy Scott, El Paso, TX; detail of an etching done for *Gray's Sporting Journal* (1979)

P. 174: William Greenbaum Fine Prints, Gloucester, MA, and Rodney Wilkinson; drypoint by Norman Wilkinson (1920)

P. 177: William Greenbaum Fine Prints, Gloucester, MA, and Rodney Wilkinson; drypoint by Norman Wilkinson (1925)

P. 178: Mark Shoemaker, Utica, NY; watercolor, *Salmon Guide Gaffing*

P. 179 (top): Meredith Long and Company, Houston, TX; oil painting

P. 179 (bottom): The Museum of American Fly Fishing, Manchester, VT; *The Salmon Fly* by George M. Kelson, *The Black Ranger* (1895)

P. 181: William Greenbaum Fine Prints, Gloucester, MA, and Rodney Wilkinson; drypoint by Norman Wilkinson (1925)

P. 182 (top): Kienbusch Collection, Princeton University Library, Princeton, NJ; oil painting by W. M. Bracken, Boston (1864)

P. 182 (bottom): The Museum of American Fly Fishing, Manchester, VT; *The Salmon Fly* by George M. Kelson, *Black Dose* (1895)

P. 183: Schoonover Studios, Wilmington, DE; *Days Off* by H. Van Dyke, illustration (oil painting, 1906) by Frank E. Schoonover from the collection of Guido R. Rahr, Jr.

P. 185: John Dodge Antique Prints and Photos, Bedford, MA; wood engraving by Dan Beard, *Harper's Weekly* (1885)

P. 186: The Museum of American Fly Fishing, Manchester, VT; *Favorite Flies* by Mary Orvis Marbury (1892)

Pp. 186–187: Kennedy Galleries, New York City; watercolor painting by A. Lassell Ripley (ca. 1955)

P. 190: The Museum of American Fly Fishing, Manchester, VT; *Favorite Flies* by Mary Orvis Marbury (1892)

Pp. 190–191: Robert K. Abbett, Bridgewater, CT; oil painting (1981)

P. 192: Francis Golden, Weston, CT; watercolor painting reproduced here in black–and–white (1981)

P. 195: Chet Reneson, Lyme, CT; watercolor painting (1981)

P. 199: Kennedy Galleries, New York, NY; oil on acrylic painting (ca. 1978)

P. 201: Sandy Scott, El Paso, TX; detail of an etching done for *Gray's Sporting Journal* (1981)

Pp. 202–203: Photo by Bill Browning, Sedona, AZ

P. 205: Franklin Jones, West Stockbridge, MA; detail of an acrylic painting reproduced here in black–and–white, appeared on cover of *Gray's Sporting Journal* (1981)

P. 206: Grand Central Art Galleries, New York City; watercolor by Tom Daly, courtesy of private New York collector (1978)

P. 206 (bottom): The Museum of American Fly Fishing, Manchester, VT; *The South Side Sportsmen's Club,* illustrations by S. F. Denton (1896)

P. 207: Grand Central Art Galleries, New York, NY; watercolor painting by Kent Day Coes (ca. 1965)

P. 207 (bottom): The Museum of American Fly Fishing, Manchester, VT; *The South Side Sportsmen's Club,* illustrations by S. F. Denton (1897)

P. 209: John Dodge Antique Prints and Photos, Bedford, MA; *Gleason's Pictorial* newspaper (1854)

P. 211: The Museum of American Fly Fishing, Manchester, VT

P. 214: The Museum of American Fly Fishing, Manchester, VT; *Fishing in American Waters,* by Genio C. Scott (1869)

P. 215: The Museum of American Fly Fishing, Manchester, VT

P. 216: Russell Buzzell, West Brookfield, MA; scratchboard drawing (1981)

P. 218: Ernest Lussier, East Meredith, NY; pencil drawing (1980)

P. 221: John Merwin, *Rod and Reel* magazine, Manchester, VT; photo by Don Gray of antique lures from Maryland collectors Dick Healy and Vernon Kirby

P. 224: The Museum of American Fly Fishing, Manchester, VT; *The Speckled Brook Trout,* illustrations by Louis Rhead (1902)

P. 225: Bernard and S. Dean Levy, Inc., New York, NY; oil painting by Richard La Barre Goodwin (ca. 1900)

P. 226: Collectors Choice, Santa Ana, CA; etching by William J. Schaldach (1930)

P. 228: Sportsman's Edge, Ltd., New York, NY; oil painting by Stanley Meltzoff (1977)

P. 229: Sportsman's Edge, Ltd., New York, NY; watercolor painting by John P. Cowan (1978)

P. 232: Sportsman's Edge, Ltd., New York, NY; watercolor painting by Chet Reneson (1976)

P. 233: Sportsman's Edge, Ltd., New York, NY; oil painting by Stanley Meltzoff (1968)

P. 236: Francis Golden, Weston, CT; watercolor painting (1975)

P. 237: The Derrydale Press, New York, NY; *American Big Game Fishing* (1935)

P. 238: The Museum of American Fly Fishing, Manchester, VT; engraving, English (nineteenth century)

P. 240: Photo by Bill Cheney, Pawlet, VT

P. 241: The Museum of American Fly Fishing, Manchester, VT; *A Book on Angling* by Francis Francis (1867), *Fishing in American Waters* by Genio C. Scott (1869), *Ogden on Fly Tying* (1887)

P. 243: The Museum of American Fly Fishing, Manchester, VT; illustration by Louis Rhead (ca. 1900)

P. 245: Kennedy Galleries, New York, NY; oil painting by H. L. Driscoll, reproduced here in black–and–white (ca. 1890)

P. 247: New York Herald–Tribune; cartoon by H. T. Webster (1940)

P. 249: Ernest Lussier, East Meredith, NY; pencil drawing (1980)

P. 250: Keinbusch Collection, Princeton University Library, Princeton, NJ; *Game Fishes of the United States* by G. Brown Goode, illustrations by S. A. Kilburne (1878)

P. 251: The Museum of American Fishing, Manchester, VT; *Fishing in American Waters* by Genio C. Scott (1869)

Front jacket: Museum of Fine Arts, Boston, MA; William W. Warren Fund, watercolor painting by Winslow Homer, *Leaping Trout* (ca. 1889)

Back jacket: Photo by Douglas Lees, Warrenton, VA

Endleafs: The Adirondack Museum, Blue Mountain Lake, NY; illustration by Frederick Remington, Spring Trout Fishing in the Adirondacks, An Odious Comparison of Weights (ca. 1900)